Manchester Studies in Religion, Culture and Gender

Divine love

Manchester University Press

Manchester Studies in Religion, Culture and Gender

edited by Grace M. Jantzen

Already published

Religion and culture
Michel Foucault
selected and edited by Jeremy R. Carrette

Representations of the post/human
Monsters, aliens and others in popular culture
Elaine L. Graham

Becoming divine
Towards a feminist philosophy of religion
Grace M. Jantzen

Manchester Studies in Religion, Culture and Gender

Divine Love
Luce Irigaray, women, gender and religion

Morny Joy

Manchester University Press
Manchester and New York
distributed exclusively in the USA by Palgrave

Copyright © Morny Joy 2006

The right of Morny Joy to be identified as the author of this work has been asserted by him/her in accordance with the Copyright, Designs and Patents Act 1988.

Published by Manchester University Press
Oxford Road, Manchester M13 9NR, UK
and Room 400, 175 Fifth Avenue, New York, NY 10010, USA
www.manchesteruniversitypress.co.uk

Distributed in the United States exclusively by
Palgrave Macmillan, 175 Fifth Avenue,
New York, NY 10010, USA

Distributed in Canada exclusively by
UBC Press, University of British Columbia, 2029 West Mall,
Vancouver, BC, Canada V6T 1Z2

British Library Cataloguing-in-Publication Data is available

Library of Congress Cataloging-in-Publication Data is available

ISBN 978-0-7190-5524-9

First published by Manchester University Press in hardback 2006

This paperback edition first published 2014

The publisher has no responsibility for the persistence or accuracy of URLs for any external or third-party internet websites referred to in this book, and does not guarantee that any content on such websites is, or will remain, accurate or appropriate.

Printed by Lightning Source

CONTENTS

Acknowledgements	page vii
Introduction: encountering Irigaray	1
1 What's God got to do with it?	7
2 Cartesian mediations	36
3 Effacements: Emmanuel Levinas and Irigaray	56
4 Love and the labour of the negative: Irigaray and Hegel	83
5 Homo- and heterogeneous zones: Irigaray and Mary Daly	102
6 Irigaray's eastern excursion	124
7 Conclusion: a world of difference	142
Notes	161
References	186
Index	199

ACKNOWLEDGEMENTS

During the years that I thought and wrote about the ideas that have come to fruition in this book, I encountered many people who supported and influenced my work. I am immeasurably thankful to all of them for the myriad ways that they fostered this demanding exercise. There are certain individuals whom I will single out for their contributions. First of all I must thank Luce Irigaray herself, who stimulated me to think beyond the limits of my enculturation, both social and intellectual. I also thank her for the careful patience she took in discussing difficult elements of her work with me. I do nevertheless take full responsibility for my own interpretations. Grace Jantzen has accompanied me from the beginning of this task, as friend, mentor and much-needed goad to bring the work to completion. There have been other friends who, by inviting me to present papers, or to contribute to publications, have enriched aspects of the project. I express my sincere gratitude to Philippa Berry, Sara Heinämaa, Ursula King, Kath McPhillips, Dorothea Olkowski, Marie-Andrée Roy and Janet Soskice. It was a wonderful experience to collaborate with Kathy O'Grady and Judith Poxon in producing two edited volumes on the ideas of the 'French feminists' and religion. The intense reading and reflection required helped to clarify much of my own thinking, particularly on the work of Irigaray. I am very much indebted to the two anonymous readers of the manuscript whose careful reading, insightful questions and suggestions made me rethink parts of chapters, and refocus certain arguments. I want to thank profusely many other colleagues, both in my home department of Religious Studies at the University of Calgary and venues in Australia, Canada, Europe and the United States. They were not immediately involved in the production of this volume, but were there for me when the going got tough. I owe so much to the many students who have helped me over the years with research and fact-checking. Thanks especially to Cathy Brehaut, Jeneane Fast, Connie Fiell Mahoney, Sheila Mann, Susan Medd, Lynn Nugent and Marcus Pankiw. In addition, I am eternally grateful to the Social Sciences and Humanities Research Council of Canada for the Research Fellowships that they have awarded me that sustained the research and writing on this project. Without their generous assistance, I would not have been able to devote the requisite time and attention needed to accomplish this project. My profound thanks as well to the Killam Foundation for granting me a Resident Fellowship at the University of Calgary in 1999. It is with sincere appreciation that I thank both the Centre for the Study of Society and Religion at the University of Victoria, Victoria, BC, Canada – where this project started during a sabbatical leave in 1995 – and Clare Hall, Cambridge University, UK, where it was finished on a Visiting Fellowship in 2003. The sustenance, of diverse kinds, provided by such institutions greatly alleviated the solitary rigours of writing. My special thanks to Professor Harold Coward, then Director at the Centre in Victoria, and to Professor Ekhard Salje, President, and Julius Lipner, Professorial Fellow at Clare Hall. Thanks also to Ann Smith for the index. Finally, I thank my partner, John King, not just for his superb editorial skills that have brought this unwieldy manuscript under control, but for having lived through this experience with me, and survived, as always, with a loving smile.

Several of the chapters in this volume appeared in earlier publications. They all appear here with permission of the publishers:

Chapter 1 as: 'What's God Got to Do With It?: Irigaray and the Divine', in K. O'Grady, A. Gilroy and J. Gray (ed.), *Bodies, Lives, Voices: Essays on Gender and Theology*, Sheffield, Sheffield Academic Press, 1998, 231–65.

Chapter 3 as: 'Levinas: Alterity, the Feminine and Women – A Meditation', *Studies in Religion/Sciences Religieuses*, 22:4, 1994, 463–85.

Acknowledgements

Chapter 4 as: 'Love and the Labour of the Negative: Irigaray and Hegel', in Dorothea Olkowski (ed.), *Resistance, Flight, Creation: Feminist Enactments of French Philosophy*, Ithaca: Cornell University Press, 2000, 113–23.

Chapter 6 as: 'Irigaray's Eastern Explorations', in M. Joy, K. O'Grady and J. Poxon (eds), *Religion in French Feminist Thought: Critical Essays*, London: Routledge, 2003, 51–67.

Introduction: encountering Irigaray

Luce Irigaray is a formidable and passionate presence, both in person and in her writings. She has charted a unique course of enquiry into the contemporary situation of women. In so doing, Irigaray has not identified herself with any particular movement. Irigaray declines the term 'feminism'. She does not accept '-isms' of any variety, as she indicates that they constrict the free play of exploration. 'Male-bashing' is also not a word that can be used to discredit Irigaray's commitment to change both the personal and social conditions that have restricted women. She believes that a new form of relations between man and women – an ethics of sexual difference – needs to be established. This ethics and its mode of mutual recognition will foster the emergence of a culture where love can flourish. Because of these ideas, Irigaray has been regarded as a utopian. In response, she has described herself as a defender of the impossible (*I Love to You*, 1996: 9–10), emphasising, none the less, that the transformation she advocates can and needs to be achieved.

It is a difficult task to introduce Luce Irigaray's work, particularly her ideas on religion and God. Primarily, this is because she does not want be identified with any orthodox religious tradition. Secondly, and more importantly, Irigaray does not want to be classified according to conventional academic categories (Hirsh and Olson 1995: 100). Irigaray is particularly averse to answering substantive questions that ask her to clarify her ideas. She believes that her work speaks for itself. Arid and tedious intellectual analysis is anathema. Irigaray has described her work as providing 'beacons' (Hirsh and Olson 1995: 102). These are to be appreciated as flashes of light probing uncharted territory that, on further investigation, will reveal multiple and unpredictable possibilities. Irigaray thus encourages creative encounters with her work, rather than reductive explanations.

Nevertheless, in various interviews, Irigaray has provided insights into her own conception of her writing and idiosyncratic style. In an early discussion, she remarks with reference to the term '*parler femme*' that has been used to describe her work: 'My writing is consonant and continuous with my loving. And my manner of loving differs, it's always different' (Amsberg and Steenhuis 1983: 202). Such an affirmation discloses Irigaray's fidelity to a manner of writing, which, while not exactly stream-of-consciousness, does not obey the requirements of intellectual exposition. It is a style at once poetic, allusive and elusive, yet also critical, ironic and playful. Footnotes are rare. This lack of documentation illustrates one of the frustrations that scholars have with Irigaray's work, but I think that this is a deliberate provocation on her part. Irigaray believes that, in academia, abstract *logos* rules. This deprives writing of its life-blood and breath, which, for Irigaray, are representative of the visceral, emotional and imaginative dimensions of existence that she wishes to incorporate in her work.

In an interview with Elizabeth Hirsh and Gary A. Olson, Irigaray describes her work as consisting of three phrases (1995: 96–7). The first, which comprises principally the books *Speculum* (1985a) and *This Sex Which Is Not One* (1985b), is a sustained criticism of the unitary male perspective that she posits as dominating western philosophy and religion. The second phase, from the period of *Sexes and Genealogies* (1993b), proposes mediations, including cultural, legal and religious aspects, that would assist in redressing this imbalance. Irigaray's final phase, which stretches from *An Ethics of Sexual Difference* (1993a) to *The Way of Love* (2002b), is devoted to establishing the philosophical and ethical contours for a new mode of relationship between women and men.

Irigaray's *oeuvre* thus commences with a critical assessment of western male philosophers and thinkers, ranging from Plato to Jacques Lacan, who have excluded women from their inner sanctum. In so far as they express any idea of the 'feminine', Irigaray understands this as a male projection. She is highly disapproving of this 'masquerade of femininity'. For Irigaray, such impositions are indicative of the dependent and inferior roles that have denied women an integral identity of their own making. She employs the tactic of *mimesis*, which involves a deconstructive reiteration of the ideas of each thinker that undermines their arguments, and exposes their blind spots, with a parodic proficiency. At the same time, according to her deliberate strategy, a space is opened up for women's own imaginative reconstructive interventions. This is not idle game-playing, as Irigaray is supremely serious in her philosophical and social purposes. For this reason, she complains that her work has been misunderstood, having been read mainly from a literary perspective in the United States (Hirsh and Olson 1995: 97). Irigaray states that an awareness of the philosophical grounding of her work is necessary for a complete appreciation of her task. There are many philosophical aspects to her work – phenomenology first and foremost – but also psychoanalytic theory, dialectics and ethics. These elements are never employed, however, in a manner that is consistent with their traditional usage. The following quotation is an illustration of her combination of certain of these approaches with specific reference to the work of Hegel:

Using phenomenology without dialectic would risk nevertheless a reconstruction of a solipsistic world, including a feminine world unconcerned with the masculine world or which accepts remaining parallel to the latter.... The dialectical method, such as I use it, is not in the service of the reassumption [sic] (*Aufhebung*) of all singularity into an absolute objectivity to be shared by any subject. My way uses the negative as a path which permits, at each moment, dialogue between subjects in respect to singularities, in particular of gender. (Pluháček and Bostic 1996: 351)

In the second phase of her work, Irigaray demonstrates that she is not satisfied with the liberal solution of equality to amend the prevailing situation. In her view, such a position can only grant women the status of token males. For Irigaray, in order for a relationship of true equivalency to be possible between the sexes, women should realise a distinct form of identity. This involves the establishment of specific legal safeguards, but it also requires a form of self-redefinition, achieved by creative explorations of the 'feminine Imaginary' (1985b: 30; 164–6). Such a process encourages women to claim specific engendered or 'feminine' characteristics, which they elect for themselves. Irigaray will herself propose certain alternative 'feminine' characteristics that she believes are beneficial to women. From Irigaray's perspective, unless women attain this state of personal plenitude or self-fulfilment, they are not ready to enter into relationships with others.

It is the matter of gender that becomes increasingly important in the books of Irigaray that have been published in English from 1993 onwards. While Irigaray initially acknowledges the somewhat simplistic division between sex as a biological given and gender as cultural acquisition, she also wishes to complicate the assumptions associated with both. Nevertheless, as her work develops, her insistence on distinct attributes as particularly appropriate for women begins to take on an insistent tone. This development in her thought has been responsible for Irigaray being described as a proponent of 'gender difference'. It needs to be noted, however, that Irigaray's usage of the term 'gender' in relation to women does not involve hostility towards men, which, by some quirk of logic, it has come to signify today (Butler 2001: 427–9). This is because Irigaray's project is one that she believes will irrevocably alter, in a positive manner, the dynamics of relationship between women and men.

This undertaking constitutes the third phase of Irigaray's work, from *An Ethics of Sexual Difference* (1993a) onwards. She believes that a constructive rethinking of the notion of 'sexual difference' is perhaps the most vital issue of our age (1993a: 5–6). It is in the prologue to *I Love to You* (1996) that Irigaray testifies to the vision she has of this new mode of relationship. '[This is a] book concerning the encounter between woman and man, man and woman. An encounter characterised by belonging to a sexed nature to which it is proper to be faithful; by the need for rights to incarnate this nature with respect; ... by the quest for new words which will make this alliance possible without reducing the other to an item of property' (1996: 11).

It is in *I Love to You* that Irigaray also develops in some detail the spiritual dimension of her work, specifically as it relates to women. This interest in women and their potentiality to experience God or, as she expresses it, 'to become divine', has been discernable in Irigaray's work from the beginning, especially in such essays as 'La Mystérique' (1985a: 191–202) and 'Divine Women' (1993b: 55–72). Charges of essentialism have also been directed at Irigaray because she has been perceived as imputing innate spiritual qualities to women. Yet it is not only women who can become divine. Irigaray depicts a heterosexual couple as also experiencing the divine in the act of love. 'I discover the divine between us, conceived by us but not combined with us, existing between each of us. We give birth to it, adults at last. Arriving at another stage of our history, God reveals himself as the work of woman and man' (2002b: 13). Human love is thus a divine and/or spiritual experience. Irigaray believes that this love, quintessentially expressed in the sexual relationship between a woman and a man, takes place in this world, not in a transcendent realm. It is located in a space that Irigaray describes as the 'sensible transcendental', and also in a mode she describes as one of 'horizontal transcendence'. These paradoxical terms denote Irigaray's rejection of oppositional dualism; of hierarchical systems; of the homogeneous resolution of the 'one and the many', as they have operated in western philosophy and theology. Irigaray shares these sensibilities with many contemporary people who are discarding former religious orthodoxies in favour of more participatory engagements with a notion of an in-dwelling divine. This replaces adherence to static metaphysical categories of an absolute Being with its doctrinaire truth claims.

In order to comprehend fully the complexity and significance of Irigaray's work, I believe that these dimensions of her religious or spiritual orientation have to be addressed. This is the principal motivation that has informed my writing of these studies on Irigaray. The questions that intrigue me as a philosopher of religion concern Irigaray's challenge to traditional religious dogmas and practices. I have selected facets of Irigaray's *oeuvre* that have not been treated in great detail elsewhere. It is the theme of love, specifically a love that is divine, that resonates in Irigaray's ethical and spiritual work. This focus takes it beyond the principally psychoanalytic and secular interests that have been the centre of most of the past attention given to her work.

Irigaray's spiritual turn, however, is not without controversy. This is because it becomes apparent that the more spiritual Irigaray becomes, as with her adoption of eastern religious practices – particularly yoga and meditation – the more conservative are her views. The love of man and woman, originally depicted in all its sensual fecundity, transmutes finally into a heterosexual family in *The Way of Love* (2002b). The divine excess of mysticism, and of women's wilful and innovative explorations of transcendental territory, are reduced to benign values of gynocratic goddesses. Irigaray's original critical outrageousness has become a domesticated quietude, though women are no longer passive objects of others' manipulations.

While I am not a proponent of neutral equality at the expense of certain sexual differences and rights, which are protected by law, I do have problems with this most recent work of Irigaray. This is not to say that I reject her work outright. For me, as for many women in philosophy and Religious Studies, Irigaray has blazed a path that has changed our lives and the way that we think and write. I am as opposed as Irigaray to ancient orthodoxies, be they philosophical or religious, that have imposed codes of conduct on women, that have excluded them from universities and ministries, that have denied them access to the echelons of power and prestige. Fortunately, I have had the great fortune to live in an era and a country where I have not been subject to such constraints. Perhaps it is because of this freedom that I have the luxury to choose to differ with Irigaray's depiction of 'feminine' ideals. Or then again, perhaps it is because I have learned too well from Irigaray's early enthusiasm to explore the infinite possibilities that she posited as open for women. For this I remain in her debt. Irigaray's encouragement to become autonomous, to become divine – understood as a search for personal integrity – instigated my own explorations of what it is to be a woman today. As it becomes apparent in my conclusion to this volume, however, these explorations have now brought me to a worldview where I have chosen to diverge from Irigaray's vision. Somehow I believe, if I have understood the challenge inherent in the early stages of Irigaray's work, that this is what she encouraged contemporary women to undertake. In this respect, I do not understand my criticism of her work as a refutation, but as promoting further discussion and an expansion of her incentive to think differently.

In recounting the various encounters that I have had over the past ten years with the work of Irigaray, I have chosen a somewhat developmental framework. Thus, in Chapter 1, I survey the first and second phases of Irigaray's work – the criticism of the western philosophical and religious tradition and the ways that she recommends for women to challenge it. The following three chapters deal sequentially with Irigaray's engagements with three philosophers, René Descartes, Emmanuel Levinas and G. W. F. Hegel, basically in the same order in which she published her reflections on their work. All of these chapters portray different dimensions of the third phase of Irigaray's work, as she refines her ideas about the new ethical relationship that can be realised by women and men. In Chapter 5, I take stock of these developments by comparing Irigaray's initiatives with those of another celebrated iconoclast of the western religious heritage, Mary Daly. It was extremely surprising to discover just how much they have in common. There is one major difference, however, and that is their attitude to heterosexuality. Chapter 6 examines and evaluates Irigaray's more recent turn to eastern religions and the impact that this has on her previous position. I see this work as in some way representing a fourth phase in the work of Irigaray, representing the spiritual culmination of her explorations. In the final chapter, as part of my own assessment of the work of Irigaray, I recount the reception of her work by feminist scholars in its different phases. I conclude by offering my own insights into the significance of Irigaray's contributions, particularly for scholars in the study of religion. I also hope that this book has something of value to offer to those many people who, when I have mentioned to them that I have been reading the work of Irigaray, wanted me to describe exactly what her work was all about. Maybe this book can help to clarify in some small way what five minutes of conversation could never begin to explain.

CHAPTER 1

What's God got to do with it?

God conceives and loves himself. That part of God has always been denied us. Thus we women have become weak, formless, insecure, aggressive, devoted to the other because unaware of our selves, submissive to the other because we were unable to establish our own order. If we are not to obey the other, we have to set a goal of our own, make our own law or laws. If we are to escape slavery it is not enough to destroy the master. Only the divine offers us that freedom – enjoins it upon us. Only a God constitutes a rallying point for us that can let us free – nothing else. (1993b: 68)

Introduction

The early work of Luce Irigaray resonates with references to God and the divine. From her first books, *Speculum of the Other Woman* (1985a) and *This Sex Which Is Not One* (1985b), Irigaray has been keenly involved with religion. She both rejects what she considers outmoded beliefs, structures and practices and explores innovative ways of (re-)introducing myths and ideals. This chapter will follow Irigaray's investigations of women and of their relation to the concept of o/Otherness, particularly as this term has featured in acts of denial that have deprived women of an identity of their own. Jacques Derrida and Jacques Lacan are major influences, but she does not accept their work at face value. Irigaray's *oeuvre* also needs to be set in the wider context of the developments in French thought since 1930, specifically the impact of such diverse thinkers as Hegel, Freud and Heidegger. Irigaray is neither a theologian nor a philosopher of religion in the traditional sense, and I think it is a mistake to try to make her one. The body of her work, especially her mythopoetic explorations and her use of mimesis – as both a critical and creative tool[1] – provide a radical opposition to received notions of divinity and the 'feminine', in what Irigaray names as patriarchy.[2] This chapter also examines Irigaray's critical response to traditional ideas of God in terms of women's o/Other, and her proposal to substitute imaginative constructs of the divine ideals. Irigaray will propose an alternative 'feminine imaginary'. She asserts that women need to affirm their status and identity as distinct from men, and to become divine. The focus of the chapter will be on certain sections from

Speculum of the Other Woman (1985a), *This Sex Which Is Not One* (1985b), and particular essays from *Sexes and Genealogies* (1993b).

Preliminary diagnosis

Irigaray's initial investigations of the situation of women and their relation to God, as well as of the notion of desire, are undertaken in *Speculum*. In this intertextual exercise, Irigaray interacts with selective themes in the work of western philosophers – Plato, Aristotle, Plotinus, Descartes, Kant and Hegel. It is the opening study of Freud, entitled 'The Blind Spot of an Old Dream of Symmetry', however, which both sets the tone and frames the issue that Irigaray discerns as critical for the position of women in the western intellectual and religious traditions. For Irigaray, it is basically a male-centred system that has prevailed, where man has been regarded as the norm or ideal of the human species. It is also the male image, with additional attributes of power and transcendence, that has been equated with God. Woman, in contrast, has been deemed inferior, if not alien to all those qualities that are associated with reason and morality, let alone with the deity. In this essay, Irigaray questions Freud's depiction of a girl's resolution to the oedipal conflict which he regards as opposite to that of a boy.

> Does 'opposite' mean 'placed over against something on the other or farther side of the intervening line; contrary in position'? Or does it mean 'opposed,' 'hostile,' or 'harmful to,' contrary like Mary in the rhyme or as the dictionary develops the meaning.
> This decisive moment in sexual structuring is then supposedly produced in the little girl's case as the 'opposite' of the (so-called) masculine economy. Or so Freud would wish, as he thinks of sexual difference from within the realm of the same, and attributes all the properties (and improprieties) of the dictionary definition listed above to the sex 'opposite' his own. (Irigaray 1985a: 83)

This explication places woman as the opposite or other of man within a framework work that Irigaray terms 'an economy of sameness'. As such, a woman's difference from man, when not deemed a deficiency, is subsumed by a model of masculine identity that incorporates any diversity into its own monolithic system – hence the notion of sameness. While such a system has definite Hegelian connections, Irigaray also places it within another context of the interplay of identity and difference – that of Greek philosophy. Here, in the work of Plato, all that is multiple issues from, and returns to the unity of the Idea or the One. In her study entitled 'Plato's *Hystera*', also within *Speculum*, Irigaray describes this process, detecting a similar unifying procedure in both Platonic and Hegelian modes of dialectical interchange: 'The Idea of Ideas, alone, is itself in itself.... It neither indicates nor indexes anything *other* than itself, however akin. And needs no heterogeneous *vehicle*, no foreign *receptacle*, in order to signify and represent itself. The idea goes beyond such mere methodological, generative procedures.

It is the end of every road, even the road of dialectic' (Irigaray 1985a: 298).

As a result, though Irigaray doesn't spell out her argument in precise detail, her implication is clear. This is that, in the western philosophic/theological heritage, a self-same unity or identity has been connected not just with the Platonic Ideas or Forms, and with the Hegelian Spirit, but also with an absolute God, most often designated in a male and paternal mode:

> The One produces the even by subsuming under it the less and the more, and the gaps between them, which are operative in the dyad, and in this way the One swells to infinity. But as sameness: the One (of) the Idea.... What is to be said, then, of him who, now and forever, through all eternity, contains all these essences, these powers, while going beyond them in a pre-existence that engenders them as such and regulates the connections between them? The Good (of) God-the-Father. (1985a: 359–60)

In Irigaray's view, this God-the-Father, particularly the god of Christianity, stands supported by religious philosophy and theology as the bulwark of a traditional system that demeans women. This model of God has been subjected to rigorous psychoanalytic scrutiny, firstly by Freud and then by Jacques Lacan. Yet though the actual existence of God may be put into question from the materialist perspectives of both Lacan and Freud, Irigaray also detects in their psychoanalytic procedures a movement that continues to 'deify' the male sex and the symbol of its power, the phallus.[3] For Irigaray, the male who accedes to his god like inheritance of phallic identity does so only as a result of a repression of the mother and, by extension, of women. In this male-focused, psychoanalytic setting, woman, as the other of men, functions both as fetish object in the guise of mother-substitute fixations and as a mirroring device, reflecting to men their own narcissistic self-preoccupations – their sameness.[4]

> What a mockery of generation, parody of copulation and genealogy, drawing its strength from the same model, from the model of the same: the subject. In whose sight everything outside remains forever a condition making possible the image and the reproduction of the self. A faithful polished mirror, empty of altering reflections. Immaculate of all autocopies. Other because wholly in the service of the same subject to whom it would project its surfaces, candid in their self-ignorance. (1985a: 136)

Within a religious setting, Irigaray detects a subtle move whereby this idealised male self-image, which from a psychoanalytic perspective is primarily an imaginary projection, becomes solidified in cultural productions as a symbolic figure of authority. In this unconscious process, the debt to the maternal other will be replaced by a projection on to an idealised Other, God. As Elizabeth Grosz explains it:

> A whole history of philosophy [and religion] seems intent on rationalizing this debt [to the mother] away by providing men with a series of images of self-creation culminating in the idea of God as the paternal 'mother', creator of the universe in place of women/ mothers. Man's self-reflecting Other, God, functions to obliterate the positive fecundity

and creativity of women. Born of woman, man devises religion, theory, and culture as an attempt to disavow this foundational, unspeakable debt. (1990: 181)

A fundamental element in the deciphering of both Lacan's and Irigaray's positions is an appreciation of the uses of the term o/Other – a borrowing from Hegel – that features as a central term in Lacan's repertoire. The o/Other is a multifaceted term.[5] In his extrapolation of Hegel's notion of difference, Lacan has reworked the Freudian transition from preoedipal to oedipal by first expanding on the what he names as the imaginary or mirror phase. Otherness plays a vital role in this process. Grosz discusses this development in *Jacques Lacan: A Feminist Introduction*: 'In the mirror stage ... the child enters an imaginary relation with the other, with others, including the mother, father, nurturer, or mirror-image (represented by *autre* [other]).... The mirror stage generates the child's ego or *moi* which is built upon its imaginary identification with the other' (74). This imaginary phase sets the scene for the development of both sexual and social identity. For Lacan, much of life a person's life is spent in a (fruitless) endeavour to re-experience this imaginary relation with the m/other figure who represents a state of primal plenitude.

This imaginary *autre*/other is distinct from *Autre*/the Other, which, according to Lacan, 'is embodied in the figure of the symbolic father, who intervenes in the narcissistic imaginary stage of total gratification' (Grosz 74). Lacan designates the shift from other to the Other as a passage from a narcissistic imaginary stage with its maternal symbiosis to a paternal symbolic one, which involves the acquisition of language and of its accompanying socio-cultural structures.[6] Grosz again elucidates:

The Other (represented by *Autre*) enters the Oedipal triangle as a point outside the dual imaginary structure. As the law of symbolic functioning, the Other is embodied in the figure of the symbolic father, who intervenes into the narcissistic, imaginary, and incestual structure of identifications and gratifications. The relation between self/*moi* and other is necessary for the initiation of social exchange, and the articulation of the unconscious. The locus of the Other is at the same time that site within the subject known as the unconscious. (74)

The o/Other in Lacanian theory has thus come to indicate two aspects of one process. It registers the change from the imaginary (unconscious) to symbolic (conscious) cultural conventions. At the same time, it indicates the site of an original maternal bond that has been repressed in this transaction. While it is the mistaken conflation of the imaginary with the symbolic representations that Lacan appreciates as the work of analysis to deflate, Irigaray will undertake her own diagnosis of this hypothesis.[7] She investigates the erasure of women that she believes underlies western civilisation. Needless to say, in her analysis of the conflation of men's unconscious fabrications with the symbolic designation of God, Irigaray is not impressed by the way that this male Ideal Other has functioned so as to limit women's spheres of activity, specifically their ability to function as independent subjects. According to Irigaray, women have been reduced to acting a masquerade of femininity that men have ordained. 'What do I mean by masquerade? In particular what Freud calls "femininity" ... whereas a man is a man from the outset ... [a] woman has to become a normal woman ... she has to enter the *masquerade of femininity*' (1985b: 134).[8] Irigaray speculates on the potential of women to oppose this designation. She also gives some intimation of the momentous upheaval that could result if this dormant force of the repressed maternal were to stir in terms of her own unconscious 'otherness', and question symbolic Otherness.

But what if the 'object' started to speak? Which also means beginning to 'see', etc. What disaggregation of the [male] subject would that entail? Not only on the level of the split between him and his other, his variously specified alter ego, or between him and the Other, who is always to some extent his Other, even if he does not recognize himself in it, even if he is so overwhelmed by it as to bar himself out of it and into it so as to retain at the very least the power to promote his own forms. (135)

Most of Irigaray's work is, I believe, vitally concerned with both the strategies and the implications involved when women refuse to support the symbolic process which determines their silencing and 'othering'. As a corollary, Irigaray is also concerned with eliciting the key elements that would support women's imaginary reclamations of a divine ideal of their own. This will entail women expressing their own unfettered desires. Inevitably, this will have repercussions for present definitions of desire and identity as well as for the nature of god and religion.

The lure of desire

Love of the other without love of self, without love of God, implies submission of the female one, the other. (Irigaray 1993b: 68)

In refusing to let women remain the basis of the male economy of sameness, Irigaray's intention is for women to recognise their own desires, which have been inhibited by their cultural conditioning. For Irigaray, these desires are not simply libidinal urges, which result from repression of a woman's relationship to the m(other). Their new formulation will result from a revision of Freud's definition of sublimation and repression, and the relation to the phallus, as it is refined by Lacan (1985b: 69–75). It will involve a woman coming to understand herself as a person in her own right, not simply as a vehicle for reproduction.[9] The reclamation of women's individuality, as distinct from her restricted maternal role, will allow women access to constructive forms of self-representation.

Irigaray describes the problem: 'Freud can discuss the little girl's relation to the place of origin only as a vacancy, a taking leave of the mother: as rejection, or hatred of the mother ... she is left with a *lack*, a lack of all representation, re-presentation, and even strictly speaking of all mimesis of her desire for origin'

(Irigaray 1985a: 42). Irigaray is, however, not only combating Freud's denial of women's desire as an active force that would allow her both a positive self-image, she also wishes to resist Lacan's further amendments of Freudian theory that associates women's fundamental lack – her being 'not-all' (*pas tout*) – not simply with the deprivation of a penis but with an absence both of awareness and of an ability to articulate her condition. In the article 'God and the *Jouissance* of the Women' (Lacan in Mitchell and Rose 1983: 137–48), Lacan expands on these opinions about women. 'The woman can only be written with The crossed through. There is no such thing as The woman, where the definite article stands for the universal. There is no such thing as The woman since of her essence … she is not all' (144).[10] In one sense, Lacan could be making a similar observation to that of Derrida – that there can be no universal definition of woman. On another level, however, Lacan is describing woman's non-existence from a symbolic perspective. As 'The woman', she exists only as a male fantasy (48). However, there is also another possible reference which elaborates on Freud's definition of women as incomplete – they lack a penis. In Lacan's reformulation of Freud, women are incomplete in so far as they lack the phallus which represents the power to function within the symbolic.

In *Speculum* Irigaray's criticisms are directed mainly at Freud, but in *This Sex Which Is Not One* (1985b), she takes direct aim at Lacan's recasting of the castration complex. Irigaray's 'Così Fan Tutti' [sic] demonstrates how Lacan's phallic frame of reference, particularly in its dry, verbal analyses of desire, is still caught in its own desire for the same. It reaffirms 'the narcissistic pleasure that the master, believing himself to be unique, confuses with that of the One' (103). She vehemently rebukes Lacan for his amendment of Freud's description of women's deficiency – her lack of the phallus (1985b: 61).[11] The ultimate inequity, however, from Irigaray's perspective, is Lacan's presumption that women do not have access to consciousness. Delegated to a role of the unconscious womb or source of man's language, women are prevented not only from being aware of their own desires but from acquiring language, the symbolic means to elucidate their condition. According to Irigaray, women are thus barred from the possibility of representing a God/Other of their own.

As for women, unless raised to the dignity of the male essence, they would have no access to the sublime circles of sameness, to the heights of the intelligible … women are incapable of realizing whether some idea – Idea – in fact corresponds to themselves, or whether it is only a more or less passable imitation of men's ideas. Unaware of the value of the names given them by the logos – assuming that some really specific names exist – women would, it seems, not know their definition, their representation, or the relationships with others, and with the All, that are maintained in this way. (1985a: 342)

To counter this muting of their voices, Irigaray posits that women need to begin to understand how Lacan manipulates the manifestations of desire. This term 'desire' will be decisive in the development of Irigaray's thought. In one sense, for both Irigaray and Lacan, it retains the associations of Platonic *eros*, which during its voyage through western thought, particularly through Hegel, and its later Freudian and Lacanian adaptations, has undergone various permutations. In her book *Subjects of Desire* (1987), Judith Butler traces its trajectory from Hegel to Lacan, especially as it was mediated in France during the 1930s by the lectures of Alexandre Kojève.[12] For Hegel 'desire signifies the *reflexivity* of consciousness, the necessity that it become other to itself in order to know itself' which is achieved by the dialectical engagement with negativity, or otherness (Butler 1987: 7). By the time of Lacan, however, 'Desire can no longer be said to reveal, express, or thematise the reflexive structure of consciousness, but is, rather, the precise moment of consciousness' opacity' (186). Desire, as it is employed by Lacan, is not an impetus to a greater awareness, but a driven, interminable movement that holds humanity in the thrall of the o/Other. As such, for Lacan, desire is a residue of the repressed maternal connection.[13]

Desire, then, is intrinsic to the complicated negotiation by which a child progresses from biological drives to the acquisition of the symbolic, in the form of language and social conventions. Kelly Oliver gives a succinct description of the somewhat intricate manoeuvres involved:

Once the infant realizes that its needs will not be met automatically by the mother, it must substitute demands (words) that indicate what it needs for the imaginary unity with the all-gratifying maternal body. Lacan calls the gap between need and demand 'desire'. Desire is unfulfillable; it is the remainder when you subtract the demand from the need. In other words, once you have to ask for what you need you cannot get what you need because what you need is to have your needs automatically met without having to ask. In Lacan's version of the Oedipal story, the infant moves from need to desire or from the maternal body to the name or law of the Father. (1995: 167)

Another description that conveys the dynamics of this mediatory exercise is that: 'man's desire is the desire of the Other' (Lacan 1977: 264). Lacan's version of Hegel's depiction of desire includes a form of psychic and emotional self-consciousness (in relation to the other) that surpasses the simple gratification of organic satisfaction. It borrows from Kojève's amendment of the Hegelian concept of recognition as self-affirmation: 'Thus, in the relationship between a man and a woman, for example, Desire is human only if the one desires, not the body, but the Desire of the other; if he wants "to possess" or "to assimilate" the Desire taken as Desire — that is to say, if he wants to be "desired or loved", or, rather, "recognized" in his human value, in his reality as a human individual' (Kojève 1969: 6).[14] In a nutshell, the development of identity depends on the manipulation of the other person to serve the purposes of the individual controlling the process. This script will have its own peculiar twist when it concerns women.

The Phallic prerogative

Lacan's ingenious denouement of this transaction depends on his controversial designation of the phallus as the key cipher in the workings of desire. While in his early works, collected in *Ecrits* (1977), Lacan kept the penis and the phallus separate, there is more of a convergence in his later work. As Kaja Silverman observes: 'while the phallus may might not be a literal penis, there is nonetheless an intimate relationship between the two' (1992: 89). The precedence accorded to the phallus is referred to latterly by Lacan as the paternal Law or the 'Name of the Father'. The unfortunate problem is that, for both Freud and Lacan, what women lack, and therefore desire, is to have this penis/phallus. For Lacan, the phallus functions within a male libidinal economy as a privileged signifier of both an anatomical and a symbolic integrity, according to which women are deemed as deficient. This results from the fact that, as Elizabeth Grosz notes, the phallus functions both as 'the crucial signifier in the distribution of power' and as 'the signifier of lack marking castration'. She then continues: 'As such, it also signifies presence or possession, for only in opposition to the absence of the term does its presence have any meaning or value. It thus signifies that what men (think they) *have* and what women (are considered) to *lack*' (1990: 125). It is from this 'phallocentric' perspective that women are doomed to desire the phallus. For if the phallus indicates the object of the various registers of lack – need, demand and desire – as they operate in a male-centred system, the phallus cannot but have an insidious relation to the penis. This relationship of the phallus to the penis, however, is a highly contested one.

Kaja Silverman has remarked that 'The Lacanian phallus depends for its libidinal centrality upon the anatomical distinction between the sexes, and it cannot, consequently, be rigorously be distinguished from the penis' (1992: 96). In defence of Lacan, however, Ellie Ragland-Sullivan claims that within the signifying system inaugurated by the oedipal resolution, 'the differences acquired/assigned are simply cultural conventions … his [Lacan's] signifier only symbolizes the learning of difference as an effect which posits a materiality in language which differentiates the word qua meaning from the word as the sense of its meaning(s)' (Ragland-Sullivan 1991: 55). Elizabeth Grosz, however, counters that 'Contrary to Mitchell, Ragland-Sullivan and others, I will claim that the phallic signifier is not a neutral "third" term against which both sexes are analogously or symmetrically positioned. The relation between the penis and the phallus is not arbitrary, but socially and politically motivated (Grosz 1990: 124). She continues: 'The two sexes come to occupy the positive and negative positions not for arbitrary reasons, or with arbitrary effects. It is motivated by the already existing structure of patriarchal power, and its effects guarantee the reproduction of this particular form of social organization and no other' (124). Silverman concludes her article with the judgement that these present gender arrangements need not necessarily continue: 'No social or psychic imperative dictates that the symbolic Law be synonymous with the Name-of-the-Father; that the phallus stand in for the subject's "very life"; or that castration be represented only by certain members of the socius. The only immutable law of desire is the one which denies to each of us the possibility of wholeness and self presence – the Law, that is, of Language' (1992: 114). Irigaray will, none the less, take issue with what she views as Lacan's inequitable designation of female lack.

Irigaray does not accept either women's relegation to a state of privation or the proposed solution to her phallic lack – a child (preferably male). She proposes an alternative procedure to that of phallic desire: 'This does not mean, however, that women's desire for herself, for the self-same – a female self, a female same is not to [be] recognized. [It does not mean that] a possible economy is not to be found or refound. [It does not mean] that this [female] desire is not necessary to balance the desire of the other' (1985a: 102; translation emended). Irigaray insists that the type of phallic economy that substitutes language, particularly the *logos* of the father/God, for the maternal body and her desire, can be changed. She not only seeks to introduce a type of corporeal language that would reflect women's desire, but one that would also disrupt the paternal law. This will lead, in turn, to further attempts to overthrow a system built on 'thoughts on divine truth that are available to man only when he has left *behind* everything that still linked him to this sensible world that the earth, the mother, represents' (1985a: 339).¹⁵ Irigaray conveys the need for women to deconstruct the male model of o/Otherness so as to be able to express their desires to counter the imposed masquerade of femininity. She also encourages women to imagine a divine figure in their own image and resist those that have been associated with their exclusion and the repression. To this end, Irigaray begins to put her mimetic twin play of deconstruction and creative construction to work. By deconstructive mimicry, Irigaray understands that one adopts the female role deliberately. She continues: 'To play with mimesis is thus, for a woman, to try to recover the place of her exploitation by discourse, without allowing herself simply to be reduced to it' (1985b: 76). In this deconstructive tactic, Irigaray is indebted to Derrida's strategy of repetition in the service of destabilising accepted meanings.¹⁶

Desire, *jouissance* and the god of excess

> Woman certainly does not know everything (about herself), she doesn't know (herself to be) anything, in fact. But her relationship to (self) knowledge provides access to a whole of what might be known or of what she might know – that is to God. (Irigaray 1985a: 231)

In the development of her work, Irigaray will expand her range of responses by employing diverse tactics. Firstly, she attempts to subvert the seemingly divinely sanctioned law of the Father. In this connection, in both *Speculum* and *This Sex*

Which Is Not One, she explores the forbidden territory of *jouissance*. This is Lacan's term for the excessive, superabundant expression of feminine pleasure, irreducible to phallic constraints (Lacan in Mitchell 1983: 145–6). For Irigaray, it refers to the myriad forms of pleasure a woman's sensuously responsive body can experience – it is not confined to a dominant sexual organ. The word 'jouissance' thus has positive connotations in that Irigaray does not restrict it simply to acts of genital sexual pleasure. As Irigaray observes: 'The whole of my body is sexuate [sexed]. My sexuality isn't restricted to my sex [sexual organs] and to the sexual act in the narrow sense' (1993c: 53). *Jouissance* is also associated with an inaccessible domain termed the Real – the unconscious in its inassimilable and uncoordinated dimensions. Elizabeth Grosz describes the Real accordingly: 'The child ... is born into the order of the Real. The Real is the order preceding the ego and the organization of the drives. It is an anatomical, "natural" order ... a pure plenitude or fullness. The Real cannot be experienced as such: it is capable of representation or conceptualization only through the reconstructive or inferential work of the imaginary or symbolic orders' (1990: 34). The Real is thus prior to the registers of the imaginary and symbolic. It also denotes domain of the alleged inarticulate pleasure of female sexuality that Irigaray will exploit. Exploring the resonances of *jouissance*, Irigaray speculates about another modality, that of 'God' – who, according to Lacan, is also not circumscribed by a phallic categorization. She suggests that there might be some form of concord, but not identification, between women and a God in this area of the Real.

Even though Irigaray will herself refer in a comparably circumspect fashion to this entity of 'God' as a 'radically autarchic unit', she does not subscribe to Lacan's scepticism. Instead, as a retaliatory device, Irigaray deliberately adopts the role of the female mystic/hysteric whom Lacan – in a condescending reference to Teresa of Avila – imputes as experiencing, but not being able to enunciate, the delights of the uninhibited erogenous zones of *jouissance*.[17] Irigaray's essay 'La Mystérique' in *Speculum* is at once a vindication of female mysticism and a prototype of the only rejoinder possible for women as long as a phallic system, which idolises the male, prevails. Her strategy is thus a concerted attempt to deflate this masculine conceit. Her approach contests not merely a generalised masculine Godlike superiority but especially the intellectual arrogance assumed by Lacan in his facile deflation of women's insight into the mystic state and her affinity with the Real.

In depicting a female mystic as a hysteric figure, Irigaray recognises her not as sexually repressed but as voicing a protest, basically through her body, against societal and religious restrictions. Elizabeth Grosz describes the hysteric: 'Hers is a mode of defiance of patriarchy, not the site of its frustration. In this sense, the hysteric is a proto-feminist, or at least an isolated individual who, if she had access to the experiences of other women, may locate the problem in cultural expectations of femininity rather than in femininity itself. The hysterics' defiance through excess, through *overcompliance*, is a parody of the expected' (1989: 135). Irigaray's mimetic strategy in much of *Speculum* is that of a hysteric in the interests of calculated subversion.[18] Again, Grosz elaborates:

> Irigaray does not naively advocate hysteria as a strategy for *women in general*. Rather, in her own *rereading of philosophy*, Irigaray herself acts as the hysteric. Her strategies are mimetic, not of organic disorders, but of philosophical and psychoanalytical texts. She imitates/ parodies women's hysterical positions in discourse. Rather than act as a mimic – the mime reproduces behaviour marked by its *difference* from behaviour (this is what distinguishes the mimic from what he or she mimes), its excessiveness over it, Irigaray mimics the hysteric's mimicry. She mimes mime itself. (136)

As a further corrective to the Name of the Father – both Christian and Lacanian – Irigaray then introduces an experiment whereby woman, as the deficient other, 'speaks' back. She finds her voice in exclusive territory, beyond the formulas of the imaginary and the symbolic. Initially women begin to explore prohibited desires – the erased pleasure of female sexuality. This is the extravagant desire of *jouissance* that meets God in a prohibited zone.

In 'La Mystérique', a mystic female, who is a composite from the writings or lives of different medieval women, is indeed exorbitant in her spiritual invocations.[19] Images of dark, shadows, fire – reflections from the Platonic cave or womb where she remains enshrouded – become the figures of a transgressive passage to an illuminative physical passion that confounds customary channels for knowing God. Beyond her standard task of being a mirror to the self-referential eye of men, an incandescent encounter awaits the eye of soul of a woman. A mutual illumination occurs, in which both God and woman in their absence or presence reaffirm the other in their fullness/nothingness. The extravagant paradoxes of negative theology are played to their extreme: 'Thus I have become your image in this nothingness that I am, and you gaze upon mine in your absence of being ... a living mirror, thus, am I (to) your resemblance as you are mine' (Irigaray 1985a: 197).

For Irigaray, this synthetic figure of a mystic, in her ecstasy, flaunts the contradictions of her condition, the abasement that is transfiguring, the lack that is fullness, the dark night that is illuminative. Her *jouissance* is at once perverse and exquisite, an exaltation of the limitless possibilities of an otherness that defies/ celebrates its escape from conscious calculations and metaphysical impositions. As Irigaray continues to eulogise women's eccentricity, she develops her infamous motif of the 'two lips' of women's sexuality as emblematic of this situation. These lips are sexual in their connotation – intimating a space of communication with God, a God who shares a similar field of extraneous forces, beyond the pale of language.

> [God] in his absolute fluidity; plasticity to all metamorphoses; simultaneous ubiquity, and invisibility, epitomises that sex which is nothing-at-all. He has not ceased to heed women, though silently, in their most secret, covered places. God knows women so well that he

never touches them directly, but always in that fleeting stealth of a fantasy that evades all representation: between two unities who thus imperceptibly take pleasure in each other. (1985a: 236; translation emended)

It is these dual lips, contiguous rather than oppositional, that defy traditional metaphysical binaries and are Irigaray's repartee to Lacan's negative designation of women as 'not-all'. They are both all and nothing, irreducible to binary logic. These lips have been variously characterised as genital, vulval, carnal, erotic. They have also landed Irigaray in controversy. She has been charged not just with essentialism but with reifying these lips to serve as a substitute or counter symbol for the ubiquitous phallus. In this early period in her work, Irigaray does not make any distinction between what, at this phase in Anglo-American feminist discussions, was referred to as the sex (biological) and gender (cultural) distinction. Irigaray's use of the term 'feminine' is a free-floating signifier. In one sense, she is trying to dismantle the established male-designated associations of the 'feminine' with biological sex. But her evocations of a counter 'feminine imaginary' (1985b: 28–33) raised suspicions of essentialism. Toril Moi's criticism from this period encapsulates this perceived offence. 'Her superb critique of patriarchal thought is partly undercut by her attempt to *name* the feminine. If, as I have previously argued, all efforts towards a definition of "woman" are destined to be essentialist, it looks as if feminist theory might thrive better if it abandoned the minefield of femininity and femaleness for a while and approached the questions of oppression and emancipation from a different direction' (1985: 148).

It is supporters such as Rosi Braidotti and Elizabeth Grosz who come to Irigaray's aid. Braidotti argues that there is no attempt (as yet) to name the feminine, rather there is an evocation of the unlimited possibilities that a woman might become. Braidotti contrasts Irigaray's work with that of Mary Daly on this point. 'It has nothing to do with a female counter-theory, reminiscent of Daly's gynocentrism, which would only be the reverse of phallocentrism; in other words fluidity, multiplicity, and so on, are not the components of a new feminine essence' (Braidotti 1991: 262).[20] Irigaray was mystified by these charges, because in her view, women had never had any input about their identity, and her intention was simply to clear a space for innovative explorations. Other defenders, such as Kathryn Bond Stockton, celebrate this immoderate move, applauding its audaciousness as perhaps the most appropriate retaliation (and deflation) of phallic pretensions. 'I want to read Irigaray against the grain of Irigaray criticism by emphasizing Irigaray's *embrace* of lack as what makes her able to convert castration into (auto) eroticism. This Irigaray – "feminist theologian of lack," as I will call her – is early Irigaray, the feminist who tangles with Freud and Lacan' (1994: 26).

The problem is, however, that even if Irigaray uses her ingenuity solely to manipulate the lacuna in the biological and structural reductions of Freud and Lacan, she could still be charged with limiting the potentialities of women to mystic interludes. Women are consigned to an ethereal assignation with a God who is encountered only in the transports of sexual abandon. While conspiratorial and indeed pleasurable, it serves only as an escape mechanism, or a consolation, but has no recourse to remedial measures to restructure society. Bond Stockton none the less vindicates such measures: 'Irigaray's uniqueness lies, if anywhere, in the explicitness with which she spiritualizes – not simply poeticizes – the bodies she would grasp. These pointedly mystical moves, which effectively locate lack and God between "women's" genital lips (no small moves, there), make possible her bold belief in women's bodies that escape the dominant constructions that would suture them' (13).

While this is indeed a positive reading of the early Irigaray in so far as she exploits women's lack, I don't think it fully captures her versatility. For Irigaray is also indicating with the emblem of two lips another facet of her work that does not want simply to react to the exclusions of male theory – however conducive to *jouissance* they may be. For Irigaray also wants, by using the play of mimesis in a productive mode, to deploy the two lips as an emblem for women's alternative constructive capabilities. Irigaray will herself admit that women's self-representation cannot remain sequestered in private mystical trysts, if it is to redress the imbalance that has, until now, distorted both human and divine relationships 'To remain within the limit of the senses in one's suffering or one's jouissance – both of them imaginary – is not the same as acceding to the creation of imagination' (1993b: 161–2). For this purpose, the 'not-all' of Lacan with its inferences of lack becomes the 'not-one' of the 'two lips' for Irigaray – a new arrangement that defies sameness, with its regenerative and unlimited abilities of metamorphosis (1985a: 233). Irigaray will develop this strategy further within a metaphysics of 'becoming', in contrast to the fixed concept of Being or God that has been the mainstay of traditional metaphysics or theology.[21]

Woman is neither open nor closed. She is indefinite, in-finite, *form is never complete in her*. She is not infinite but neither is she *a* unit(y), such as letter, number, figure in a series, proper noun, unique object (in a) world of the senses, simply ideality in an intelligible whole, entity of a foundation, etc. This incompleteness in her form, her morphology, allows her continually to become something else. (1985a: 229)

Irigaray's conception of a women's morphology is one that refuses to identify women's bodies simply with the biological. As Elizabeth Grosz notes: '[Irigaray] sees them [women's bodies] as the bearers of meanings and social values.... Her emphasis on morphology in place of anatomy indicates she has stepped from the register of nature to that of social signification' (1989: 112). For Irigaray, women's manifold, even infinite (in the sense of indeterminable) possibilities are not just of a sexual nature. Irigaray asserts that, thus far, she has not been concerned with producing a logic of the 'feminine', or a substitute female subject/object (1985b: 78). Her work in *Speculum* and *This Sex Which Is Not One* has rather been an exploration of women's non-linear, not absolutist, 'not-one' modes of subjectivity. As she elaborates: 'Our horizon will never stop expanding; we are always open. Stretching out, never ceasing to unfold ourselves, we have so many voices to invent in order to express all of us everywhere, even in our gaps, that all the time there will not be enough. We can never complete the circuit, explore our periphery: we have so many dimensions' (1985b: 21).

It is in *Sexes and Genealogies* (1993b) that Irigaray moves into a specifically constructive mode. This change is crystallised in the essay, 'Divine Women' (1993b: 57–72). It marks her first attempt to formulate a version of a feminine divine or other. Irigaray's principal undertaking is to indicate women's difference or otherness in a positive way – disputing the misrepresentations of Christianity and of the Freudian-Lacanian psychoanalytic coalition. 'We women, sexed according to our gender, lack a God to share and to become. Defined as the often dark, even occult mother-substance of the world of men, we are in need of our *subject*, our *substantive*, our *word*, our *predicates*: our elementary sentence, our basic rhythm, our morphological identity, our generic incarnation, our genealogy' (1993b: 71).

Irigaray identifies the task at hand as not only one of 'destroying the master' (1993b: 68) but also of conceiving an alternative mode of the divine to the patriarchal deity. This is not a simplistic undertaking of reinstalling goddess figures of the past (1993b: 81). In distinct contrast to such facile literalism, Irigaray is well aware that the creative project of portraying the otherness of women is a manifold one. It will have reverberations that are revolutionary in their psychic, emotional, political, ethical, philosophical and theological effects. Irigaray acknowledges that these diversifications will initiate radical reformations of the way that otherness or difference will be construed, particularly in three areas. These are: (1) a notion of a divine/other along feminine lines; (2) mother/daughter relationships (genealogy) that are divine; and (3) an innovative ethical standard of loving interaction with (an)other human being that also has the status of divine. In this chapter I will be concerned with the first of these three topics. The other topics will be discussed in the following chapters.

Imaginative possibilities

Irigaray's complex interweaving of these ideas converges round the notion of otherness that is to be rescued from a fixated ideal or predetermined object. God can no longer continue to be located on high as a remote, authoritarian figure. God must figure as an integral part of the mode of 'becoming' as a mode of human existence, in contrast to the former static metaphysical categories of God or Being. 'Why do we assume that God must always remain inaccessible transcendence rather than a realization – here and now – in and through the body?' (1993a: 148). Thus, the figure of the divine that Irigaray seeks to express will be an incarnate one. In her explorations of this topic which begin in 'Divine Women' (1993b), Irigaray will insist not only on a more positive form of female identity but on a new form of relationship to her own otherness. This is because women have not had a positive relationship to an other of her own. 'Woman scatters and becomes an agent of destruction and annihilation because she has no other of her own that she can become' (64). In this movement, otherness begins to take on aspects for women that are distinct from primarily repressed masculine or negative sublated forms. God will emerge for women: 'As an other that we have yet to make actual, as a region of life, strength, imagination, creation which exists for us both within and beyond, as our possibility of a present and a future' (72). In her evocation of a feminine divine, it is patently obvious that Irigaray's intention is to avoid both the intransigent transcendence of Christianity and the psychoanalytic orthodoxies described by Lacan. This is even more clear when Irigaray, in a paradoxical way, refers to women's divine other as 'their Other without capital letters' (Irigaray 1993b: 115). This evocation of a 'feminine' divine will thus introduce, instead of the permeable 'two lips', more explicit designations of qualities appropriate for women.

By way of introducing a 'feminine' divine other, Irigaray makes some deliberate definitional moves. She will clarify her use of the terms 'sex' and 'gender' and their relation to her use of the imagination. The French words *le sexe* and *le genre* are extremely problematic to translate. *Le sexe* has a specific reference not just to biological sexuality but to the male and female sexual organs. *Le genre* refers to the human race as well as to grammatical gender. Irigaray has thus far been extremely circumspect in her use of *le sexe*, making sure that it is not simply associated with genitality. In a rare footnote in *Sexes and Genealogies*, Irigaray now consolidates her usage of these two terms. She states 'The word *sex* is used in regard to male and female persons and not only to male and female genital organs' (1993b: 128). Previously, in relation to the emblem of 'two lips', Irigaray had also specified that: 'the/a woman who doesn't have one sex organ, or a unified sexuality ... cannot subsume it/herself under one generic or specific term [i.e., male gender]' (1985a: 233). In connection with the biological sex, Irigaray expands on her notion of a new morphology for women beyond the maternal: 'The issue is to to learn to discover a different kind of magnetism and the morphology of a sexualized body' (1993b: 180). This is because Irigaray appreciates that 'Women do not obey the same sexual economy as men' (200). It is in connecting this understanding of sex with the term 'gender', however, that Irigaray will effect her most significant development. Given her analysis of women's subjugation in terms of the French language, it is no surprise that Irigaray claims: 'Gender is confused with species. Gender becomes the human race, human nature, etc. as defined from within patriarchal culture. Gender thus corresponds to a race of men who refuse, whether consciously or not, the possibility of another gender: the female' (1993b: 3). As a result, Irigaray supports an emergent female gender in both language and life, but, given centuries of suppression, it is not immediately clear, after her move beyond *jouissance*, how it is to be represented.

Irigaray presents her case in a number of essays in *Sexes and Genealogies*. She refers to gender as an 'index and mark of the subjectivity and the ethical responsibility of the speaker' and says that it 'constitutes the irreducible differentiation that occurs *on the inside of the human race*' (169–70). This appears to imply that, as a result of sexual differentiation, there are specifically gendered tasks and traits for women only, in the sense that there is a distinct 'female gender' (120). Thus, when Irigaray begins to describe the gendered ideals that are to represent the divine for women, it becomes apparent that she is now proposing specific values that she regards as appropriate for women. The total picture of this development emerges only slowly, as there is no organised argument. There is, instead, a subtle change, as Irigaray ceases to describe the way the 'masculine' symbolic has functioned, and proposes a new 'feminine' modality will alter the way the world is ordered. (When Irigaray begins to ascribe certain qualities to actual women, there now begins a constant slippage in her ideas between women, the female gender and 'feminine' attributes. My own use of the term 'feminine' is designed both to keep conceptual clarity and to indicate my understanding of the constructed nature of these qualities.)

In presenting this new direction, Irigaray first asks: 'This God, are we capable of imagining it as a woman?' (63). While such an enquiry could be taken to indicate that Irigaray is simply seeking to establish an alternative possibilities for a divine female figure, she then qualifies this implication by posing further rhetorical questions: 'How is our God to be imagined? Or is it a god? Do we possess a quality that can reverse the predicate to the subject as Feuerbach does for *God* and *man* in the analysis of the *Essence of Christianity?*' (67). Such a statement marks a definite change in Irigaray's use the term 'imagination'. Whereas Irigaray has described her task in *Speculum* as one of rediscovering 'a possible space for the female imaginary' (1985b: 164), she now moves beyond this limited Lacanian viewpoint. Irigaray conceives of the need for a creative imagination, which opens up a future, rather than staying within the constraints of the Lacanian imaginary. 'The work of analysis destroys, deconstructs, and allows no room for resynthesis [sic]. Synthesis can come only out of the *imagination*, not the faculty of analyzing.... Furthermore, the knowledge we gain from analysis is probably man's weakest resource if it is cut off, on the one hand, from a receptive affect or sensoriness, and, on the other, from the imagination as a synthetic faculty' (1993b: 162-3). Irigaray's dual position is reflected in her appeal to an intervention of the imagination that, together with perception, is sexed: 'That which is sexed is linked to perception, to its specific imaginary creation as well as regeneration, procreation, and more generally, life' (163).

I agree with Margaret Whitford in her book entitled *Luce Irigaray: Philosophy in the Feminine* (Whitford 1991) when she remarks that, though Irigaray restricts herself in *This Sex Which Is Not One* to Lacan's postulate of the *imaginary*, in order to undertake a mimetic subversion of the psychoanalytically framed symbolic, she later construes the term to fit her own designs. In *Sexes and Genealogies* (1993b), and in her later work, however, Irigaray indulges in experimental permutations of a purely imaginative nature that I consider to be work of a mythopoetic nature. This is in keeping with Irigaray's recognition that, unless a mode of a female divine can be imagined, women will not be able to affirm their own identity in a way that liberates them from their previous symbolic confinement.[22] Whitford detects elements of the thought of Jean-Paul Sartre, Gaston Bachelard, Cornelius Castoriadis, Louis Althusser and Maurice Merleau-Ponty in the composite model of imagination that informs Irigaray's work. (Unfortunately, because of Irigaray's reluctance to employ footnotes, it is extremely difficult to document such sources with any accuracy.) Whitford then continues by remarking: 'Whenever we find the term "imaginary" in Irigaray's work, then, we have not only to look for the network of associations within her work that give the term its meaning, but also to bear in mind the network of associations circulating in the intellectual context within which she is writing and being read' (Whitford 1991: 56). This is sound advice. Perhaps of all these scholars, it is Merleau-Ponty who has had the greatest influence on Irigaray.[23] Similarly to Irigaray, Merleau-Ponty questioned traditional dualism and sought to recast philosophy. Irigaray is in agreement with him on this matter: 'We must go back to a moment of prediscursive experience, recommence everything, all the categories by which we understand things, the world, subject–object divisions, recommence everything and pause at the "mystery ... which ... remains at its source in obscurity"' (1993a: 151).

Imagination was central to Merleau-Ponty's depiction of perception. He allowed that it enables one to move from the visible to the invisible, from the real to the virtual. As such, it underlies Merleau-Ponty's phenomenological procedure in *The Visible and the Invisible* (1968), which, similarly to Irigaray's, rejects both Cartesian dualism and Husserl's transcendental idealism. In his attempt to be faithful to lived experience, Merleau-Ponty also modified Heidegger's notion of *Dasein*, because he believed that it did not succeed in incorporating the world of the senses. Merleau-Ponty strove to portray the intimate interaction of two previously irreconcilable terms, the immanent and the transcendent, by his appeal to the word 'flesh'. This charged term did not simply refer to corporeality but to the expressiveness of all sensibility in contact with the world, inchoate in its ability to articulate an intertwining that is, at once, vast and intricate. Such ideas will become of profound importance to Irigaray in developing her own philosophical position, especially her similar construct of the 'sensible transcendental'. (This topic will be treated in the following chapter.) In adapting Merleau-Ponty's ideas, however, Irigaray will find him lacking on two interrelated counts. These amount to a charge that he is gender-blind. First, Irigaray will find concealed in Merleau-Ponty's lush evocations of fleshly embodiment, with its mysterious source that escapes exact definition, a womb-like plenitude. For Irigaray, this is the repressed mother with her fleshly substance that subtends all existence (1993a: 159) – the unacknowledged mother that haunts all men's philosophic undertakings, even in their efforts to redeem her. Irigaray chides Merleau-Ponty: 'He tries to establish a *continuum*, a duration, between the most passive and the most active. But he cannot manage it. Especially without the memory of that first event where he is enveloped-touched by a tangible invisible of which his eyes are also formed, but which he will never see: neither visible nor visibility in that place' (154).[24]

At the same time, Irigaray ponders Merleau-Ponty's reluctance to see beyond himself. She finds his work marked by a solipsism as he examines phenomenologically the situation of one who cannot be conscious of both touching and being touched at the same time. She questions the ontological status of the other person, of the one who is touching him (157). All too often this other is a woman – not necessarily erased like the mother, but ignored in men's self-referential reflections on reality. From Irigaray's perspective, both of these omissions have to be repaired if women are to take their proper place in the world.

Irigaray investigates different aspects of imaginative (re-)productions that would encourage women's participation. Her first inquiry concerns the viability of reappropriating divine projections in the manner of Feuerbach. Irigaray's argument appears to be that women have never had a divine ideal of their own, which has prevented them from fulfilling their potential – 'the wholeness of what we are capable of being' (1993b: 61). Her ideas are in keeping with Feuerbach's when she advocates that any divine portrayals need to be reclaimed by humanity in a concrete and practical manner, rather than simply idolised. Yet, in one sense, if a female divine is simply a projection (albeit a positive and conscious one), it cannot but appear to be a female equivalent of male self-idealisations. It now appears as if Irigaray first deconstructs male transcendence, only to supplant it with a female version. Women scholars in religion, such as Serene Jones (1995) and Amy Hollywood (2002), are critical of Irigaray's employment of Feuerbach, specifically her unproblematised adaptation of his notion of projection. Amy Hollywood describes the problem: 'If Irigaray's argument for the destruction of hierarchy and the creation of new divinities seem paradoxical, or at least circular, it is because she insists that before they can be destroyed "it is necessary that God or the gods exist" [Irigaray 1993b: 62]. This claim leaves us with the apparently paradoxical task of both positing and deconstructing a feminine divine' (Hollywood 2002: 213). Serene Jones is also concerned that Irigaray is simply following in the steps of the fathers who constructed a god in their own image: 'Although her new god may be clothed in the garments of female desire, this God still occupies the space of an empty sign, a blank screen of transcendence who can finally author nothing but the same. And when woman meets this God, she is really only meeting herself' (Jones 1995: 65). It does indeed seem that, if Irigaray were to remain within this interpretation of Feuerbach, her imaginative variations would not hold much weight, but I think her infinite designs are leading her in other directions.

There is a distinct possibility that Irigaray may not even be interested in positing an actual divine figure that is in need of deconstruction. She appears at times to be seeking a way to express how the divine can to be realised in the world, without mediations. This becomes apparent when Irigaray specifies that, by 'divine women', she intends that women should achieve the 'perfection of their subjectivity' (1993b: 63). It is as if, at the one and same time, Irigaray is proposing an imagined sex-specific mode of existence, where the practical achievement of this ideal is itself a divine process – a 'becoming divine'. Irigaray's model of 'becoming' is in sharp contrast to the stasis of Being. Thus, instead of a regression to goddesses who fight against male gods in quest of the supreme divinity, Irigaray begins to formulate certain cultural and ethical practices as appropriate for women only. In an enigmatic phrase, Irigaray introduces one feature of these recommended procedures – a 'return to the cosmic' (60).

As Irigaray depicts the task of becoming divine women within this cosmic perspective, it will require a marked change of disposition and conduct. 'We climb toward God and remain in Him, without killing the mother earth where our roots lie, without denying the sky either. Rooted in the earth, fed by rain and spring waters, we grow and flourish in the air, thanks to the light from the sky, the warmth of the sun' (69). This connection to nature would seem to be in contrast to the disembodied ideal of a transcendent understanding of God. Irigaray acknowledges the alteration in her approach: 'I was anxious to go back to those natural matters that constitute the origin of our bodies, of our life, of our environment, the flesh of our passions. I was obeying a deep, dark, and necessary intuition, dark even when it is shared by other thoughts' (57). Irigaray does not, however, develop the implications of this intuition in any detailed way in the essay 'Divine Women'. While she does refer to certain values 'of our own' (72), apart from the phrase 'return to the cosmic', in the concluding section of 'Divine Women', she does not as yet specify a comprehensive vision. To become 'God for ourselves' (71), thus does not involve any form of apotheosis. Instead, it is concerned with a way of living that is in connection with the basic elements of life. Irigaray envisages that this return will help effect a new modality of the divine and at the same time introduce 'a new chapter in history.... Still to be discovered? To be incarnated? Archi-ancient and forever' (72).

In the light of this evolution in Irigaray's thought, the question arises as to what form of belief, if any, remains operative in this process. In the essay 'Belief Itself' (1993b: 23–54) – which precedes 'Divine Women' in *Sexes and Genealogies* – Irigaray strives to avoid traditional formulas of belief as well as dogmatic proclamations of a remote deity. She allows that, for those who abandon such obstacles, a new life is possible where belief is replaced by a relationship of trust and openness 'which gives flesh to speech: air, breath, song' (52). Central to this new orientation of trust is a connection with the repressed 'maternal elemental substrate' (46), which has obvious affinities with 'the return to the cosmic'. In the place of traditional faith, Irigaray is thus encouraging a practice of trust in oneself and in one's ownmost possibilities, which now have an intimate relation to the natural world. This move is in keeping with Irigaray's belief that women should be able to find herself in 'the images of herself already deposited in history' (1993a: 10). Yet, there is no clear indication in 'Belief Itself' or 'Divine Women' as to how exactly this is to be achieved. For this reason, I agree with Amy Hollywood and her concern about the ambiguous status of belief and its relationship to Irigaray's understanding of the divine at this juncture in her work. Hollywood remarks: 'Irigaray does not articulate clearly the mechanism by which religious ideals emerge and by which they might be appropriated as one's own' (2002: 229).[25]

Mythopoetic divinations

Though absent in 'Divine Women' and 'Belief Itself', there are further indications of what is entailed in the imaginative reclamation of elemental values by women in other essays in *Sexes and Genealogies*. In this second phase of her work, Irigaray becomes fascinated with a purported gynocratic community that predated patriarchy. She begins to develop these insights in 'Body against Body: In Relation to the Mother' (1993b: 9–21). Here Irigaray harkens back to the Freud of *Totem and Taboo* and his own mythic rendering of an original patricide. She faults Freud for the 'forgetting of an even more ancient murder, that of the woman-mother' (11). In support of the fact that our imaginary is still held in thrall by this matricidal schema, Irigaray cites Clytemnestra's murder in the *Oresteia* (1993b: 11). 'Orestes kills his mother because the empire of the God-Father, who has seized and taken for his own the ancient powers (*puissances*) of the earth-mother, demands it.... Electra, the daughter, will remain mad. The matricidal son, on the other hand, must be saved from madness so that he can found the patriarchal order' (12–13). For Irigaray, the fate of Clytemnestra in the *Oresteia* represents, in the Greek tradition, one of the founding myths of patriarchal society and the eradication of an earlier gynocracy.

This interest in gynocracy also indicates an alteration in the focus of Irigaray's attention. In 'The Universal as Mediation' (1993b: 125–49), Irigaray emphasises a version of mythic beginnings that differs from Freud's. 'Our societies began as gynocracies. Primary to our cultures is a female religious power linked to the cult of Aphrodite' (129).[26] Irigaray then describes the attributes that were associated with this era: 'In the rule of Aphrodite the earth's fruitfulness remains spontaneous, linked to water, dampness [and] valued for its flowering' (129). This mythic scenario is further elaborated in *Thinking the Difference* (1994). 'Aphrodite thus holds a very special place between nature, gods and human manifestation. She represents the embodiment of love ... but still close to the cosmos ... In Greek, Aphrodite's specific attribute is that of *philotes*: tenderness. It therefore is not a matter of agape without eros, both of the two combined in a love that is both carnal and spiritual' (1994: 94). In another essay in *Sexes and Genealogies*, 'Women the Sacred and Money' (1993b: 73–88), Irigaray refers to other goddesses, such as Gaia, Kore, Persephone, Diana, and asks: 'How can we affirm together those elementary values, those natural kinds of fruitfulness, celebrate them, keep them, preserve them, make currency of them while becoming or remaining women?' (81).[27] Then, in the final essay in *Sexes and Genealogies*, 'A Chance for Life' (185–206), Irigaray definitely identifies this gynocratic mythological period as a time of love, peace and tenderness, where there was respect for the body and nature in communion with the divine. It is a somewhat perplexing move in that, in her imaginative reclamation of a founding 'feminine' mythology, Irigaray seems to embrace literally the attributes she has assigned to the goddesses.

In her descriptions of gynocracy and its successive Aphroditean and Demetrian stages, Irigaray has been heavily influenced by the work of J. J. Bachofen (1815–87), a controversial nineteenth-century scholar of the romantic school. Bachofen wrote *Das Mutterrecht* (1861), selections of which appeared in English as *Myth, Religion and Mother Right* (1976). In this work, Bachofen postulates a primordial gynocracy that was inevitably surpassed by patriarchal ideals and structures. Irigaray does cite other Greek texts, such as Hesiod and the *Homeric Hymns*, in connection with her interpretation of Aphrodite as 'the embodiment of love becoming human freedom and desire ... the spirit made flesh' (1994: 95). Nevertheless, her placement of the two succeeding gynocratic stages of Aphrodite and Demeter are indebted to Bachofen, though her own characterisations of the goddesses differ at times from his.[28] Irigaray's uncritical adoption of such a discredited authority is somewhat puzzling, given her previous trenchant condemnation of patriarchal texts, of which, ironically, Bachofen's work would be a prime example.

Feminist archaeologists Margaret Conkey and Ruth Tringham have assessed Bachofen's claims and are troubled by his unilinear evolutionary model. They worry that such a model cannot account for the diversity of human development. At the same time, they believe that much of the contemporary goddess-centred appropriation involves a projection backwards of twentieth-century sex and gender issues (1995: 215). Mary Lefkowitz, a classical scholar who has written on women in Greek mythology (including Aphrodite and Demeter), is also critical of Bachofen. She observes that there is a need to return critically to the source material that he cites only partially, and to also consider other documentation that both Bachofen and his modern followers omit (1986: 28). While Irigaray does seek to redress elements of Bachofen's version, by questioning the reason for the mandatory triumph of patriarchy over a primordial matriarchy, she does not interrogate the basic structure of his idealised mythological structure, or his omissions and distortions of the original material.

One reason for this is that Irigaray is sympathetic to Bachofen's overly romantic perspective, which appreciates mythology as the most authentic representation of the past (see Bachofen 1967: 75–7). Irigaray echoes his sentiments: 'For myth is not a story independent of History, but rather expresses History in colourful accounts that illustrate the major trends of an era' (1994: 101). Stella Georgoudi regards such an understanding of myth as constituting its own form of myth-making: 'Bachofen and his followers clearly saw this legendary "reality". Their error was to take the Greeks at their word, to mistake myth for history. In so doing, they created a myth of their own, itself a worthy object of study: the myth of the matriarchy' (1992: 463). The adoption of this self-serving view of myth becomes somewhat disturbing when Irigaray further confirms: 'History as expressed in myth is more closely related to female, matrilineal traditions' (1994: 101). Such an assertion is extremely problematic in that it indicates mythology as a specifically 'feminine' way of depicting the world, as distinct from actual history, which is depicted as the sole preserve of men. This attitude simply reinforces gender stereotyping. As Helene Foley remarks: 'A myth whose content may well be largely shaped by and responsive to a patriarchal context cannot be made to reveal a historically prior core imagined to be untouched by it; it is important to recognize the degree to which such "pre-Olympian" myth runs the risk of perpetuating the estrangement of women from the mainstream culture' (2001: 230). Judith Ochshorn, though she is undertaking a more comprehensive criticism of the historical claims regarding the actual existence of goddess-like attributes in a purported Golden Age, voices many of the reservations that could be applied to the prototype of gynocratic harmony and peace that Irigaray approves:

> Are we to believe that in this thousands-of-years era of co-operative, peaceful, egalitarian, artistic, one-with-nature living, no bad things ever happened? ... There was no dark side to human nature, none of the complex irrational forces, along with life-enhancing impulses and struggles we know as part of the ambiguity of being human? Can we make the claim that the rule of the Goddess, linked to the leadership of women in human societies ... was based on female preeminence both symbolically and in real life? Is there something inherently nurturant of life in women? In Goddesses? Valuable as nurturance is, do we come by it naturally or through socialization? ... Are all women alike, and will nurturance free us from male domination? (1997: 389)

These problems with Irigaray's use of myth demonstrate quite dramatically that, in this mythopoetic stage of her work, Irigaray seems to have left behind the extreme critical acuity with which she deconstructed the patriarchal precedents. There is no appreciation of the different theories by which myth can be studied, nor of the problematic history of the way mythic interpretation has been employed.[29] I do not wish to engage in the contentious argument as to whether or not there was ever a Golden Age of a matriarchal or gynocratic or matrilinear nature. The present polarization of the debate in terms of the truth claims of history versus myth seem at an impasse. This does not mean that I am against women imaginatively exploring alternative forms of religious or philosophical ways of being. From a religious perspective, it is only honest to admit that, whatever the actual foundational event, most religions have resorted to mythological embellishments in their histories and scriptures. Contemporary religions, including those of the goddess, are no different. What are deeply troubling, however, are uncritical claims to myth as a form of history that insists on promoting genuine 'feminine' values.[30] This leads to the advocacy of particular qualities and practices, derived from a selective reading of mythology, as being especially beneficial to women.

While Irigaray's aim is not the restitution of the goddesses themselves, her unqualified recommendation of ideals such as tenderness and love sound naive at best.[31] They are also troublesome in that they would curtail the infinite possibilities that she has previously proposed as integral to women's explorations of new identities. Whitford aptly describes what has happened: 'despite her disclaimer – women should not be attempting to construct a logic of the feminine – that is exactly what she has ended up doing' (1991: 96). Judith Poxon describes the situation in even stronger terms: 'I want to suggest, then, that even if Irigaray had succeeded in deconstructing the totalising transcendence of the father God of Christianity in her linking of divine transcendence with the bodies of women ... she has effectively foreclosed the possibility of women's infinite becoming, understood as the multiplying of actual differences among women, by re-enacting a dynamics of idealization as the ground of subjectification' (2003: 46).

Irigaray will link these gynocratic values with an alternative form of eastern spirituality which, in her more recent work *Between East and West* (2002), she claims as being intrinsically 'feminine'.[32] In the essays in *Sexes and Genealogies*, however, Irigaray provides only intimations of this later direction, but it is in this work in particular that a significant shift can be detected from her former patriarchal preoccupations to an elaboration of a gynocratic or divine mode of regeneration. There appears to be a marked inconsistency with her work in *Speculum* and *This Sex Which Is Not One*, where Irigaray used this emblem of 'two lips' to propose an 'infinite becoming' of women as the ground of a new 'feminine imaginary'. Her endorsement of finite gynocratic values, based on a presupposition that 'In the history of women religion is mixed up with a culture of the earth, the body, life, peace' (1993b: 190), marks a provocative change in the evolution of Irigaray's thought. It will provide the foundations for her promotion of 'sexual difference' which is of a different order from the plurality of the 'two lips'.

The conundrum of sexual difference

Irigaray declares that the western tradition, in its obsession with sameness, 'knows nothing of sexual difference, in the sense of the difference between men and women' (1993b: 45). If a definition of sexual difference is to be established, it must affirm, on Irigaray's account, a 'physiological and morphological complementarity between the sexes' (107). In her attempts to describe this sexual difference, Irigaray is initially preoccupied with the significance of a naturalised biological distinctiveness for women (108), as she does not want them to be remain neutralised by a dominant male gender. As a corollary of this, Irigaray is also vitally concerned with establishing a new mode of relationship between the two sexes. She is apprehensive that women will be unable to relate to the male gender, 'if we have no definition of [feminine] gender as gender' (123). Such a positing of sexual difference is well and good if, as Irigaray states, it is lived so as to encourage growth or fecundity of each person. Obviously, there are both biological and cultural components to be negotiated in this new pact. Women's task is to develop their own forms of morphology, rather than have them inscribed on their bodies:

> For women, the issue is to learn to discover and inhabit a different kind of magnetism and the morphology of a sexualized body, particularly of the mucus particularities and qualities of that body.... The issue for women is ... to discover gestures that have been forgotten, misunderstood, gestures that are also words, that are different from the gestures of maternity and shed a different light upon generation in the body, in the strict sense of the term. (180–1)[33]

As a result, cultural and social changes will be required to allow women to embody the 'fulfillment of her gender'.

What is quite fascinating about this shift in the direction of sexual difference by Irigaray is that it is approved, even condoned, as essentialist, by her erstwhile defender against this charge, Rosi Braidotti. Earlier in this chapter, I discussed how Braidotti, together with Grosz, supported Irigaray's use of the motif of 'two lips' not as essentialist but as a deconstructive device. In this context, however, the ground has shifted, and Braidotti now supports use of the word 'essentialism', as it is linked with sexual difference. This is a remarkable change, and in need of a detailed assessment, for I believe that it can provide insights into both the mixed reception of Irigaray and a discrepancy at the heart of her enterprise.

Braidotti will now claim that the postulate of sexual difference is a crucial and critical tool needed to establish women's integrity. 'The starting point for the project of sexual difference – level one – remains the political will to assert the specificity of the lived, female bodily experience; the refusal to disembody sexual difference into a new allegedly "postmodern" and "antiessentialist" subject, and the will to reconnect the whole debate on difference to the bodily existence and experience of women' (1994: 160).[34] Braidotti's opinion is that this affirmation of women's sexual difference, which she will also refer to as 'ontological difference', should not be regarded as antithetical to the struggle for equality, and bemoans the fact that it has been positioned this way by feminists.[35] 'Ontological difference is a political strategy aimed at stating the specificity of female subjectivity, sexuality and experience' (131). In Braidotti's view, there should be no separation 'of the empirical from the symbolic, of the material from the discursive, or of sex from gender' (177). Braidotti appreciates that thinking and acting in this non-divisive way is inseparable from an ontological stance that mandates a distinct form of difference for women. It is from this perspective that she defends Irigaray.

In arriving at this position, Braidotti has been influenced by her collaboration with the Italian scholar Adriana Cavarero, who has in turn been influenced by Irigaray. (From the 1970s Irigaray had been active in Italian feminist politics.) Cavarero herself documents her own political views that are indebted to the ideas of Irigaray: 'Thinking in terms of sexual difference ... is thus not simply a philosophical exercise, but the inaugural act in a political project that assumes women to be subjects capable of freedom and self-signification' (1992: 45) While Cavarero's own interests are basically materialist, she does make some astute observations regarding historical or anthropological research that is in quest of 'an "original" femininity ... that had rightly belonged to her [woman] at the beginning' (1993: 203). She makes two comments in relation to such searches. One is that while she regards such undertakings as helpful and legitimate utopian explorations, she is concerned that a mistaken nostalgia can project present desires backwards on to a supposedly forgotten heritage. The other is that such retrospective pursuits can detract from the present political commitment.[36] Perhaps these remarks have been made by Cavarero with Irigaray in mind, for she does seem to be drawing a distinction between herself and Irigaray's primordial pursuits. Because her concerns are pragmatic, Cavarero concentrates, as does Braidotti, on those aspects of Irigaray's work that are most useful for political recognition. As such, their main references are *Speculum* (1985a), *This Sex Which Is Not One* (1985b) and *An Ethics of Sexual Difference* (1993a).[37]

Neither woman discusses in any detail *Sexes and Genealogies* (1993b), the work where Irigaray speculates about a primal gynocracy and reveals her advocacy of particular 'feminine' traits as constitutive of women's identity. Cavarero identifies the main task for contemporary women as a determination by each woman to realise her own situatedness, and her need for self-representation, both in her commonality with, and her difference from other women. This is an essentialist undertaking for Cavarero, in that she accepts an originary empirical sexual difference, but allows for differentiated expressions, and does not endorse stipulated behavioural or attitudinal characteristics. In discussing sexual difference, Cavarero observes: 'This foundation defining the being a woman of every woman [sic], is the same for every women, but since every woman is this unique woman, the same foundation is revealed to be always and necessarily incarnated in the infinite unique existents who are alike in it, but who do not correspond to it like monotonous replicas of a mould which allows no variations' (1993: 216).[38]

This is where I believe that careful distinctions need to be drawn. What both Braidotti and Cavarero are respectively describing as ontological difference and 'essentialism', in connection with sexual difference, are not 'essentialist' according to its classical metaphysical definition of timeless, innate qualities. Braidotti even states that she understands ontology as an unfinished project that does not entail static and eternal essences (1994: 177). Cavarero and Braidotti are both concerned with those biological differences of women that lead to distinct experiences, and that, in certain cases need the protection of the law. Irigaray herself defends this forcibly, observing that the law, as it stands, despite some recent gains in the area of equality, does not defend the life, rights and properties of women. She postulates that 'what is needed is a full-scale rethinking of the law's duty to offer justice to *two genders that differ* in their needs, their desires, their properties' (1993b: 4). These changes will ensure women's subjective liberties.[39] Such gains, however, are not sufficient for Irigaray, as she believes that another dimension, that of personal identity, needs to be cultivated. Irigaray will posit that 'the impotence, formlessness, the deformity associated with women' needs to be replaced by 'their own physical, bodily beauty, their own skin, their own form(s)'. For this task they need 'a female god who can open up the perspective in which their flesh can be transfigured' (1993b: 64). It is in this connection that Irigaray does begin to recommend specific ideals and conduct for women that are not in accord with Braidotti's idea of ontology as an unfinished project that does not entail eternal essences.

Braidotti's and Cavarero's use of the terms 'ontology' and 'essentialism' needs to be evaluated because basically they are subsuming them within their own political categories. Irigaray, however, has other ideas in mind. She hearkens back, as do most romantic theorists of myth, to a time of origins, and the values that are subsequently invoked, in the name of tradition, are inherently conservative.[40] Irigaray reinforces the idea that, when patriarchy did supersede gynocracy, it appropriated its values and manipulated them to suit its own ends. For Irigaray, it is now time to reinstate these gynocratic ideals.

There is no explicit reference in either Braidotti or Cavarero to Irigaray's mythic claims where she introduces these attributes of the 'feminine'. For this reason, I do find Braidotti and Cavarero somewhat selective in their usage of the terms 'essentialism' and 'ontological difference'. This creates difficulties, as it precludes further discussion of this topic in Irigaray's work, particularly of her more recent publications, such as *Between East and West* (2002a), which I think does exhibit signs of what I consider to be traditional metaphysical essentialism. (The question of essentialism, and Irigaray's relation to it, will recur in this book. Further discussions concerning sex/gender and essentialism will appear in a number of the chapters that follow as other facets of the debate become relevant.) Braidotti's and Cavarero's lack of commentary on this aspect of Irigarary is symptomatic of a number of secular theorists who refuse to examine the spiritual dimensions of Irigaray's work. While it is understandable that there is a certain distaste on their part to deal with Irigaray's appeal to 'feminine' or gynocratic paradigms, I believe that it inevitably results in a failure to come to terms with her *oeuvre* as a whole – in its richness, its complexities, its contradictions, its idiosyncrasies. As it becomes apparent, over the course of her work, Irigaray is at heart a religiously, or rather, a spiritually inclined person – to use a contemporary term for a person who is non-aligned with traditional religions. This is at once Irigaray's greatest strength and greatest weakness. It is a strength in that she realises that established religion has been at the heart of the formation of the male-centred western symbolic order, and that any attempt to change it, even at the legal and political level, cannot be successful without taking religion's deeply ingrained symbolic controls into account. It is a weakness in that Irigaray herself, in attempting her reform of the religiously dominated symbolic structure of western culture, gets caught in a bind of her own making. She has succumbed, in fact, to a new idealisation of women, which ultimately introduces a gynocratic, nurturing modality as a property of a divine orientation. Even though this change may have certain affirmative consequences, such as an acknowledgement of maternal repression, it remains a complementary model, consonant with the paternal order. The promotion of fecundity and other nurturing values is also hard to differentiate from patriarchal clichés of motherhood.[41] It is ironic that Irigaray wishes to break down such binaries but, by setting up certain qualities as appropriate to the female gender as divine, she runs the risk of simply reinstating conventional stereotypes. Thus, while Irigaray cannot be accused of promoting actual maternity – for there is no glorification of traditional biological motherhood – her exaltation of mother earth's primal elements is troublesome.

There are strong criticisms today by feminists, both within and without Religious Studies, who argue that by affiliating women with nature, even in a positive elemental way, there is a danger that the nature/culture bifurcation as well as other binaries will be perpetuated (Roach 2003). I do not think, however, that in this instance Irigaray's recommendation of maternal values can be identified with the conventional definition of metaphysics. This is because these values, whether gynocratic or patriarchal, are constructed, not inherent. Accordingly, Braidotti, and Cavarero's unqualified advocacy of ontological essentialism is somewhat inadequate. This is, after all, the age of gender-bending and sophisticated debate concerning the mutually implicated influences of sex and gender, as well as of other differences.[42] 'Feminine' ontological differences may be recommended as a propaedeutic exercise for strategic political purposes, such as claiming rights, but this does not necessarily mean that such differences are essential according to orthodox metaphysical conventions.

Conclusion

It is a fascinating undertaking to speculate about the reasons why Irigaray, who seemingly embarked on a radical, even revolutionary, programme, wants to convince women to become affiliated with 'feminine' ideals. While it is impossible to provide any definitive answers, I think there is a flaw lurking in Irigaray's presuppositions that provides a clue. In her delineation of a biological distinction of the sexes, Irigaray positions herself within an inflexible dimorphism that does not leave her much room to manoeuvre. This is because she insists on a natural heterosexuality – something that even Freud himself was loath to assert after his initial forays into this territory (Mitchell 1983: 12). At times it is difficult to discern whether Irigaray's intent is to maintain the primacy of a psychoanalytically derived normative heterosexuality, while refining its perceived phallic distortions, or to totally reform existing gendered arrangements with a revised prescription for normative heterosexual relations. None the less, whichever of these options is chosen, Irigaray begins from a dualist position. This is because she identifies everything that she connects with patriarchy with rationality and the symbolic. Women are consigned to the mythic and imaginative, without recourse to their rational capabilities. This forces Irigaray, in her attempt to re-establish a 'feminine' sexual difference, to reinstall 'maternal' or gynocratic ideals. These, in turn, depend on a myth of gynocratic origins.

Such a response is as unsatisfactory as Freud's own oedipal myth of patricide by the primal horde – and is a dubious tactic at best. This is not the revolution that is needed, as ironically women remain the exemplars of all the stereotypical features that patriarchy has conferred on them. The ideals Irigaray promotes would seem to indicate her own mythopoetic fantasy of a feminine divine writ *large*. These ideals inhibit a free play of ideas where women explore innovative ways of envisaging and embodying their own ideals. There are thus two paradoxical forces at work in Irigaray's explorations regarding the way in which women become divine. One approves a mode of becoming for woman that is unfettered by patriarchal constraints, with indefinite possibilities, while another uncritically prescribes self-selected imaginative assumptions as the most appropriate for women to pursue. The endorsement of these explicit attributes by Irigaray indicates a prescriptive undertone in her work, something that is also apparent in her insistence on the primacy of sexual difference. Thus, despite the revolutionary impetus of Irigaray's early work, which has brilliantly broken with the old dream of symmetry that has held women in its phantasmagoric spell, Irigaray's further imaginative speculations on the nature of the 'divine' foreclose the in(de)finite imaginative ways by which women can envision the fullness of their manifold identities. In addition, Irigaray seems to be eliminating women from any connection to rationality. While 'masculinity' may have been associated with rationality in the history of philosophy (Lloyd 1993b), especially in its instrumental form, this does not imply that such imaginary alliances, of a constructed nature, need to continue. Contemporary feminist scholars have proposed gradated models of the interaction of reason, imagination and emotion, which also acknowledge corporeality. Such models are not regarded as inherently 'feminine'. Irigaray does not mention these revised models of knowing. Ultimately, while Irigaray deserves tribute for her discernment and articulation of women's oppression, it is now time for women, in full awareness of their compromised heritage, to construct a worldview that honours their new-found integrity, and that acknowledges their powers of both reasoning and imagination.

CHAPTER 2

Cartesian meditations

Because the pleasures of the body are minor, it can be said in general that it is possible to make oneself happy without them. However, I do not think that they should be altogether despised, or even that one should free oneself altogether from the passions. It is enough to subject one's passions to reason; and once they are thus tamed they are sometimes the more useful the more they tend to excess. (Descartes 1991: 265)

And it can be said in particular of Wonder that it is useful in making us learn and retain in our memory things we have been previously ignorant of. For we wonder only at what appears rare and extraordinary to us. (Descartes 1989: 59)

The passions have either been repressed, stifled, or reduced, or reserved for God. Sometimes a space for wonder is left to works of art. But it is never found to reside in this locus: *between man and woman*. (Irigaray 1993a: 13)

If you talk to the guardian of the church of Saint-Germain-des-Près in Paris, where Descartes' final resting place can be found, it becomes evident that, in death, Descartes' head has been separated from his body. The head – or rather his brain – is stored deep in the vaults of the Musée de l'Homme.[1] Is this the ultimate irony, or is it just deserts for the man who is often characterised as a major culprit in the disconnection of mind from matter, of body from soul? This designation is usually made on the basis of Descartes' pronouncements in the *Meditations* (Descartes 1984) and *Discourse on the Method* (Descartes 1985) but it does not take into account a small volume written in the last few years of his life, *Passions of the Soul* (Descartes 1985). A recent book by Susan James, *Passion and Action* (James 1997), contends that, once Descartes' depiction of the passions is taken into consideration, the simplistic dichotomy of mind and body often attributed to Descartes can no longer stand. It is intriguing to locate where Luce Irigaray stands in this debate, for in her work there are two distinct treatments of Descartes' ideas. Firstly, in *Speculum*, there is the chapter entitled '… and if, taking the eye of a man recently dead …' (1985a: 180–90), and, in *Ethics of Sexual Difference*, there is 'Wonder: A Reading of Descartes' *Passions of the Soul*' (1993a: 72–82).

Both of these reflections are quite short, and in each of them Irigaray introduces the topic of women – a subject that was notably absent from Descartes' own deliberations. In the first essay, Irigaray aligns herself with interpretations that associate Descartes' suspension of bodily connections and impulses with the suppression of women. At the same time, her deconstructive mimetic reading of Descartes also seeks to establish a site for women. The difference, or otherness of women, will thus disclose itself in Irigaray's first reading of Descartes as a mode of interrogative disturbance of the mind's certitude. In the second, more constructive reading, women feature as an instance of otherness that initiates an experience of the passion, wonder, which is nominated by Descartes as a primary passion. In this second reading, Irigaray will employ her construct of sexual difference with telling effect. For Irigaray, wonder, as a passion, is inextricably linked with love and the divine. Yet Irigaray does not make any explicit connections between her two essays, though she does recommend that Descartes needs to be reread in the light of his work on the passions. She does not comment, however, whether Descartes' later treatise on the passions might mitigate the criticism of his earlier dualistic experiments. It is illuminating nevertheless to compare Irigaray's two separate treatments of Descartes so as to establish certain trajectories in her own thought, with specific reference to philosophy and religion, and also to situate her work with reference to contemporary women's (re-)evaluations of the work of Descartes.

Descartes' certainty

The *Meditations* of Descartes were a self-styled exercise of liberation. In a narrow sense, they described a quest for epistemological certainty that involved a repudiation of the evidence of the senses as untrustworthy. On a larger scale, they constituted a rebuttal of the dominant Scholastic tradition and its Aristotelian-Aquinas lineage.[2] Yet Descartes' sceptical withdrawal into a mode of self-interrogation as the only means of affirming his own conviction of his rational capability, and thus his existence, is ultimately dissatisfying from a rationalist position. For it presumes the existence of a steadfast God who vouchsafes the validity of Descartes' own conclusions.

At first glance, it appears that all Descartes' empirical experiments are in the service of demonstrating the physical operations of the body function as an intricate machine, but a machine none the less. The brain is simply a conduit for messages, relaying impulses from the nerves to the 'common' sense which resides in the pineal gland. In the brain, these sensory transmissions are transmuted into a suitably rarefied form by the 'animal spirits', so as to allow knowledge to occur (1985: 102).[3] Thus, the pineal gland, situated in the brain, basically functions as a transfer mechanism from sense perception (body) to thought (mind). This ingenious, though bizarre, explanation is necessary because Descartes posits that there is a mind/soul continuum within the brain that is the sole agency of knowledge. Descartes states that 'The mind is not affected by all parts of the body, but only by the brain' (1984: 59). The mind/soul is thus permitted to be affected by the brain alone from which it receives the sense impressions. It is this mind/soul, whose existence is immortal, however, that constitutes for Descartes the essence of a person's being. 'I can infer correctly that my essence consists solely in the fact that I am a thinking thing' (1984: 54).

This last quotation is from the *Sixth Meditation* where Descartes elaborates at some length on both a mind/body interaction and the distinction between them. This builds on a differentiation he has made in the *Fifth Meditation* between innate ideas – such as that of God's existence – and sensory experiences (1984: 44–6). The innate idea of God as a perfect being is a truth which validates Descartes' own certainty: 'I think therefore I am' (1985: 126–31).[4] As he declares: 'I know that everything which I clearly and distinctly understand is capable of being created by God so as to correspond exactly with my understanding of it' (1984: 54). Descartes' proof of certainty rests on the notion that a beneficent God, who is not a deceiver, is at the core of his enterprise. But there is no absolute certainty here, except for Descartes' own conviction that his own thought processes, and the world's conformity to them, as guaranteed by God, are incontrovertible. This is a form of circular reasoning.[5] At this stage in Descartes' work, the body appears to have absolutely no role in this method of self-justification, except as a potential source of error because it supplies unreliable sense data.

Of the presumptions that sustain this undertaking, it is the division of the res cogitans (mind/soul) and res extensa (matter/body) which has remained Descartes' most influential legacy. This division and its manner of operation, however, have received strong criticism. Marjorie Grene registers one version of a classical objection to Descartes' position, particularly with reference to later philosophical developments:

> Most philosophers have abandoned the traditional God as the guarantor of knowledge, yet they retain the notion of the 'real distinction' to which only God's veracity could give metaphysical or even solid epistemological support and fails to recognise the richer bodily being of mental life that marks, not an abstract and outworn vision of the world, but the texture of experience as we live it both before philosophy begins and after the collapse of the Cartesian enterprise. (1985: 21)

In the light of Grene's remark, it is interesting to observe that certain present-day Cartesian proponents tend to conflate the mind with the brain of Descartes, thus discarding the soul which is the linchpin of his whole theory.[6] Descartes is thus treated primarily as a rationalist, while the crucial idealist dimensions of his work are disregarded. This tactic avoids having to deal with Descartes' extraordinary mediation between the mind and body by means of the pineal gland. Because he has characterised the mind/soul as without location, and the body as having extension in space, Descartes has to resort to this awkward contrivance as the medium of exchange of these two incompatible entities. He is thus at pains to demonstrate that there are interactions, if not any union, between mind and body. They are, none the less, 'closely joined' (1984: 54). Yet, at the same time, Descartes also organises his data so as to be able to declare that rational knowledge cannot derive directly from sense knowledge and corporal agency.

> We know for certain that it is the soul which has sensory perceptions, and not the body. For when the soul is distracted by an ecstasy or deep contemplation, we see that the whole body remains without sensation, even though it has various objects touching it. And we know that it is not, properly speaking, because of its presence in the parts of the body which function as organs of the external senses that the soul has sensory perceptions, but because of its presence in the brain, where it exercises the faculty called the 'common' sense. For we observe injuries and diseases which attack the brain alone and impede the senses generally, even though the rest of the body continues to be animated. (1985: 164)

What is particularly intriguing about this programme is that one of Descartes' strongest supporters, though also a critic, especially from a theological perspective, was Antoine Arnauld, who was associated with Port Royal and the Jansenist movement.[7] This puritanical group, which would have had no interest in Descartes' empirical studies, found his views on the body congenial. This is because Jansenism was strongly imbued with an Augustinian suspicion of the body and the senses, and an equally strong emphasis on the will. While Descartes himself was not an advocate of either Augustinian thought or Jansenist philosophy, and its recommended bodily practices of mortification, he shared their attitude of suspicion of the body. Marjorie Grene draws a striking comparison:

> Descartes' chief aim is to understand 'nature', in the sense of geometrically intelligible extended matter; Port Royal's chief aim is to live in Christ, in the hope of grace. What aims, what existences, could be more different? Yet they have in common a fateful bond: the denial of nature in the traditional, Aristotelian-common-sensical sense ... the alienation of mind from nature is its Cartesian liberation. And the alienation from nature is, just as fundamentally, the necessary starting point for the asceticism and penitentialism of Port Royal. (1985: 190)

For Irigaray this alienation from the body, from the senses, and from nature, is an indication of the suppression of the maternal. The triumph of reason is achieved at a high cost. Irigaray's responses to Descartes will attempt to undermine his security in the superiority of the reasoning mind over an unsound body.

Women and the rational

Irigaray does not concern herself, as does Grene, with Descartes' affinities with Jansenism or with the issue of the questionable legacy of a Cartesian God in philosophy. Instead, she focuses on Descartes' solipsistic preoccupation that wants to protect his own boundaries of knowledge against the possible deviations of a capricious natural world. It is in response to this distrust of the senses that Irigaray shares Grene's resistance to Descartes' abstract model of the Cogito with its reified subjectivity:

> The 'I' reifies itself, attests to itself in a reality that is eminent from the word go. Reality is formally and objectively demonstrable as thinking substance. It follows immediately that: the 'I' is in him who cogitates, here and now, without any possible flaw in his proof.... That is, in clear and distinct fashion, without the profusion of nerve impulses that jumble the parts of the body and the environment all up together: sensations, imaginations, memories, ... these need to be suspended during the aseptic procedures accompanying this surgical dissection. (1985a: 184)

Irigaray's disquiet comes from her appreciation that Descartes' quest for certainty, with its rejection of the body and its aberrations, is symptomatic of a pattern that she believes permeates western culture. From a psychoanalytical frame of reference, Irigaray likens Descartes' quest for self-sufficiency and self-assertion to an adolescent need to establish independence. This gradual task of separation from the mother, with its cumulative testing of limits, entails constant repetition. 'The "I" is still a child, an infant, when it comes to manipulating logic. On the other hand, there is a touch of adolescence when self-identity has to be constantly re-affirmed' (1985a: 181; translation emended). There are, however, further implications in that Irigaray detects in this oedipal script both the rejection and repression of the mother and, by implication, all things concerned with women. 'Once *the chain of relationships, the cord* has been *severed*, together with his maternal ancestry and the mysteries of conception, then there is nothing left for the subject but to go back and continue to sever them. He does this in a speculative act of denial and negation that serves to affirm his autonomy' (182; translation emended).

According to Irigaray, women thus remain the unacknowledged substratum of the edifice of masculine rationality. Women, as such, have never defined their own subjectivity. Whatever definitions of both 'women' and the 'feminine' have circulated in the different cultures of the western world, for Irigaray, they have always been male-ordered. Irigaray declares that a natural and maternal alliance with living body and matter has been circumscribed by rational reifications that deny women their fecundity, their own generative energy. As a result, body or matter serves only as material to be analysed and rendered tractable to reason's redirections. 'The "I" thinks, therefore this thing, this body that is also nature, that is still the *mother*, becomes an extension at the "I's" disposal for analytical investigations, scientific projections, the regulated exercise of the imaginary, the utilitarian practice of technique' (1985a: 186).

These ideas find echo in Susan Bordo's assessment of the Cartesian project (Bordo 1987). This is because Bordo also appeals to a psychoanalytic model. She describes Descartes' security-seeking mechanisms as manifestations of a 'cultural anxiety', which results from the modern intellectual emergence from an organic medieval world that had no problem with an intimate union of soul and body. As well as sharing a psychoanalytic approach with Irigaray, Bordo explicitly associates a disembodied rationality with the male and 'masculine' qualities in contrast to a corporally related worldview with the female and 'feminine' characteristics.

The basis for Bordo's claims, which are somewhat similar to Irigaray's, is that in Descartes' work – where her principal reference seems to be the *Meditations* – the corporeal is no longer connected with the spiritual (Bordo 1987: 99). Thus, whatever is relegated to matter becomes identified with the *res extensa* and the physicalist dimensions of nature. 'Cartesian objectivism and mechanism ... should be understood as a *reaction-formation* – a denial of the "separation anxiety" ... facilitated by an aggressive intellectual flight from the female cosmos and "feminine" orientation' (100).

This anthropomorphising of mind and matter, particularly on a grand scale, is somewhat problematic. At the same time, the generalisation of a psychoanalytic diagnosis, with its gendered connotations writ large, also raises issues regarding literal and metaphorical usage. In her book *The Man of Reason* (1993a), Genevieve Lloyd struggles to clarify the various interests involved in gendered constructs, especially with reference to the absence of women from the philosophical enterprise. As a constructivist, Lloyd primarily views the 'gendering of knowledge' as historically determined, without any essentialist characteristics. 'Men have conceptualized reason through Woman, symbolizing what is opposite to maleness and, to that extent, what is opposite to themselves as men. The symbolization of reason as male derives historically from the contingent fact that it was largely men – to the literal exclusion of women – who devised the symbolic structures' (1993b: 73).[8] The issue that Lloyd then raises was the major concern that predominated in the sex/gender debate when her book was first published in 1984. 'How does the symbolic content of maleness and femaleness, revealed through the exploration of philosophic texts, bear on the ways we think of ourselves as male or female? How does symbolic maleness or femaleness interact with the cultural formation of gender identity?' (1993a: xi).

Lloyd is concerned with Irigaray's universal applications. She remains dissatisfied with Irigaray's inclusive psychoanalytic explanation for the exclusion of actual women from philosophy, and of 'feminine' attributes from the definition of reason. As she says, 'The maleness of reason is not a unitary representation; rather it is a network of symbolic operations – some relatively simple, others deeply embedded of our conceptualizations of what it is to think at all' (1993b: 82). Lloyd's solution is that these matters need to be contextualised, and reflected upon in the light of present day interdisciplinary scholarship (1993a: xi). Lloyd does acknowledge the effectiveness of Irigaray's deconstructive and ironic tactics, yet she remains suspicious of their potential for concrete social change. And although she agrees that Irigaray is not an essentialist, in the metaphysical sense of the term, Lloyd does anticipate certain dangers that are involved in Irigaray's position. As she states:

Clearly, symbolic Woman is not to be identified with an essential feminine. What concerns me, however, is a general lack of clarity about the status of this nonessential feminine. In claiming it as a new conceptualization of both reason and the feminine are feminists perpetuating the link between sexual difference and the symbolization that is at the heart of the problem? Does this Irigarayan mode of criticizing the maleness of reason perpetuate a symbolic use of sexual difference that we would do better to part company with altogether? (74)

Lloyd was not alone in this position. Her work is symptomatic of many feminist thinkers' early questioning of Irigaray, but Lloyd's reaction was not, as were those of other feminists, an utter dismissal of Irigaray's work on the grounds that it was essentialist. It is necessary to note that Lloyd was making these statements with specific reference to the works of Irigaray that appeared in English in the 1980s. At that time, Irigaray remained at her deconstructive and tantalising best, and had not yet moved on to her constructive programme.

Taking Descartes to task

Irigaray's tactic of critical mimicry is extremely evident in her first essay on Descartes '... and if, taking the eye of a man recently dead ...' (1985a), where she is in a deconstructive and mimetic mode. By inserting herself in his text, Irigaray's subtle interventions constitute an ironic undermining of Descartes' assurance. This assurance is that by following his directives for the dissection of an eye, his anatomical and physicalist theory of vision will be corroborated, thus confirming the divine rules at work in the universe.[9] Irigaray will protest against the alleged invincibility of the *Cogito* and the manufactured conditions of the experimental method.[10] 'The eye/"I" ... is closed to the charms of seductively deceptive things and, once the mechanism has been analysed, it will frame and reproduce only what is technically set up in front of it' (184). She also challenges Descartes' notion of a self-serving God: 'I think, *therefore God* is: infinite being who at every moment gives a new impetus for the formation of my subjectivity and, what is more, confers upon my words the truth of the objective realities that they aim for in ideas' (1985a: 186). For Irigaray, Descartes, by constructing God and thereby reinforcing his own subjectivity in this mirror image, is just one more man who enlists God either as an ego-ideal or as a surety of his own system of (self-)justification. For Irigaray, 'God' may not necessarily prevail in the way Descartes assumes. In a mimetic voice, Irigaray indicates all too plainly the fragility of Descartes' hold on certainty. 'I shall remain in ignorance of the fact that, in this embrace of truth that I covet above all else, I am seeking, in simplest terms, to be united with *an image in a mirror*. This is how I am. At last alone, copula, I-me, coupled together in an embrace that begins over and over again. And fails equally often, because of the glass that separates us' (189–90). Irigaray astutely discerns that it is God who is at the heart of Descartes' project. 'God at least leaves me the hope that it will be different. One day' (190). This future God, from Irigaray's perspective, may have, however, very different resonances from those Descartes anticipates.

In her book *Cartesian Women* (1992), Erica Harth discusses Irigaray's treatment of Descartes. She ventures that Irigaray, specifically in her own deployment of doubt and suspicion, may be the last in a long line of Cartesian women, employing rationality against itself so as to advance the position of women – practically and/or intellectually. Harth depicts these Cartesian women, e.g., Princess Elisabeth of Bohemia, Madeleine de Scudéry, Emilie du Châtelet and Olympe de Gouges, as intelligent women all living in the seventeenth and eighteenth centuries, adopting the Cartesian ideal that 'the mind has no sex', yet floundering in social milieux that were not supportive of women's intellectual achievements (1992: 63, 121, 212, 234). Harth demonstrates that all of these women, in their different settings, were caught in something of a double-bind. While extolling the virtues of a neutral mind, in consequence of Descartes' pronouncement that the mind has no sex, they were also variously involved in striving to appreciate and express a form of 'feminine' sensibility that honours emotions and virtue.[11] As Harth observes:

> Irigaray's seventeenth century predecessors were half in love with the logocentrism that she defies because it offered them an escape from imprisonment in their bodies. To think was to be ungendered. By the eighteenth century, dualism had worn out its welcome for women who had gained no significant recognition as thinking subjects. Women such as Emilie du Châtelet and Olympe de Gouges wanted equality in difference, but the only discourse they possessed for laying claim to it was one that in the name of nature either denied difference altogether or made it an insuperable barrier to equality. (237–8)

Harth wonders if Irigaray is caught in a similar predicament: 'Does she write a new feminist alternative, an infinite potentiality of non-universal "eyes," gendered and socially located, or does she simply rewrite the masculine as feminine, resuscitating the dead man as the universal feminine?' (Harth 1992: 237). Harth's concerns are somewhat similar to those of Lloyd. I believe, however, that Irigaray, at this early stage of her work, is somewhat more subtle than Harth and Lloyd allow, though they do detect incipient problems in her work on gender that will become obvious only in her more recent constructive work.

In her deconstructive phase, Irigaray is seeking to expose the repression or omission of women that she believes is endemic to philosophy. She is also seeking to reveal the male prerogative of ordering the world – both his own and that of women (1993a: 121). Basically Irigaray is expressing the need for forms of knowledge different from those that have flourished in traditional western modes of philosophy and religion. In her early work, women are 'otherwise' for Irigaray. They represent something beyond the current parameters of knowledge. This is a 'feminine' difference that, as yet, waits to be disclosed. Only when they attain subjectivity will women be able to express their identity. It is perhaps Drucilla Cornell who, in retrospect, captures the early allure of Irigaray.

Well, I started out in a romantic relationship with Irigaray.... First, the unabashed utopianism that she associated with the feminine within sexual difference.... I did not see Irigaray at all as an essentialist. If anything, the feminine was a kind of radical otherness to any conception of the real or reality. More than anything else, here I found someone who was deploying the feminine unashamedly in a utopian manner, saying that there is a beyond to whatever kind of concept of sense we have. (Cornell 1998: 20)

Irigaray is not in love with logic or logocentrism, as were the eighteenth-century women described by Harth. She does not consider the mind, as it is employed by Descartes, to be neutral. For her, it is definitely a 'masculine' mind, in the tradition of Plato, Aristotle, Kant, Hegel, Heidegger, Levinas – to name some of Irigaray's most celebrated interlocutors. Irigaray appreciates that this gendered differentiation has led to a certain exclusion of women, or of whatever attributes are associated with their lifestyle, from admittance not just to the inner sanctum of knowledge but to genuine self-expression.

While Irigaray does not especially comment on whether Descartes' separation of mind and body is one of radical non-interaction, she is alarmed by the mode of the separation. 'In this ascetic ellipsis of the body ... the "I" believes its field of operations has been simplified, cleansed of all stains: dreams, insanities, disordered passions' (1985a: 185). Her work is at once a parody and a refutation of Descartes' following statement, which renders the mind distinct from the body:[12] 'From this I knew that I was a substance whose whole essence or nature is simply to think, and which does not require any place, or depend on any material thing, in order to exist. Accordingly this "I" – that is, the soul by which I am what I am – is entirely distinct from the body, and indeed is easier to know than the body, and would not fail to be whatever it is, even if the body did not exist'. (Descartes 1985: 127).

Irigaray, however, is not the only woman who has interrogated Descartes on this matter. Even in his own time, Descartes was not destined to remain unchallenged in this rather barren worldview. Princess Elisabeth of Bohemia intervened somewhat dramatically.[13] In their six-year correspondence, from 1643 until the year before his death in 1649, she questioned Descartes on his notion of the soul/body relation as well as on the role of the emotions.[14] Their exchange culminated in his writing of *The Passions of the Soul* (1985: 325–404), which features wonder as the first of the six primary passions.[15] It is this late volume of Descartes' *oeuvre* that provides the basis of Irigaray's second exchange with Descartes.

Certain aspects of Princess Elisabeth's responses to Descartes are not all that different from those voiced by Irigaray and other feminist critics today (See Bordo 1999). As Erica Harth observes:

For Elisabeth, the thinking subject is grounded in the materiality of the body. She does not understand the effacement of the subject behind abstract reason or the bracketing of subjectivity. When Descartes insists that a certain kind of positive thinking will help cure her vapors (although he reluctantly admits that the waters too can help obstructions), she digs in her heels. A stoicism that promises victory over the power of the passions and the body is not a realistic solution. (1992: 77)

Elisabeth's acute questions perhaps led to a modification of Descartes' views. Over the years, he tended to become more expansive in his letters to her regarding the body/mind interaction, and the problems of a purely rational explanation. His answers are not quite as absolutist as his early defence of reason. Elisabeth, however, does not ever seem to have received a satisfactory response to her view that the senses and emotions played a significant role in acts of knowing. The following is typical of Descartes' replies. '[T]he union of the soul and the body is known only obscurely by the intellect alone or even by the intellect aided by the imagination, but it is known very clearly by the senses' (1985: 227). Because of his deliberate avoidance of the issue, Andrea Nye describes Descartes' work in the treatise on the passions as simply reinforcing his established ideas, emphasising the mind or soul as the agency for mastering the passions.[16]

In *Passions*, the theoretical separation between mind and body that Elizabeth had questioned in her first letter to Descartes becomes a way of life. The key to the achievement, as Descartes presents it, is in the scientific understanding of passion as a variety of bodily 'mechanisms'.... this is the main lesson to be learned from studying the passions scientifically – in man, or in a man like Descartes who has achieved philosophical detachment, the separation between body and soul holds [firm].... The key to removing any possible deleterious effect of passions on the soul, therefore, is the fostering of mental separation and the proper understanding and regulation of passion, so that the soul suffers only those passions that are pleasurable and helpful. (1999: 90)

Irigaray and the world of wonder

Irigaray chooses not to focus on Descartes' reaffirmation of a sterile rationalism, as Nye does, in his book on the passions. In contrast to her first critical essay, Irigaray's second response, in 'Wonder' (1993a: 72–82), is itself a paean to wonder, situated by Descartes as the first of the six major passions. Irigaray's essay is a celebration that, while acknowledging Descartes' primary placement of wonder, expands his ideas by venerating its expressive dynamism and its grounding in the body.

For Descartes, wonder, with a direct connection to the brain (Descartes 1985: 353), does not have as influential a role to play as do the other five passions. Wonder is alone in being of a prereflective nature (Descartes 1985: 350). It is an autonomic reflex that reacts in a non-discriminatory way to novelty. Its containment is therefore not necessary to achieve a rationally ordered life, as it does not excite the appetites.[17] Wonder's pre-eminence is thus neither temporal nor spatial, but an acknowledgement of a special status.

Irigaray appreciates this nomination of wonder as a passion. Nevertheless, while Irigaray concurs with Descartes' depiction of wonder's innocence and initiative, she questions its restriction to psycho-physiological descriptions. For Irigaray, in contrast to Descartes, wonder is not confined to cerebral impulses that do not activate human urge to know. It is pervasive in its initiatory effects. 'Wonder is the motivating force behind mobility in all its dimensions. From its most vegetative to its most sublime functions, the living being has need of wonder to move' (1993a: 73). In a compelling variation, Irigaray will also insist that wonder is not something that occurs simply extemporaneously, as it does for Descartes. Irigaray declares that wonder needs to be cultivated, not in the mode of an artificial enhancement of virtuous behaviour but as a conscious refinement of habitual responses which have desensitised a person's capacity for spontaneous delight.

Irigaray's appraisal of Descartes' wonder is situated in the context of her creative mimetic responses to 'masculine' reason. Irigaray believes that there must be a revolution in both thought and ethics: 'We need to reinterpret everything concerning the relations between the subject and discourse, the subject and the world, the subject and the cosmic, the microcosmic and the macrocosmic' (6). For Irigaray, this deliberate revision will alter particular modes of thinking and relating, so as to redress the dualistic framework of subject and object. Among the revisions Irigaray recommends is a rethinking of space and time so that they are no longer viewed as discrete concepts which demarcate and isolate. 'The transition to a new age requires a change in our perception and conception of *space-time, the inhabiting of places*, and of *containers*, or *envelopes of identity*. It assumes and entails an evolution or a transformation of forms, of the relations of *matter* and *form* and of the *interval between*' (1993a: 7). A special tactic employed by Irigaray is the introduction of an intermediary place that she terms 'the interval'. It indicates an interstitial space between a subject and an object. This space ensures that there is a movement away from the encapsulation and reduction of a rationalist model that imposes its divisive categories on the world of matter – be it the earth or human beings. According to Irigaray, wonder inhabits this mediatory space of freedom: 'Wonder is the moment of illumination – already and still contemplative – between the subject and the world' (77; translation emended).

One of Irigaray's preliminary creative explorations in 'Sexual Difference' (1993a: 5–19), involves the implications of such a space for women. Primarily, it will free them from their containment or 'enveloping' by men. 'Once there was an enveloping body and an enveloped body … The one who offers or allows desire moves and envelops, engulfing the other' (12). An interval or interstitial space liberates women from such envelopes to explore the indefinite possibilities that Irigaray envisioned for them, as we saw in Chapter 1. There are no limits to their potential. 'Woman, insofar as she is a container, is never a closed one' (1993a: 51). Irigaray will also propose that, because of this interval, a woman can experience sexuality as a form of transcendence. 'Nothing more spiritual, in this regard, than female sexuality. Always working to produce a place of transcendence for the sensible' (53). Thus, Irigaray will also locate a mediatory sensible-spiritual construct, which she names the 'sensible transcendental', in this interval.

It is difficult to convey the exact meaning of this apparently contradictory postulate, the sensible transcendental, which incorporates two seemingly exclusive dimensions. This is because Irigaray evokes it in different guises in the specific context of her discussions with certain philosophers. Yet Irigaray's rejoinder, ostensibly made with reference to Descartes, is, at the same time, a deliberate rebuke to all male philosophers who place mind and body in opposition and then devalue the body. Thus wonder, as the passion of illuminative insight, designates a locus where these two co-ordinates of the sensible and the transcendent can find expression. For Irigaray, this postulate is not simply a figurative form but a mode of physical manifestation that allows for a *coincidentia oppositorum* – of the sensible and the transcendent, of the material and spiritual, of mind and body – where their interaction does not result in a blending, but a flourishing co-existence:

Wonder would be the passion of the encounter between the most material and the most metaphysical, of their possible conception and fecundation one by the other. A third dimension. An intermediary. Neither the one nor the other. Which is not to say neutral or neuter. The forgotten ground of our condition between mortal and immortal, men and gods, creatures and creators. In us and among us. (1993a: 82)

Wonder and sexual difference

In contrast to Descartes' estrangement of empiricism from metaphysics, for Irigaray the meeting with another person initiates an encounter that is both sensible and metaphysical.[18] In this model, it is to the notion of sexual difference, specifically as it is exemplified by the person of the opposite sex, that Irigaray will accord the special characteristic of the new, of the extraordinary, that stimulates wonder. 'This other, male or female, should *surprise* us again and again, appear to us as *new, very different* from what we knew or what we thought he or she could be' (74). For Irigaray there must be two sexes to interact in pluralistic ways that witness to a new ontology. Wonder and mystery are essential components of this ontology. As Irigaray attests in the opening essay of *An Ethics of Sexual Difference*: 'Who or what the other is, I never know. But the other who is forever unknowable is the one who differs from me sexually. This feeling of surprise, astonishment, and wonder in the face of the unknowable ought to be returned to its locus: that of sexual difference' (1993a: 3).

From this perspective, wonder is crucial to Irigaray for the establishment of sexual ethics. She claims: 'To arrive at the constitution of an ethics of sexual difference, we must at least return to what is for Descartes the first passion: wonder' (12). This is because the other of sexual difference contains not simply a rebuttal of existent, self-referential modalities but an element of delight and surprise in its unfamiliarity. This wondrous, non-reductive encounter with difference, which does not assimilate to an existing frame of reference, becomes for Irigaray the prototype for all sexual relationships: 'Always for the first time' (75). Yet, as Irigaray notes, sexual difference is absent from Descartes' own reflections. His description of the object of fascination is neutral. For Descartes, wonder at difference is simply of something that captivates the mind, whereas for Irigaray it embodies, in its tensional energies of attraction and expansion, an ethical orientation of respect that decreases the proprietary aims of desire.

It was obvious from our discussion in Chapter 1 that Irigaray was extremely critical of a Lacanian version of desire which denied women any access to a conscious expression of their own (1985b: 61; 131). Irigaray wishes to liberate women from such repression but proposes that their new expressions of desire will not engulf the other person. For Irigaray, desire will also be regarded as a principal passion, not a secondary one, as Descartes designated it. Thus desire, instead of its Lacanian connection to the phallus as an indicator of lack (61), is now intimately connected to wonder: 'In a way, wonder and desire remain the spaces of freedom between the subject and the world' (1993a: 76).

There is, in addition, a deliberate and significant juxtaposition by Irigaray of these mediatory revisions with the terms 'vertical' and 'horizontal'.

> The link uniting or reuniting masculine and feminine must be horizontal and vertical, terrestrial and heavenly.... It must forge an alliance between the divine and the mortal, such that the sexual encounter would be a festive celebration and not a disguised or polemical form of the master–slave relationship. Nor [should it be] a meeting in the shadow or orbit of a Father-God who alone lays down the law, who is the immutable spokesman of a single sex. (17)

In this setting, the term 'transcendental' has a specific reference to the transcendent realm, which, in a conjunction with the horizontal, suggests an interface that prevents the vertical from assuming a position of either precedence or dominance – something it does in the conventional understanding of transcendence.[19] At the same time, the term 'transcendental' carries allusions to Kant's and Husserl's employment of the word. Though their respective definitions of the terms had distinctive applications, both involved a separation from the sensible in a way that favoured forms of intellectual abstraction. Again, Irigaray wishes to effect a reconciliation of such a split in a relationship of parity. Another implied reference concerns the lack of reciprocity in a scopophilic worldview which privileges the male's specular gaze. This gaze can regard woman, from its loftier perspective, as a blank surface on to which it can project fantasies but also as an object to be manipulated. Such a rift reinforces for Irigaray the sensible/intelligible split exploited by Descartes. '[W]e interpret at each "moment," the *specular make-up* of discourse, that is, the self-reflecting (stratifiable) organization of the subject in that discourse. [This is] an organization that maintains, among other things, the break between what is perceptible and what is intelligible, and thus maintains the submission, subordination, and exploitation of the "feminine"' (1985b: 80; translation emended).

Finally, Irigaray will appreciate this revised notion of desire with love: 'Desire, as it inhabits the space of the interval, is reconfigured and becomes love' (1993a: 89). She queries Descartes' disconnection of wonder from love, which is also one of the six major passions. 'Why would these passions be separated? Do we love with the heart and blood, and not through thought? Do we wonder with the head and not with the heart?' (79–80). Descartes himself defines love as 'an emotion of the soul caused by a movement of the spirits, which impels the soul to join itself willingly to objects that appear to be agreeable to it' (1985: 356). Amorous activity is thus initiated by a volition that results from a rational evaluation of the beneficial consequences. This somewhat apathetic description of love belies the perturbations of the soul caused by the allied emotions of attraction and repulsion, noted by Descartes. Such sensual connections must be carefully monitored. Excess is discouraged in the name of moderation. Yet informing Descartes' dissection of the physiological and psychological dimension of love is an incipient philosophy of fusion whereby 'we imagine a whole, of which we take ourselves to be only one part, and the thing loved to be the other' (1985: 356). Annette Baier remarks approvingly on this implied *telos* of union and its intentional operations (1986: 51–2). But Descartes does not make any distinction between human beings and objects in relation to the desired outcome of this passion. There is no acknowledgement of mutual exchange, let alone the possibility that the passions of the other party might not be similarly engaged.

In contrast, for Irigaray it is in this vibrant interval of interaction of the sensible and transcendent, where desire has transmuted into love, that the divine becomes manifest. God is no longer a disembodied principle of ethical ultimatums or an artificial hypothesis of humanity's pretences to perfection but a dynamic presence incarnated in an ethical relationship of love.

> This creation would be our opportunity, from the humblest detail of everyday life to the 'grandest,' by means of the opening of a *sensible transcendental* that comes into being through us, of which we would be the mediators and bridges. Not just mourning for the dead God of Nietzsche, not waiting passively for the god to come, but in conjuring him up among us, within us, as resurrection and transfiguration of blood, of flesh, through a language and an ethics that is ours. (1993a: 129)

Contemporary Cartesian women

It is obvious that though both Irigaray's and Descartes' work examine the mind/body relation, Descartes' undertaking is of a different order from Irigaray's. For Descartes the passions are a fascinating phenomenon, basically because of potential beneficial effects, but they are of concern principally because of their possible harmful effects. It would seem that Descartes' whole enquiry is ordered to domesticate the passions and thus to delimit their cognitive value. His conclusions have implications for their bodily connections. The body or brain appears as a sensate and even mechanistic system for receiving and conveying messages. It is dependent on evaluative directives from the mind or soul – in the form of volitions – for instigating further activity. For Susan James, it is this interpretation that has resulted in an erroneous accusation often made against Descartes to the effect that he portrays the passions and body as passive, while the mind alone is active. In her book *Passion and Action* (1997), James describes the Cartesian project as involving a more complex interplay.

> Descartes strives to combine his metaphysical division between body and soul with the view that there are states which 'cannot be referred to the body alone'. And among these he includes, in best Aristotelian style, both sensory perceptions and passions. While passions are thoughts, and therefore allocated to the soul, their dependence on the body pulls them across the boundary so that, in order to understand what they are and how they work, one has to take account of their bodily causes. To this extent they straddle the very divide Descartes has created, and in so doing they place a question mark against his doctrine that body and soul engage in different sorts of activity: matter moves and soul thinks. (1997: 106)

The metaphysical and phenomenological accounts depicted here, nevertheless, remain somewhat at odds. In conceding the cumbersome nature of Descartes' exposition, James still insists that this ability of sense perceptions to transpose and diversify their effects to both mind and body mitigates the rigid dichotomy so often assigned to Descartes. Though this defence is persuasive in ameliorating any harsh anti-corporeal or anti-affective denunciation of Descartes, it doesn't consider the contrivances of the pineal gland that make this situation tenable. Nor does it acknowledge the fact that the body is still considered as 'the lesser part' (Descartes 1985: 377), and is the subject of strictly functional descriptions. The impression left by Descartes' work is that though the passions, when rightly managed, can be pleasurable, and even a source of great joy, their bodily attachment is a source of disquiet. Their proper expression is always in need of the regulation of the mind and/or ministrations of the soul. It is this situation that Irigaray contests.

Another contemporary philosopher, Amélie Oksenberg Rorty, specifically defends Descartes' work on the passions:

> The passions, especially wonder and joy, provide the impetus and the direction for thought. Without the passions to direct the principles of association, the mind would not be motivated to think one thing rather than another: it might just reproduce the *cogito* or some mathematical proof over and over. The passions introduce *value, utility,* and *importance,* as well as the criteria of benefit and harm. Although they are not essential to the mind's thinking, they do indeed provide the life of the mind, and the benefits and harms that do affect it. (1986: 529)

Oksenberg Rorty, in supporting this integrative model of mind and body, justifies the awkwardness of Descartes' treatment of the passions as due to a conflict of traditions that Descartes was striving to reconcile, particularly with reference to the will. Oksenberg Rorty views the will as pivotal for the relation of the mind and body. Yet, she observes that one tradition discernible in Descartes' work is a modified Platonism, replete with innate ideas, where the body is the material expression of a formal principle in the mind. This model is devoid of any ontology that would invest it with a teleological direction. Matter is thus identified within mathematical physics so that it operates according to observable principles. This model downplays the agency of the will, depriving it of its discriminating functions. Such a model is in conflict with Descartes' attraction to the Enlightenment tradition with its emphasis on the autonomy of the will. In this tradition, the will operates as the co-ordinator of the various activities that co-operate between mind and body. Its volitions, issuing from the mind or soul after due reflection, are responsible for the bodily responses. The trouble occurs with the attempt to integrate these two incompatible models. Oksenberg Rorty does not believe there is a successful merger. Nevertheless, she concludes: 'Even if we have reservations about Descartes' solutions, we can at least admire the bold ambition of his enterprise. Far from being a dogmatic dualist, Descartes suffers from an unexpected *générosité* in his respect for the conflicting traditions that his system attempts to reconcile' (Oksenberg Rorty 1986: 530).

Irigaray, however, is not concerned with this lack of consistency in Descartes' system, nor with any putative generosity in his attempt at integration. Her focus is on wonder, which she celebrates as the advent of something new – particularly of the other. Irigaray also contests both the divisions that Descartes draws between mind and body, and his negative view of the body. She combines these two interests when she expands the domain of wonder to embrace the motif of sexual difference, and sets it in an ontology of becoming. 'Wonder is a passion that maintains a path between physics and metaphysics, corporeal impressions and movements toward an object, whether empirical or transcendental. A primary passion and a perpetual crossroads between earth and sky, or hell, where it would be possible to rework the attraction between those who differ, especially sexually' (Irigaray 1993: 80). This new ontology, with its sentient references, is in stark contrast to the epistemology of James and Oksenberg Rorty, who maintain a Cartesian neutrality in their discussions of the passions and mind/body relations.

Ethical orientations

It is from their respective delineations of the ethical that the most cogent comparison can be drawn between Descartes and Irigaray. From a comprehensive perspective, ethics, for Descartes, bespeaks a well-tempered life. This is the result of deliberative volitions which demonstrate a sound mind moderating an unreliable body.[20] Ethics is related to epistemology in a way that emphasises the primacy of the will as the executor of a mind that has the power to master and, if necessary, overrule the passions.[21] In contrast, for Irigaray, whose project is to engage ethics with ontology, it is sexuality and love that play vital roles in configuring conduct. The owning and expression of passions, such as wonder and desire, need no longer conform to abstract, authoritative regulations issued by men. This is not to say that Irigaray is promoting unfettered release of repressed emotions without an exercise of deliberation, for her ethics of sexual difference will demand its own discipline.[22] Such an ethics respects the integrity of the partner as a subject in his or her own right.

Irigaray's celebration of the body with its interconnected perceptions and passions aims at a wondrous correlation of body and mind. There is no special case, as there is for Descartes, where the passions establish a specific mode of mind/body interaction (1985: 328–9, 339). Focusing on wonder, Irigaray invests it with a particular emphasis of the moment, of an in-stance (1993a: 75), of a non-assimilative ideal that ultimately should inform all our encounters with otherness – not simply those with the other of sexual difference. For Irigaray, such an infinite openness is primarily represented by woman, a figure of an unconditional and boundless horizon of knowing, as distinct from her former restricted and repressed roles. But this is not to be her privilege alone. In Irigaray's ethical orientation, her ideal is that woman and man will both henceforth journey alone and together, honouring wonder – the passion of non-possessive attraction and reciprocal fecundity (78). Irigaray's treatment of the primary passion of wonder is an insistent questioning of Descartes' priorities which, though they honour wonder, reduce it to a propaedeutic condition. Wonder does not generate for Descartes, as it does for Irigaray, a momentum of becoming that marks a unique location of opening and openness to difference. For Irigaray, wonder is an expression of mind/body collaboration with its own loving mode of awareness.

Love is intimately involved with wonder in the mediatory space of the sensible transcendental in Irigaray. She wishes to retain the fertile tension between a man and woman that is not changed into a sterile transcendence or immobile immortality. Neither does she want a child to be the token of the relation's generativity (1993a: 33). Irigaray understands love as the active agent that fosters mutual flourishing. Love thus sustains an ever-mobile process of becoming that bestows each encounter with the radiance of wonder and originality. Such a love both requires and nurtures the ethics of sexual difference that is at the heart of Irigaray's later work, particularly I Love to You (1996). For Irigaray, love is situated as a place-time composite that is not constrained by categorical divisions that organise diversity according to discrete temporal or spatial units. As a result, love as carnal knowing is where corporal and intellectual dimensions are intertwined, not hampered by their consignment to separate spheres with appropriate norms and rules. Love rejoices in its magnanimous and abundant resources – both bodily and spiritual – and heralds the advent of a continuous transformation. Irigaray will crystallize an appreciation of this love in *I Love to You*: 'Love, even carnal love, is therefore cultivated and made divine. The act of love becomes the transubstantiation of the self and his or her lover into a spiritual body. It is a feast, a celebration, and a renaissance, not a decline, a fall to be redeemed by procreation. Love is redemption of the flesh though the transfiguration of desire' (139).

Serene Jones is worried about the heretical implications of Irigaray's move. She believes that the transcendence of God, as woman's incommensurable Other, has been removed from the spiritual scene, and replaced by a mere mortal. In Jones's orthodox position, the act of love cannot, of itself, generate divinity. 'From a Christian perspective, such an ethic of wonder is made possible through the concept of a divine, transcendent (and immanent) agent who comes into relation with the world and thereby with women through the promissory act of unmerited love – through grace' (1995: 67) For better or worse, I do not believe that Irigaray herself is bothered by the niceties of theological doctrine such as those of unmerited grace, any more than she is preoccupied with the law of Moses, and the person of Jesus Christ as mediums of an utterly other God's purposes for this world (85). I believe that Irigaray's position as to the existence of a God, particularly as conceived by western religions, is one of agnosticism. From this perspective, while Irigaray's work may offer rich material for further theological reflection by feminist scholars, it is not, of itself, intended as a theological document.

Questions will be also be asked as to whether Irigaray's presentation involves an acceptable characterisation of Descartes. Certain contemporary women philosophers, such as Baier (1985; 1986), James (1997) and Oksenberg Rorty (1986; 1992), whose philosophical background is Anglo-American, would definitely take issue with much of Irigaray's portrayal. Baier, James and Oksenberg Rorty none the less do call attention to the salutary effects of the passions. For James, it is important to acknowledge how intellectual emotions can produce sympathetic passions that sustain the desire for knowledge (1997: 206–7). Oksenberg Rorty appreciates the positive motivational directions that the passions, rightly channelled, can provide, concentrating the mind while also protecting the body from harmful excess (1992: 386–7). Yet they both give priority to the mind, and the passions are subordinate to the principal task of intellectual inquiry and volitional judgement. And perhaps this marks the place where Descartes' system is most vulnerable to feminist criticism. This is because his work presupposes a monolithic man, secure in his world – as Descartes certainly was by the time of his writing *The Passions of the Soul* – who presumes to speak for all humanity.[23] Perhaps this is an oversight, however, as Descartes cannot be faulted for his treatment of Princess Elisabeth, though it has to be admitted that he regarded her physical infirmities as due to a weakness of mind and will. Thus, Descartes' dualistic and rationally controlled definition of love is lacking according to Irigaray's standards in her discussion of Plato (and Diotima) in *An Ethics of Sexual Difference*:

> If the pair of lovers cannot safeguard the place for love as a third term between them, they can neither remain lovers nor give birth to lovers. Something becomes frozen in space-time, with the loss of a vital intermediary and of an accessible transcendental that remains alive. A sort of teleological triangle is put into place instead of a perpetual journey, a perpetual transvaluation, a permanent becoming. (1993a: 27)

Conclusion

Ultimately, the difference between Irigaray and Descartes could be described as resulting from their disparate designs. Descartes is concerned with establishing an epistemological foundation that will provide the disciplined mind/soul and body with the essentials of a harmonious life. The existence of a God that is both perfect and infinite, though incomprehensible, is guaranteed by a form of the ontological argument – in the *Third Meditation* – which, in turn, guarantees all finite efforts to establish its credibility. Irigaray, in contrast, has infinite designs. Her project is an ontological one that seeks to replace the desiccation of the Cogito with an unbounded genesis of becoming. God is endlessly incarnated in living love. For Irigaray, wonder will never cease.

There are those, however, who would argue that, despite her largesse of spirit, Irigaray does not avoid the sexual stereotypes that have pervaded the anthropomorphism of reason, and that, rather than abolishing them, she even perpetuates them in her heterosexual ideal. This can indeed denote a shortcoming in Irigaray's work but it does not detract from her depiction of embodied wonder. There are also those who discern in Descartes' final work, *The Passions of the Soul*, an amelioration of the somewhat austere ratiocination that marked his early writings. They find there an optimism in a form of co-operation of the mind and body that refutes any caricature of Descartes as the philosopher who epitomises a facile division of mind and body. As a result, it is mistaken to attribute to Descartes any deliberate intention to promote a rational masculinity at the expense of an emotional and aberrant femininity.

None the less, Descartes remains a supreme rationalist and it is his unapologetic stance that reveals the nature of Irigaray's radical break. This is an awareness that wonder, with its shock of the new, has productive corporal (as well as cerebral) revelations. These revelations, as they express the vivifying energy and insight that the body and its emotions can provide, will continue to confound reason's presumption to be the sole agent of cognition. It is from this perspective that Irigaray can also be considered as theologically transgressive (or heretical). Dogmatic consistency is neither Irigaray's intent nor her forte. The word is made flesh for Irigaray, and this embodiment is now sanctified not by attempts to flee the flesh but by embracing it. Perhaps the most powerful development in Irigaray's revisions of Descartes for philosophy and religion is her vindication of the flesh and the passions as having divine dimensions. Henceforth, women's bodily associations need no longer be symptomatic of instincts that have to be subdued. Wonder, in its gratuitous incarnation, and acceptance of an embodied other, does not just introduce an infinite horizon of knowing and becoming. It promotes, in a passionate relationship of sexual difference, a revolutionary rereading of the doctrine of transfiguration, as well as that of transubstantiation.[24] Happily, today Irigaray does not have to worry about witch-hunts and an *auto-da-fé*.

CHAPTER 3

Effacements: Emmanuel Levinas and Irigaray

The alterity of which I am speaking is alterity of the face, which is not a difference, not a series, but strangeness – strangeness which cannot be suppressed, which means that it is my obligation that cannot be effaced. (Levinas 1988: 179)

He is the Subject, he is the Absolute – she is Other ... I suppose that Levinas does not forget that woman, too, is aware of her own consciousness, or ego. But it is striking that he deliberately takes a man's point of view, disregarding the reciprocity of subject and object. When he writes that woman is mystery, he implies that she is mystery for man. Thus his description, which is intended to be objective, is in fact an assertion of masculine privilege. (Beauvoir 1975: xvi)

It is not that we can step outside male language, any more than we can step outside metaphysics. But we can try to think our otherness not *simply* as different from the sameness of male language. And that is why Levinas, by taking to the extreme the otherness of the feminine, can be said at the same time to have recognized a space for some kind of thinking of the other outside its opposition to the same. (Chanter 1988: 53)

The other sex, then, would represent the possible locus of the definition of the fault, of imperfection, of the unheard, of the unfulfilled, etc. But this fault cannot be named except by my other or its substitute. More precisely there are at least two interpretations of the fault: that which corresponds to the failed fulfilment of my sex, to the failure to become the ideal of my gender, and that which is defined in relation to the ideal of the other gender. These faults are not the same. For centuries, one has been cruelly masked by the other. (Irigaray 1991b: 112, translation emended)

Introduction

Luce Irigaray and Emmanuel Levinas (1906–95) share a commitment to reconfigure contemporary ethics. They both wish to move beyond the predominant model of a subject/object relationship which has led to the effacement of the other. They both also envisage a revised male and female relationship as paradigmatic for the changes they wish to introduce. This relationships will be heterosexual, where there are specific qualities that are 'feminine' and distinctive roles for women. Finally they both employ similar terms to describe vital aspects of the radical transformation of ethics: desire, *eros*, infinite, transcendence, mystery, virginity. They have much in common, including the influence of Martin Heidegger. Irigaray, however, has chosen to disapprove of certain aspects of Levinas's work – specifically those which concern his depictions of women, the 'feminine' and the relations between men and women.[1] Levinas himself stated that he had been criticised by feminists,[2] and would seem to be trying to respond to this in a number of interviews (1998: 113; 2001: 115). From his responses, it is very clear that there is no intention of exploitation of, or animosity towards, women on Levinas's part. In fact he attempts to clarify, if not enhance, his original depiction of the 'feminine' as the paradigm of the situation of the other (2001: 115; 1998: 113). Yet there remains something problematic with this description for many women readers. One task of this chapter is to explore the writings of Levinas on women and the 'feminine'. The principal writings that will be treated in this chapter are those on the o/Other; the woman as 'feminine', 'beloved' and 'fecundity', as they occur in *Totality and Infinity* (1969, published in French in 1961). Then the topic of maternity in *Otherwise than Being* (1981) will become an important source for reflection. In concluding, the responses of contemporary women thinkers, of Luce Irigaray in particular, will provide a basis for evaluating Levinas's work which, from his own perspective, is a homage to women. This exercise in comparative ethics will also help to illuminate Irigaray's own ideas on the 'feminine' and women.

To undertake a comparison and contrast of Levinas's and Irigaray's work is to enter into a labyrinth. I am not using this word in a pejorative sense, but to indicate the extremely intricate and interconnected, as well as divergent and impassable, strategies that are involved. In part, this is due to the lack of precision in Levinas's work of the notions of 'sex' and 'gender' – is he referring to actual women, to simply 'feminine' attributes, or to both at once? Irigaray, who will not agree with Levinas, has her own complex ideas on the interaction of sex and gender, on the 'feminine' and on relationships between men and women. It is in an interview with Amsberg and Steenhuis, published in *Hecate* (1983) that Irigaray makes reference to the fact that she is writing an article on Levinas. The critical article that resulted, 'The Fecundity of the Caress', which appeared originally in French in 1984, is published as the final essay in *An Ethics of Sexual Difference* (1993a: 184–217). From this time on, it is Levinas who becomes Irigaray's primary conversation partner on the topic of the o/Other, rather than Lacan – though Hegel is always hovering in the background. Levinas's ideas, particularly those depicting the ethical encounter, help to modify Irigaray's previous predominantly psychoanalytic orientation. Levinas's impact on Irigaray's work is noticeable, particularly in her approach to the other of sexual difference, though she does not admit to this (2004). On this issue, I am in agreement with Tina Chanter when she states that 'Irigaray's work as a whole is profoundly influenced by Levinas's conception of ethics' (1995: 214). In the end, however, Irigaray finds Levinas wanting on the subject of women and subjectivity.

The work of Levinas

In the aftermath of the Holocaust, or Shoah, Emmanuel Levinas has contemplated the bankruptcy of the western ethical tradition that did not prevent such devastation. 'The essential problem is: can we speak of an absolute commandment after Auschwitz? Can we speak of morality after the failure of morality?' (1988: 176). A Lithuanian-born Jew, who spent most of his adult life in France, Levinas studied in Germany with Husserl and Heidegger in the late 1920s and early 1930s. Although he esteems Heidegger's *Being and Time*, and considers Heidegger 'the greatest philosopher of the [twentieth] century', he can never forget Heidegger's affiliation with the National Socialist Party in 1933. It is only Heidegger's early rethinking of ontology that impressed Levinas.[3] Levinas worked without scholarly prominence for many years and it is only in the last thirty-five years that his work has received acclaim in Britain and North America. It is now being mined for insights to help formulate a new orientation to ethics.

Levinas wishes to reclaim a metaphysical position that establishes an originary ethics of relationship towards an irreducible other human being. Ethics is primary, it precedes ontology. This non-objectifying ethical disposition recognises the priority of the other person. It denotes a form of knowing that cannot be confined to rational reflection, thereby designating a domain of excess that confounds established categories. Levinas, like Irigaray, is highly suspicious of the reigning philosophy of the same, which has not respected the integrity of the other: 'Ontology, as a first philosophy, which does not call into question the same, is a philosophy of power, a philosophy of injustice' (Levinas 1969: 46; translation emended). For both Levinas and Irigaray, it is the infinite as unlimited possibility and as mode of transcendence – a sphere that cannot be reduced to a rational explanations – that informs their undertakings. Yet it is in their understanding of 'God' – as an unrealisable absence for Levinas, as a realisable divine presence for Irigaray – that their work manifests a primary dissimilarity. For both of them, nevertheless, it is in the relations of human intersubjectivity that God or the divine is realised, though in different guises.

For Levinas, God, as infinite, is that which exceeds all bounds; that which is irreducible to rational categories; that which has not and never will be present; that which, in Levinas's words, is 'Otherwise than Being' (Levinas 1981). With such a conjecture, Levinas interrogates the need to impose conceptual closure, which has been the hallmark of western philosophy and theology. To name, to contain, to control – these are the rational tendencies that have sought to subdue the manifold by reducing it to an imposed unity. Difference has had to be displaced, eradicated. In traditional western metaphysics, multiplicity has always been treated not as an integral otherness but as a variant of the same. It has been God as an Absolute, and as presence that has presided over this monotonous landscape. Thus, an oppressive system, which Levinas names totality, has been dominant. Levinas intimates that, in acquiescing to totality, we have lost our infinite inheritance.

At once uncompromising and enigmatic, Levinas is one of those seminal thinkers whose work is not simply provocative but deeply disturbing. To take his work seriously is to be dislodged from the securities and complacencies characteristic of western thought. Is he then another Derrida, an erstwhile debunker of the metaphysics of presence who could leave us ambivalently languishing with the remnants of our former ideals and certainties? The answer must be no – for Levinas is not afraid to evoke a notion of transcendence as an incomprehensible mystery. Thus, Levinas cannot be simplistically categorised as a deconstructionist who trades in undecidability for its iconoclastic value. Is he postmodern? Perhaps. Modernity's ideals are definitely displaced, but in the name of a more primordial orientation towards an infinite possibility.

The fact that ontotheology and logocentrism (as Heidegger and Derrida have respectively characterised the two monolithic impulses of metaphysics) may have suffered a setback as a result of contemporary challenges is not a cause for pessimism for Levinas. This is because he does not believe that metaphysics needs to be abandoned. Ultimate questions are still posed. The radicalism of the questioning, however, does not permit easy assurances. A new path is being charted that is a vital reorientation rather than a simple readjustment.

> We cannot obviate the language of metaphysics, and yet we cannot, ethically speaking, be satisfied with it: it is necessary but not enough. I disagree, however, with Derrida's interpretation of this paradox. Whereas he tends to see the deconstruction of the Western metaphysics of presence as an irredeemable crisis, I see it as a golden opportunity for Western philosophy to open itself to the dimension of otherness and transcendence beyond being. (1986b: 28)

This statement implies that, for Levinas, ontology as a philosophy of Being, in its Greek and Christian variations, has not respected the worth of the other. It has been a power trip. As an alternative, Levinas's work looks to the God of the Bible, not simply to the God of the philosophers.[4] Jerusalem and Athens, however, do not conclusively part company. Levinas postulates transcendence as that which is previous to philosophical reflection. It is the excluded, the 'unthought' of western philosophy and theology. We are back with an absent God, a God of absolute Otherness, a God who cannot be revealed in accordance with prescribed imagistic or definitional forms. This God at once surpasses yet permeates any attempts at designation. Levinas depicts this omnipresent yet elusive God: 'I can never have enough in my relation to God, for he always exceeds my measure, remains ever incommensurate with my desire' (32).

While this form of transcendence forever evades objectification, it does not preclude signification. It is just that this signification does not have any traditional ontological resonances because, prior to any ontology, Levinas postulates ethics. This primal ethical orientation displaces traditional understandings of ethics as dependent on philosophical or religious foundations. In this context, for Levinas, transcendence will disclose itself according to an ethical modality of an interior summons rather than an overt verbal communication (Levinas 1987b: 171). There are no preordained rules. Instead there occurs, in a mysterious fashion, a profound personal witnessing of the utter incompleteness, yet infinite potentiality, of the human condition. In Levinas's estimation, we have not heeded the invitation to this form of transcendence. To reclaim it, all former false certainties are to be discarded. It is not just our intellectual predispositions but also the narcissistic preoccupations that inform all our actions that are in need of transformation.

Irigaray is just as uncompromising as Levinas in her demands for a new beginning that will have repercussions for women and their relationships to men and God. She believes that 'a revolution in thought and ethics' has to take place (1993a: 6). Similarly, she has serious reservations about the domination of an absolute God figure, as well as the metaphysical concepts that sustain him. A new god needs to be disclosed. Echoing Heidegger she states: 'We still have to await the god, remain ready and open to prepare a way for his coming. And, with him, for ourselves, to prepare, not an implacable decline, but a new birth, a new era of history' (129). Irigaray will also affirm that 'Who or what the other is, I never know' (13). This, however, for Irigaray does not mean that God or the divine cannot be grasped, but that any understanding that takes place will not be achieved by intellectual means. In fact, it will be within a dynamic of personal relations – specifically a heterosexual one – that this will occur. As with Levinas, Irigaray's ethics will be concerned with another who cannot be reduced to the same. '[T]he other who is forever unknowable is the one who differs from me sexually' (13). It will be in the sexual relation of a woman and man that the divine will be realised. It is in this recognition of the divine within an interpersonal and carnal communion that will distinguish Irigaray's solution from that of Levinas.

For Levinas, the ethical domain is also situated within a dynamics of personal relationship, but the initial characterisation of the other person as 'the stranger, the widow and the orphan' (1969: 77) would not seem to be revolutionary. Benevolence towards the outsider is the grand (if unfulfilled) gesture of traditional Jewish and Christian morality which failed at Auschwitz. What Levinas intends, however, is an extreme exteriority whereby the other person will always take precedence over me. Simplistic injunctions to charitable conduct are thereby eclipsed. For Levinas, ethics connotes an integral situation where philanthropy and even reciprocity are rejected in the name of a transparent openness in approaching another human being. As an illustration of his extreme requirement,

Levinas feels that Martin Buber's model of an I–Thou relationship is insufficient. 'I must always demand more of myself than of the other; and that is why I disagree with Buber's description of the I–Thou ethical relation as a symmetrical copresence' (1986b: 31). This primacy of the other presupposes a complete realignment of justice: 'The effort of this book [*Totality and Infinity*] is directed towards apperceiving in discourse a non-allergic relation with alterity ... where power, by essence murderous of the other, becomes, faced with the other and "against all good sense", the impossibility of murder, the consideration of the other, or justice' (1969: 47).[5]

The actual relationship with another, or alterity, as depicted by Levinas, is not self-sufficient. Nor is it a relationship where the subject dominates the other. It has also nothing to do with the 'absolute knowledge' of Hegel. Levinas will describe this otherness in a number of ways. In *Totality and Infinity*, he will declare that 'The absolutely other is the Other' (1969: 39) ('L'absolument Autre, c'est Autrui' (1961: 9). By this condensed statement, Levinas indicates that the other person, 'Autrui', marks a location of the Absolutely Other, God.[6] For Levinas, however, this God can never be known in person, because it is transcendent. Levinas remarks: 'Alterity is not at all the fact that there is a difference, that facing me there is someone who has a different nose than mine, different colour eyes, another character. It is not difference but alterity. It is alterity, the unencompassable, the transcendent. It is the beginning of transcendence. You are not transcendent by virtue of a certain different trait' (1988: 170). Such a dispensation does not conform to a conventional act of knowledge, or a conventional idea of a transcendent Absolute. Levinas locates the signification of the Infinite in the ethical exercise of responsibility for the other, which is witnessed by saying: 'Here I am!' [*MeVoici*] (1981: 146) – which could be loosely translated as 'Here I am at your disposal'. This implies a witnessing on the part of a subject 'to the Infinite, to God, about which no presence or actuality is *capable* of testifying'. The dynamics of this asymmetrical relationship witnesses to the Infinite. As Levinas observes: 'For he [the witness] has said "Here I am!" before the Other, and from the fact that before the Other he recognises the responsibility which is incumbent on himself, he has manifested what the face of the Other signified for him. The glory of the Infinite reveals itself through what it is capable of doing in the witness' (1985: 109). In this manner, Levinas's ethics of alterity, communicated as radical responsibility, opens on to the Infinite.

In this complex interaction, it is the face of the other person that is the medium by which signification occurs, but this must not be construed as fathoming the depth of the Infinite. The witness, in recognising in the face of another person his or her own responsibility for this unique and irreducible other human being, is party to an exchange whereby 'The face *signifies* the Infinite' (105). This attestation, however, before/of the face is not to be equated with the presence of the Infinite. 'It is not a *manifestation* in the sense of a *disclosure*, which would be adequation to a given. On the contrary, the characteristic of the relation to the Infinite is that it is not disclosure' (106).

By discriminating in this delicate way, Levinas strives to ensure that the transcendent is not conflated with the immanent, that absence is not submerged in presence. 'The other proceeds from the absolutely absent. His relationship with the absolutely absent from which he comes *does not indicate, does not reveal* this absent; and yet the absent has a meaning in a face' (1986a: 355). The meaning conferred in the encounter with a face depends on Levinas's somewhat obscure designation of constituting the face as a *trace*. This latter term, evocative of vestiges which remain, marks for Levinas the immemorial passage, but never the presence of God.[7] Such a reference to God as trace expresses Levinas's own Jewish inheritance. Another term Levinas uses to refer to this non-present God is *illeity*, which refers to 'the origin of alterity' (1996: 64). In this guise, it indicates 'the beyond from which a face comes signifies as a trace. A face is in the trace of the utterly bygone, utterly passed absent' (1996: 60). The face is thus the trace, which witnesses to the evidence, but never a complete revelation of God. 'He shows himself only by his trace, as is said in Exodus 33. To go toward Him is not to follow this trace which is not a sign; it is to go toward the Others who stand in the trace of *illeity*' (64).

In other words, God cannot be encountered directly, but only in a relationship where I am responsible for the other in a mode beyond the will, beyond any self-centred intentionality. This dispossession is activated in the encounter itself, in a movement that at once elicits and responds to a capacity which otherwise would remain latent. It cannot be instigated at will. 'This order steals into me like a thief, despite the outstretched nets of consciousness, a trauma which surprises me absolutely, always already *passed* in a past which was never present and remains unrepresentable' (Levinas 1987b: 171). Thus, the stimulus of this ethical command is not the result of an external imposition, but is actually an interior realisation. This summons is not to be confused, however, with a Kantian categorical imperative that dictates its purposes in accordance with a given universal law. And it is perhaps here where Levinas is at his most profound and most enigmatic. 'The command is stated by the mouth of him whom it commands. The infinitely exterior becomes an "inward" voice, but a voice bearing witness to the fission of the inward secrecy that makes signs to another, signs of this very giving of signs. The way is crooked' (1981: 147). This obscurity emphasises Levinas's belief that the ways of God are not directly decipherable. He quotes Paul Claudel: 'God writes straight with crooked lines' (147).

Given this indecipherability, such a radical dispossession of self-determination can occur only because, according to Levinas, it is prompted by a desire for the Infinite – for that which calls us beyond any finite concerns. This refutation of egocentric needs in deference to the other is portrayed by Levinas in hortatory tones. 'But the moral priority of the other over myself could not come to be it if were not motivated by something beyond nature. The ethical situation is a human situation, beyond human nature, in which the idea of God comes to mind' (1986b: 25). A crucial distinction between desire and need is basic to Levinas's discussion of the wellspring of our infinite aspirations. Need is identified with preoccupations for self-gratification, for assimilation to selfish requirements. Desire, in contrast, is inordinate in the sense it can never be fulfilled. But this does not have a negative connotation of indulgence, for it is a sublime hunger, an infinite momentum unto the other, which constantly replenishes itself. 'The relationship with another puts me into question, empties me of myself, and does not let off emptying me – uncovering for me ever new resources. I did not know myself so rich, but I have no longer any right to keep anything. Is the desire for another an appetite or a generosity? The desirable does not fill up my desire but hollows it out, nourishing me as it were with new hungers' (1986a: 350–1).

Neither the epiphany of the face nor the dynamics of alterity can be thematised according to traditional ontological categories. This is because for Levinas, from a metaphysical perspective, the Infinite is anterior to Being. From this perspective, an encounter with the alterity will always confound any idealised, self-sufficient or pre-existent ontological notion of Being as identity. For Levinas, the other/Other thus instantiates a relationship of proximity, not a metaphysics of presence. Proximity designates a relation that is not confined by autonomous subject/object predications. '[T]he Other is not simply close in space, or close to me like a parent, but he approaches me essentially insofar as I feel myself – insofar as I am – responsible for him' (1985: 96). The ethical relationship of responsibility for an other indicates at once a religious and a metaphysical disposition. It is religious in the sense that it literally embodies a ceaseless search for the Infinite – a going towards God: '"Going towards God" is not to be understood here in the classical ontological sense of a return to, or a reunification with, God as the beginning or end of temporal existence' (1986b: 23). Levinas wishes to stress that we are not on a quest for that which can be named or defined, either prior to or as the culmination of our enquiry. The journey itself marks the absent/present which informs, but neither institutes or directs proceedings in an executive way.

Although this infinite scenario does not favour causal or teleological principles, it obviously does not altogether avoid the language of metaphysics. Thus, while Levinas strives to modify the claims of Greek ontological and epistemological categories, he remains dependent on them. Levinas himself admits the inevitability of their inclusion.[8] Thus, in Levinas's work, the interpersonal becomes the interface of two completely different forms of discourse – Greek and Jewish. In this endeavour, Levinas is as influenced by aspects of Descartes and Kant as by the Jewish thinker Franz Rosenzweig (Levinas 1987b: 159–66), by Husserl and Heidegger as much as by Jewish Talmudic and Midrashic thought (Levinas 1986b: 13–21). Yet these are not the only relevant traditions, for Levinas also acknowledges his Lithuanian and Russian background.[9] None the less, when Levinas seeks to convey the immeasurability that can never be contained by finite human proportions, he finds his main sources in the biblical tradition. In the biblical frame of reference, the recounting of human experience is couched in polyphonic voices that testify to an infinite dimension: 'The existence of God is not a question of an individual soul's uttering logical syllogisms. It cannot be proved. The existence of God, the *Sein Gottes*, is sacred history itself, the sacredness of man's relation to man through which God may pass. God's existence is the story of his revelation in biblical history' (18). At the same time, Levinas will also refer to this dimension by the philosophic phase 'otherwise than Being'.[10] Ultimately, however, both religiously and metaphysically, God is realised (albeit incompletely) only in and through the vicissitudes of human interaction. This is depicted metaphysically as a modality of existence where the ontological self-complacency of Being is interrupted by Otherness. This Otherness elicits an ethical response from humanity.

The 'feminine'

There have been many books and essays of appreciation and evaluation of Levinas's work that respond to the proposal of ethics as first philosophy. However, few of these deal with the imagery of woman that Levinas employs, both with reference to the situation of the other and of the subject who responds to the summons of the other. Over the years, a number of women scholars have investigated this usage, and examined its weaknesses or strengths, not simply from a feminist perspective but from the standpoint of contemporary women, both Jewish and secular, e.g., Ainley (1988); Chanter (1995; 2001); Chalier (1982; 1991); Grosz (1987); Handleman (1991); Katz (2001a; 2001b; 2003); Sandford (2000; 2002); Wright (1999); Wyschogrod (2000 [1974]). It is not my plan to simply recount their observations in detail, but to revisit an essay I wrote on Levinas in 1994 and revise its claims in the light of more recent insights, as well as of Irigaray's responses to Levinas.

Both Levinas and Irigaray share an important orientation in their intention to move beyond an economy of the same. Both take the love relationship between a woman and man as the prototype of an ideal interaction in their ethics, where neither partner is absorbed by the other. For Levinas, this stance was particularly obvious in his work *Time and the Other*, published originally in France in 1947. As he states: 'I have precisely wanted to contest the idea that the relationship with the other is fusion' (1987a [1947]: 90). He develops the implications of this insight in the Preface: 'Finally there is what is said of the relationship with the Other ... neither an ecstasis, where the Same is absorbed in the Other, nor a knowledge, where the Other belongs to the Same.... This idea should make the notion of the couple as distinct as possible from every purely numerical duality' (35–6). In her early work *Speculum* (1985a), Irigaray also reflected on the economy of sameness, and she investigated ways in which women could escape from being absorbed by it. This led to her development of an ethics of sexual difference (1993a). In a more recent book, *To Be Two* (2001), Irigaray reflects on the significance of her solution: 'It is not, therefore, in the fusion or the ecstasy of the One that the dualism between subject and object is overcome, but rather in the incarnation of the two, a two which is irreducible to the One: man and woman' (2001: 59). The fact that woman is of a different gender from the male of the species is central to both Irigaray's and Levinas's formation of a new ethics. They will differ markedly, however, in their ultimate ethical emphases.

Both Levinas and Irigaray wish to exalt women. But there are disparities. While Irigaray wishes to liberate woman from her inferior otherness – as 'femininity', in the masculine economy of sameness – Levinas initially proposes the 'feminine' as the ideal exemplar of the other. In *Time and the Other*, the 'feminine' is described as *of itself other*; as the essence of the very concept of alterity (1987a: 85, originally published in French in 1947). Here Levinas aligns the 'feminine', in a seemingly neutral connotation, with the other, as transcendence that can never be known. (It is noteworthy that Levinas will never use the upper case when he utilizes the 'feminine' as a figure for the other as transcendent.) In this usage, the 'feminine' is evocative of mystery – as that which is inaccessible and elusive. In a later interview with Philippe Nemo, Levinas reflects on the 'feminine', and adds a further observation: 'The feminine is other for a masculine being not only because of a different nature but also inasmuch as alterity is in some way its nature' (1985: 85, originally published in French in 1982). Here there is an evident change of inflection, from a figurative to literal sense, in that the reference is now the male and female of the species. Alterity is now named as a constituent of the female nature, not just a 'feminine' attribute assigned to otherness in general.

In an essay, 'Judaism and the Feminine', Levinas strives to distinguish his definitions of the 'feminine' from that of woman. Within the context of Judaism, 'the feminine is the original manifestation of these perfections, of gentleness itself, the origin of all gentleness [and goodness] on earth' (1990a: 33, originally published in French in 1960).[11] These natural 'feminine' attributes, however, do not interfere with a woman's essence, which is, as a person – both distinct from and not in opposition to man – 'to stand in a relation of equality with man' (35). For Levinas, this reading is in accord with the text of Genesis where man and woman were created equal in the eyes of God.[12] Then, in contrast, Levinas defers to another Talmudic commentary on the second version of creation in Genesis where woman is created from the rib of Adam. In a somewhat disingenuous way, Levinas interprets this to indicate that a certain priority needs to be accorded to the man. From a religious perspective, a man's life is to be honoured as it is ordered towards eschatology. Women are also to be honoured, but their role is one where 'maternity is subordinate to human destiny' (35–6). As a result, men are concerned with the public matters of God, while woman's lot is to maintain the family as essential to the flourishing of the Jewish people. Although Levinas concedes that the essential and cultural differences between male and female are 'blurred' in a messianic age, in the human world there must be a distinction, even if it leads to sexual inequality. This is made only too clear in another essay, 'And God Created Woman': 'To create a world, he [God] had to subordinate them one to the other. There had to be a difference which did not effect equity: a sexual difference and, hence, a certain pre-eminence of man, a woman coming later, and as woman, an appendage of the human ... Society was not founded on purely divine principles: the world would not have lasted' (1990b: 173, originally published in French in 1973).

There is absolutely no doubt that Levinas respected and admired women, but I believe that his Jewish orthodoxy influenced his attitudes of the place of women in the order of creation. The reason this happens is that Levinas employs the 'feminine' in a dual sense. For Levinas, in a divine or messianic age there will be no sexual difference, and in one sense, the 'feminine' reflects both the perfection and the utter inscrutability of this divine dimension, but this is a time that is yet to be realised (1990a: 35). Thus, in an earthly, and all too human, existence, women bear the burden of a lower status in the order of creation. Thus the 'feminine', in addition to depicting utter alterity, graphically illustrates women's mundane condition. Whether Levinas is conscious or unconscious of his intended meanings, the 'feminine' here represents all the compensatory virtues with which women have been endowed as a form of recompense for the autonomy and transcendence that they have been denied.

Irigaray is extremely suspicious of any use of the term 'feminine' by men and its ascriptions to women. She understands these associations as an inevitable symptom of a male ordering of the world. In Levinas's case, she does not find fault with the 'feminine' per se, but she takes issue with a perceived imbalance in Levinas's portrayal of the expression of heterosexual relations, and especially in his description of *eros*. Irigaray, however, does not fully appreciate the religious reasons that lie behind Levinas's denial of autonomy to women. Her difference in approach, however, is immediately apparent in her usage of the term 'mystery'. While also assigning the stature of mystery to a transcendent other – and I believe that Levinas's influence on her is evident in this move – Irigaray will not view it as necessarily a prerogative of the 'feminine'. Irigaray declares: 'The other, whose mystery will never be a shared secret, the other who will always remain a mystery to me, is the other of sexual difference' (2001: 111). Thus, in Irigaray's view, mystery inheres in both male and female in an intersubjective relationship. Irigaray's egalitarian dynamics displays a different sexual arrangement from that of Levinas in the love relations that can exist between women and men.

Eros exalted

For Levinas, in *Time and the Other* (1987a, originally published in French in 1947), it is *eros*, in a relationship of voluptuosity, that fosters and protects the mystery of the other. Levinas makes clear that this profound mystery must not be associated with ethereal romanticism, or the vagaries of all too human women. 'The pathos of voluptuousness lies in this fact of being two. The other as other is not here an object that becomes ours or becomes us; to the contrary, it withdraws into its mystery. Neither does this mystery of the feminine – the feminine: essentially other – refer to any romantic notions of the mysterious, unknown, or misunderstood woman' (1987a: 86).

On first reading, these are quite exceptional words to have been written in 1947, as a vindication of love. Yet, it is this reference to the 'feminine' as 'other' to which Simone de Beauvoir took exception. On a closer reading, this otherness need not simply be a reinforcement of women's otherness and immanence, as Beauvoir's rejoinder suggests. This is because, if Levinas is taken at his word, 'the feminine' is identified with transcendence, which cannot be comprehended by reason. In this sense, otherness, as the 'feminine', may indeed slip 'away from the light' or consciousness (Levinas 1987a: 87). But this is not quite the type of transcendence that Beauvoir had in mind for women. For Beauvoir, transcendence is to be linked with an autonomous woman's ability to question and change her given situation. Nevertheless, Beauvoir's criticism is actually indicative of an obvious problem that most feminists detect at the heart of Levinas's work, no matter what the standing of the term 'feminine': it is Levinas who assigns women their position, rather than allowing them the right to question or choose their 'feminine' role.

It is from this perspective that Irigaray will censure Levinas's depiction of the caress as the gesture of non-possessive love. This is because his ambiguous position leads to the impression that the caress belongs solely to the male quest for transcendence. Levinas seems to be aware that his description might be problematic when he states: 'The seeking of the caress constitutes its essence by the fact that the caress does not know what it seeks. This "not knowing", this fundamental disorder, is essential ... This intentionality of the voluptuousness – the sole intentionality of the future itself, and not an expectation of some future fact – has always been misunderstood by philosophical analysis' (1987a: 89).

For Levinas, the caress, as the movement of desire that seeks the Infinite, does not indicate a possessive attitude, nor attempt to control the outcome in any way. The caress, as the token of love, represents the ideal moment of an ethical relation with the other. This selfless gesture of love needs to be stressed because, in *Time and the Other*, such *eros* is honoured without qualification. 'There is nothing of this ['grasping', 'possessing', 'knowing'], in *eros*. If one could possess, grasp, and know the other, it would not be other. Possessing, knowing and grasping are synonyms of power' (90). In this model the 'feminine', as a model of alterity, is portrayed as pure, nude, empty. This is where the trouble begins, for it is evident that the other is a passive recipient of the ministrations of the subject. Thus, though there is no mention of actual women, Levinas could easily be interpreted as extrapolating from the role of women in his society. The implication for women who read this text is that the caress expresses a form of imposition, and indeed, this is how Irigaray understands it. For her, the caress is not a disinterested gesture.

To caress, for Levinas, consists, therefore, not in approaching the other in its most vital element, the touch, but in the reduction of that vital dimension of the other's body to the elaboration of a future for himself.... the caress ... is a good example of the way in which the temporality of the male subject, of Emmanuel Levinas at any rate, makes use of the support of the feminine in the intentionality of pleasure for its own becoming. In this transformation of the flesh of the other into his own temporality, it is clear that the masculine subject loses the feminine as other. (1991b: 110)

Although such a criticism might not reflect Levinas's own stated intentions on the matter of the caress, the terms that he has used to describe the 'feminine' do provide a basis for such an interpretation.

Eros as suspect

Things, however, become even more complicated. By the time of *Totality and Infinity* (1969), Levinas himself seems to have had some misgivings about the nature of the caress and untainted voluptuousness that he described in *Time and the Other*. The paradigm of selflessness no longer holds. Eros appears to have fallen from its exalted state and can also indicate a path to perdition. In *Time and the Other*, eros, as desire, is free from all expectations in a continuous initiation unto the Infinite. Now, in *Totality and Infinity*, eros, aligned with need, can degenerate into possession. Voluptuousness, if not treated with care, can become profanation. Levinas describes his suspicions. 'If to love is to love the love the Beloved bears me, to love is also to love oneself in love, and thus to return to oneself. Love does not transcend unequivocably – it is complacent, it is pleasure and dual egoism. But in this complacence it equally moves away from itself; it abides in a vertigo above a depth of alterity that no signification clarifies any longer – a depth exhibited and profaned' (1969: 266).[13]

It is difficult to conclude with any accuracy what could have occurred for Levinas to reverse his position on love so drastically. The only evidence that I can offer for this alteration is that, since approximately 1945, Levinas had been studying the Talmud.[14] An article on women in the Jewish tradition, 'Judaism and the Feminine', also displays this shift in his attitude. It is here that Levinas states, after confirming that the 'feminine' has a spiritual dimension, that the romanticisation of women as a love object – as in the 'Eternal Feminine' – can lead to her downfall. The 'feminine' as woman, no longer represents goodness and gentleness.

The feminine also reveals itself to be the source of all decline. This appears in an ambivalence in which one of the most profound visions of the ambiguity of love itself is expressed. The delicious weakness which, in the swoon of inner life, saves the human being from rootlessness takes place on the verge of letting go. Woman is complete immodesty, down to the nakedness of her little finger. She is the one who, *par excellence*, displays herself, the essentially turbulent, the essentially impure. (1990a: 37)

Perhaps the most alarming aspect is the alteration in the words he now uses when he describes the 'feminine' as profane. Thus, in *Totality and Infinity*, *eros* will appear in two modes: there is *eros* as a positive desire for the Infinite Other, signified by voluptuousness, and there is *eros* as a negative need, where voluptuousness has gone awry and degenerated into concupiscence (1969: 256–66). For Levinas, the potentiality of *eros* to appear in either of these two modes exemplifies a state of equivocity. '[T]his simultaneity of need and desire, of concupiscence and transcendence, tangency of the avowable and the unavowable, constitutes the originality of the erotic which, in this sense, is *the equivocal* par excellence' (255). For reasons that remain unclear, Levinas will nominate the 'feminine' as representative of this state of equivocity. 'Equivocation constitutes the epiphany of the feminine' (264).

This same strange logic then allows Levinas to depict the 'feminine' as able to represent both the positive and negative dimensions of *eros*. The 'feminine' as the Beloved ('*L'aimé qui est Aimeé*' (1961: 233)) remains virginal and untouched: 'The Beloved, at once graspable but intact in her nudity ... abides in virginity. The feminine, essentially violable and inviolable ... is the virgin or an incessant recommencement of virginity, the untouchable in the contact of voluptuousity' (258). Yet profanation lurks behind this appearance of integrity: 'In the feminine face the purity of expression is already troubled by the equivocation of the voluptuous' (260). The 'feminine' thus comes to bear simultaneously the burden of all that is chaste and all that is corrupted, within the context of sexuality. It is perhaps for this reason that Levinas is hesitant to draw on the 'feminine' in any allusion to God. As he has stated: 'The feminine will never take on the aspect of the Divine' (1990a: 37).

It is none the less somewhat perplexing to appreciate why Levinas apportions the blame for this indeterminacy between need and desire on the 'feminine'. It is need as possession that appears most worrisome to him. In so far as *eros* becomes uncontrolled, given the gendered nature of Levinas's graphic descriptions of the passive beloved, would it not be 'masculine' passion that is responsible? At the very least, it would appear that it is Levinas himself who is the one who is equivocal in his attitude to women, seemingly torn between his attitude of reverence, as initially evident in his idealisation of the 'feminine', and a conservative religious attitude that is troubled by women who may not conform to the ideals of chaste womanhood.

Redeeming *eros*

From these descriptions, it could be surmised that, though woman or the 'feminine' is still granted an integral part in ethical proceedings by Levinas, she is appreciated as having merely an ancillary role. As an equivalent of the face or the trace of transcendence, she simply initiates the lover (or ethical agent) into its mysteries, without any access of her own. The 'feminine' permits, indeed encourages, transcendence, but does not achieve it. Catherine Chalier also notes this discrepancy: 'Intimacy and gentleness do not comprehend *height* which is, according to Levinas, the only authentic ethical dimension. It means that the feminine (and he often says "the woman") would be excluded from the highest destiny of human being. This highest destiny would be reserved for the masculine once it has been converted to ethics thanks to the feminine' (1991: 123).

Irigaray has the same misgivings as Chalier, and the modifications that she introduces are of significance. Irigaray insists on the fact that women are to be acknowledged in their full human freedom and dignity. She will both reject 'feminine' characteristics imposed by men and suggest her own. For Irigaray, the task of women today is to achieve their own autonomy, to reclaim their own otherness, i.e., those aspects of women's lives that have been denigrated, neglected or discarded as inconsequential. When women act to rectify this, they establish their virginity. For Irigaray, virginity has to do not with chastity, as for Levinas, but with women's autonomy. It is not just a civil autonomy, however, but a form of wholeness where a woman realises a spiritual identity. 'For me, becoming a virgin is synonymous with women's conquest of the spiritual. And it's not always a matter of gaining something more but one of being capable of being something less. [It is] feeling more free vis-à-vis your fears, fantasies about others, freeing yourself from useless knowledge, possessions, and obligations' (1993c: 117; translation emended). In this way, for Irigaray, women also cease to be the other of men, and become divine. This is in contrast to the traditional propensity of envisaging God as male.

This personal wholeness and autonomy does not permit women to remain the objects of men – civilly, emotionally, ethically or spiritually. Passivity is no longer acceptable. Irigaray posits that 'This relationship between the two genders cannot be reduced to passivity for the female and activity for the male, as still happens in our tradition.... This division annuls one's identity: the two genders, the two people in relationship with each other no longer remain' (2001: 35). If women cannot be active, for Irigaray there is no basis for a relationship. There has to be a genuine reciprocity. Irigaray stresses this by insisting that a woman is not only the Beloved but a lover. She describes her intervention: 'In "Fecundity of the Caress," I used the term "woman lover" (*l'amante*) and not only, as Levinas does, the word "beloved" (*aimée*). In this way, I wanted to signify that the woman can be a subject in love (*un sujet amoureux*) and is not reducible to a more or less immediate object of desire' (1991b: 115). Love has to be acknowledged as the meeting of two responsible beings, where both are animated by desire. Neither is the passive recipient of the other's attentions. In her declaration of the amorous couple, however, she is not an apologist for intemperate sensuality, nor for narcissistic pleasure. As a result, Irigaray, in her own study, reads the caress in a manner that contrasts with Levinas's. 'The caress is an awakening to intersubjectivity, to a touching between us that is neither passive or active; it is an awakening of gestures, of perceptions which are at the same time acts, intentions, emotions. This does not mean that they are ambiguous, but rather, that they are attentive to the person who touches and the one who is touched, to the two subjects who touch each other' (2001: 25).

Desire is thus transformed. It is not associated with need or instinctual indulgence. For Irigaray, the return to the self is marked by an interiority whereby each person consciously disciplines their instincts, so as not to burden the other with impulsive projections. This is a work of self-knowledge and restraint that is undertaken both individually and as a couple.[15]

Desire and pleasure are then cultivated by and for each sex with the intention of accomplishing the perfection of its gender. The man trains his instincts and drives so as to become fully man and the woman does the same in order to accomplish the perfection of her gender. The man and woman can thus form a human couple. In the couple sexuality finds its actualization, its realization, an *in-itself* and a *for-itself* corresponding to the poles needed for the perfect incarnation of every man and woman's humanity. This task is realized both separately and together. (Irigaray 1996: 28–9)

This mutual management of desire, as far as Irigaray is concerned, will not lead to equivocation, as love is no longer driven by unconscious urges (2001: 28). Love thus cannot become needy or possessive. In this way, Levinas's fear of concupiscence is eliminated. Irigaray will situate her criticism of Levinas's equivocation within a context of other male scholars who have also found the bodies of women to be a troublesome obstacle in matters of love.

For this reason, the sexuate body and the sexual relationship are not bewitching or possession, submersion or nausea (as Sartre writes in *Being and Nothingness*), they are not ambiguity (according to the language of Merleau-Ponty in *Phenomenology of Perception*, 'The Body in its Sexual Being'), and the feminine body, or the feminine, is not equivocation (as Lévinas suggests in *Totality and Infinity*). (28; translation emended)

Irigaray indicts Levinas for thinking only of himself and not of the other, who is woman. 'This description of pleasure given by Levinas is unacceptable to the extent that it presents man as the sole subject exercising his desire and his appetite upon the woman who is deprived of subjectivity except to seduce him' (1991b: 115). In contrast to Irigaray's celebration of a disciplined yet sublime love, Levinas, suspicious of self-preoccupation, and of a lack of openness to the other, appears to set up the 'feminine'/woman as a scapegoat for a sexual excess. This impasse in their understanding of the dynamics of male and female relationship accentuates their divergent diagnoses and remedies for curing the malaise in the contemporary ethos. For both, a heterosexual relationship is understood as the model of regeneration, but the corrective erotic and ethical model is conceived in entirely divergent ways.

Maternal compensation

In *Totality and Infinity*, Levinas proposes another solution to equivocation in order to retrieve the 'feminine'/woman from erotic decline. This solution is an appreciation of the love relationship as ordered towards fecundity. 'Fecundity evinces a unity that is not opposed to multiplicity, but, in the precise sense of the term, engenders it' (1969: 273). This ensures that the relationship is productive of a child, so that love is never an end in itself. Levinas further explores this facet of the 'feminine' in *Otherwise than Being or Beyond Essence* by means of the motif of maternity (1981: 75–81). In doing this, Levinas turns from an examination of the other to the responsibility of the subject in an ethical relationship. It also marks a turn from *eros* to *agape* as the expression of responsibility. Tina Chanter notes: 'Eros has no place in the later texts of Levinas. And as eros disappears, so does the feminine, only to be replaced by the maternity, which is apparently the only acceptable face of the feminine' (1995: 208). *Agape*, as 'love without concupiscence', involves an unconditional mode of responsibility on the part of a subject towards the other. Certain commentators have argued that, in this later work, Levinas's appeal to maternity, and its link to an extreme form of *agape* as absolute responsibility, compensates for Levinas's accentuation of the 'masculine' in *Totality and Infinity*. Yet it seems that maternity functions both figuratively and literally to support an adulation unto effacement of women. 'It is being torn up from oneself, being less than nothing, a rejection into the negative, behind nothingness; it is maternity, gestation of the other in the same' (Levinas 1981: 75). Such a description by Levinas of maternity as abandonment and annihilation, while illustrative of the exigency of his ethics, is a further application of the 'feminine' and woman that entails unthematised prescriptions of women's behaviour.

One possible explanation for this disproportionate description is that, in order to wake people out of their ethical lethargy, Levinas, by invoking a self-sacrificing maternity, intends to express an extreme responsibility that expends itself to an exorbitant (if almost incomprehensible) degree. 'Is not the restlessness of someone persecuted but a modification of maternity, the groaning of the wounded entrails by those it will bear or has borne? In maternity what signifies is a responsibility for others, to the point of substitution for others and suffering both from the effect of persecution and from the persecuting itself in which the persecutor sinks. Maternity, which is bearing par excellence, bears even responsibility for the persecuting by the persecutor' (75).

Such an unprecedented notion of responsibility provokes an exclamation from one interviewer, Philippe Nemo: 'You go that far!' (Levinas 1985: 99). Levinas then tempers his seemingly self-effacing imperative, by allowing that this admonition is to be understood as a personal alert, always in need of contextualisation, and never absolved from the demands for communal justice. In all contexts, however, it is responsibility that is foremost. Identity can be realised only within the parameters of this excessive responsibility. 'I speak of responsibility as the essential, primary and fundamental structure of subjectivity. For I describe subjectivity in ethical terms. Ethics, here, does not supplement a preceding existential base; the very node of the subjective is knotted in ethics understood as responsibility' (1985: 95).

The personal expenditure that Levinas portrays obliterates any smug appeals to self-righteousness. Yet, in demarcating maternity as an instance of such unrestricted responsibility, Levinas nevertheless enters on a contentious area for contemporary women. For what he seems to portray — even if as a figurative description — is not just an idealisation of traditional motherhood but a caricature of its overwhelming demands. But do contemporary women, whatever their stand regarding the 'feminine', still wish to be acclaimed as the epitome of self-sacrifice? A corollary of this question is whether women also wish to be solely identified with motherhood. Catherine Chalier again makes a telling observation on Levinas's use of the 'feminine'. 'Maternity is the ultimate meaning of the feminine, the very metaphor of subjectivity and of course, not only a metaphor.... The maternal body knows in its flesh and blood what subjectivity means. But we have to take note of the fact that, according to Levinas, ethics in its feminine achievement means to be a mother and nothing else. Can we agree?' (1991: 127).

In recent years, in the wake of such books as Carol Gilligan's In a Different Voice (1982), Sara Ruddick's Maternal Thinking (1989) and Nel Noddings' Caring (1984), women have passionately debated these issues. Several topics are involved in the controversy. Firstly, Gilligan's work raises the question as to whether women make ethical decisions more along the lines of an ethic of care and responsibility rather than one of justice. She contests the evaluation of women as morally inferior because they do not measure up to the standards of moral maturity established by alleged 'masculine' norms of justice (1982: 64–105). Ruddick is more concerned with the reaffirmation of what she regards as neglected maternal values. Her advocacy of maternal thinking and its virtues of protection, nurturance and training are set in opposition to the impersonal categories of reason. The rehabilitation of these maternal attitudes and their adoption by both men and women are considered by Ruddick as essential to a peacemaking enterprise needed to counteract masculine militarism (1989: 13–27, 224–51). Finally, Nel Noddings wishes to institute caring (identified with mothering) as a comprehensive standard to displace absolute principles of goodness, justice and autonomy which she associates (though not exclusively) with men (1984: 1–5, 36–7). All of these women insist on relationship as the definitive ethical medium.

In many ways, then, these women and Levinas have much in common. In their commendation of care and responsibility Gilligan, Ruddick and Noddings will still insist on intersubjectivity and reciprocity as the ideal form of relationship. (On this score, all have responded to their critics that, though at times there is dependency involved in such a caring and maternal condition, this should never condone exploitation, submissiveness or simply a desire for approval.) Yet they would seem to be reluctant to endorse an unmitigated displacement in the service of others such as Levinas proposes. It would seem that Gilligan, Ruddick and Noddings (though it would be a mistake to state their programmes are identical) hesitate to formulate a comprehensive position by extrapolating from the early months of selfless service towards a totally dependent child. For them, maternity is not, as it is for Levinas, an invitation to abandonment to the claims made by the other. For these women thinkers, maternity involves a qualified response.[16]

There are other feminists, however, who are extremely suspicious of any such wholesale support for such imputed maternal ideals as care and responsibility, detecting therein a compensatory idealisation of women. They also fear that this form of rehabilitation, though laudatory, if it is pursued unilaterally, will merely reconfirm women's allocation as an emotional factotum in the service of men as well as children. Their objections can also be appreciated as a caution, not just of Gilligan's, Ruddick's and Nodding's unquestioning acceptance of the designations of 'feminine' and 'maternal' but also of Levinas's usage. As Sara Lucia Hoagland says: 'A truly radical ethics will challenge not only the masculine but also the feminine, for the feminine is born of a masculinist framework and so does not, at a deep level, represent any change' (1990: 112). Elisabeth J. Porter echoes this when she states: 'When actions have developed as responses to subjugation, any uncritical appropriation does not challenge this subjugation' (1991: 158). In the light of this discussion, it is undeniable that Levinas's use of both the images and roles of women as beloved and as mother both serve to emphasise women's traditional positions in relation to men. What also becomes increasingly obvious in these depictions of women, which have more to do with actual women than the 'feminine' per se, is that Levinas is constrained by his esteem for the traditional roles of women within the confines of an orthodox Jewish position.

Irigaray disputes Levinas's portrayal of maternity and fecundity. She faults Levinas for viewing the child as the main creative outcome of love, rather than viewing love as creative in its own right. Irigaray is just as apprehensive of possessive pleasure as Levinas, and would agree with his attempts to free it of compulsive romanticism. Irigaray's concern is that marriage, within religious traditions, is none the less principally mandated to reproduction. While she does not reject the outcome of children by choice, Irigaray wants to reconceive the purpose of marriage. She envisages another form of birth as the expression of fecundity. 'I discover the divine between us, conceived by us but not combined with us, existing between each of us. We give birth to it, adults at last. Arriving at another stage of our history, God reveals himself as the work of man and woman' (2001: 13).

Finally, Irigaray will dispute Levinas's assumption that, when the child is born, it is always a son. She contemplates an alternative possibility that it is the woman who is 'transfigured' by the birth of a daughter. 'Giving herself to nature to be reborn from there, made fecund – within herself. Pregnant with a son, perhaps (but why a son and not a daughter, her other self?), but also with herself by him' (1993a: 197, translation emended). The proposal of a daughter in this context is a sharp reminder of the male perspective that dominates Levinas's reflections. Whether this depiction is intended as empirical, or whether it belongs only in a figurative register, the fact that the woman/'feminine' is supplanted in the final scheme of things by Levinas's automatic assumption of a male child, leaves Levinas open to Irigaray's charge of patriarchal bias.[17] To appreciate Levinas's position fully, however, it is important to take Levinas's religious background into consideration.

Levinas's Jewish influences

It is evident that, in his responses to questions in interviews, Levinas became aware that his employment of the terms 'woman' and the 'feminine' have become problematic. He makes different attempts to try and improve the situation. In response to one question, in an effort to elucidate his understanding of the 'feminine' in relation to alterity, he states:

At the time of my little book *Time and the Other*, I thought that femininity was this modality of alterity – this 'other genus' – and that sexuality was this non-in-difference to the other, irreducible to the formal alterity of terms in an ensemble. Today I think it is necessary to go back even further and that the exposition, the nudity, and the 'imperative demand' of the face of the other constitute this modality that the feminine already presupposes: the proximity of the neighbor is the non-formal alterity. (2001: 115)

Even in this qualification, the 'feminine', as the other genus, still retains the presuppositions of vulnerability, abandonment, poverty as the representative of alterity. A further reflection by Levinas, however, indicates that he has become aware of the distinction between sex and gender, and that gender attributes need not necessarily be restricted to a specific sex. 'Perhaps ... all these allusions to the ontological differences between the masculine and the feminine would appear less archaic if, instead of dividing humanity into two species (or into two genders), they would signify that the participation in the masculine and feminine were the attribute of every human being' (1985: 68). None the less, such a modification need not mean that gender stereotypes, traditionally connected with qualities and behaviour of either sex, lose their influence – something that is very conspicuous in the continuing popularity of C. G. Jung's ideas of male and female archetypes in his complementary model.[18]

Levinas wants both to use the 'feminine' as a model of alterity and to uphold woman as the guardian of values and the begetter of progeny. At the same time, with the human couple as a model for ethical exchange, he wants to sanctify love as *agape*. He appears to be caught in a conundrum. This is because Levinas is unwilling to move beyond certain Jewish religious ideals that designate women's responsibilities from a male viewpoint. This restricts his view of the 'feminine'. Levinas's distrust of love comes from his religious belief that selfish immoderation contaminates *eros*. This interferes with the grave responsibility of 'love without concupiscence' – *agape* – towards the other. Because of this untoward influence, he rejects any romanticisation of woman and love, even that depicted in the Song of Songs.[19]

The dimension of the romantic, in which love becomes its own end, where it remains without any 'intentionality' that spreads beyond it ... is foreign to Judaism.... Doubtless the mysterious interiority of feminine existence will be used to experience, like a betrothed, the Sabbath, the Torah itself; and sometimes the divine Presence in the nearness of men, the *sheckhinah*. The images do not in any way become feminine figures. They are not taken seriously. (1990a: 37)

Yet it is another step to associate both the 'feminine' and women with the ambiguity that marks degeneration of love (1990a: 37). Levinas's motives seem mixed, though they are no doubt well-intentioned.

In his rejection of a 'feminine' or female-centred interpretation of the Song of Songs, Levinas has been influenced by the work of Franz Rosenzweig, particularly by *The Star of Redemption* (1970). Susan Handleman notes the impact of Rosenzweig on Levinas's work. She observes: 'For Rosenzweig, the Song of Songs is the book that describes revelation "literally"; it is not an allegory or an analogy but the focal point of revelation, of the I and Thou of God and humanity ... because the revelation of this love is both worldly and spiritual at the same time' (1991: 266–7). Humanity thus witnesses to this revelation of love by leaving behind voluptuous love, in an expansive gesture of love towards another, one's neighbour. This is marked by the response: 'Here I am', which specifies a love that is neither profane nor self-indulgent. Levinas commends Rosenzweig and the strenuous demands to be placed on love in human relationship (Levinas 1990a: 195). Claire Katz comments on the parallels between Levinas and Rosenzweig, noting that that it is 'love [that] brings us out of ourselves through the desire that cannot be fulfilled but which longs for eternity' (2001a: 129). She also declares that, within the marriage relation, such love is manifested primarily in maternal care and responsibility for a child. It should not be understood as a mandate for women 'to become pregnant and sacrifice their lives' (Katz 2003: 143). Yet the maternal ideal predominates in his descriptions of women.

Levinas's position is amply demonstrated in 'Judaism and the Feminine', where Levinas extols the strength and valour of the biblical women – Miriam, Debora, Tamar, Naomi, Ruth, Abigail, Bathsheba, Sarah, Rebecca, Leah and Rachel – all of whom were central to the destiny and sacred history of the Jewish people (1990a: 31). He understands their place, however, as that of wife and mother, wellspring of the people of Israel. From this perspective, however, any personal or maternal relation 'is subordinate to a human destiny which exceeds the limits of "family joys": it is necessary to fulfil Israel, "to multiply the image of God" inscribed on the face of humanity' (35–6). A woman's manifest destiny is thus to tend the hearth, to secure the amenities of life, to provide the requisite support that makes men's valiant deeds possible. In the same vein, he reverts to a type of reverie, where he muses as to where the world would be without the existence of these women – 'without the secret presence, on the edge of invisibility, of these mothers, wives and daughters; without their silent footsteps in the depths and opacity of reality, drawing the very dimensions of interiority and making the world precisely habitable' (31). Thus, while Levinas allows that the 'the feminine figures among the categories of Being', and that she is a necessary participant in co-creation – 'as two totalities complete one another' (35) – he continues to support the priority of man in the created, as opposed to the messianic world. When he asks the rhetorical question 'Maybe the masculine is more directly related to the universal?' – it is difficult to disagree.

In her book *Levinas, Judaism and the Feminine*, Claire Katz cautions that Levinas's ethical pronouncements are not to be taken normatively. This is because they are providing an 'argument for understanding the possibility of the ethical in the shadow of a world that seems to make ethics impossible' (2003: 143). She none the less concedes that Levinas is stepping into dangerous territory in his employment of 'feminine' and maternal imagery. Katz also counsels against taking a blunt feminist approach to Levinas's work, allowing that Levinas is not proposing an essentialist view of women. While acknowledging that he does single out the role of maternal responsibility, Katz affirms that he appreciates the multifaceted dimensions of women (154). I am basically in agreement with these recommendations offered by Katz, but I am still worried that Levinas himself remains somewhat equivocal in his views on woman, alternating between extremes of exaltation and abasement. While such polarised descriptions of women are not foreign to western culture as a whole (e.g. the Madonna/harlot complex), Levinas may well be taking such imagery from his own Jewish tradition, as in Isaiah's graphic description of Israel as an errant wife.

Irigaray's divine interventions

In her response to Levinas, Irigaray will strive to give equal status to woman as the other of sexual difference. 'Who is the other, if the other of sexual difference is not recognized or known?' (1991b: 112). She rejects Levinas's notion of the 'feminine': 'For him, the feminine does not stand for an other to be respected in her human freedom and human identity. The feminine other is left without her own specific face. On this point, his philosophy falls radically short of ethics' (113). Irigaray is also unhappy with Levinas's compromised attitude to the flesh. 'He invokes his God but does not perceive him in the here and now, where God is already to be found and lost: in the sensibility of the female lover. [God is found] in the creation that she perpetuates while preserving her intimacy, her inviolability, her virginity. God of the universe, God of the fecundity of a future coming, is also preserved in the female lover' (1993a: 196–7; translation emended). The fact that women cannot become divine and that God or the divine cannot be realised in an erotic relationship of a woman with a man is something that, for Irigaray, interferes with Levinas's exemplar of the face. 'The God of Levinas is not incarnate, sensible, perceptible to the senses; he remains faceless. How does one see the face of the other through this invisibility?' (2001: 109).

The principal consideration of Irigaray's engagement with Levinas is to ameliorate the condition of women who she understands are being denied their autonomy, their right to love. Irigaray does not believe real change can be introduced without recognising women in a way that transforms both their identity and society (Irigaray 1993b: 45–50). As far as Irigaray is concerned, if there is no equivalence between men and women, there can be no ethics.[20] For Irigaray it is also the freedom of both partners that alone constitutes a true marriage. 'Love is accomplished by two, without dividing the roles between the beloved and the lover, between objectival or animal passivity on the one hand, and generally conscious and valorous activity on the other. Woman and man remain two in love. Watching over and creating the universe is their primary task, and it remains so' (1996: 138). Claire Katz interprets Irigaray's allegation that the lovers 'do not marry' (2001a: 27) to mean that marriage is unconsummated in Levinas's work. In her justification of Levinas against what she takes to be Irigaray's charge of puritanism, Katz states that, in Levinas, there is indeed a consummation, and that the couple do marry (2001a: 127). But this is to misunderstand Irigaray. What Irigaray is actually arguing is that there is no real marriage. This is because, for Irigaray, the conditions of parity between the sexes have not been met. These alone establish a true meeting of man and women. In acknowledging that Levinas has the same goal of disciplined love as she does, yet fails to accord the divine as present in the other, Irigaray remarks: 'For Lévinas the man, the passage through his God is perhaps, an imposition of limits upon his instincts, upon his natural intemperance, but does not represent a way of respecting the other as other. Instead it might lead to the other's subjection' (2001: 108).

In Levinas's ethics, God remains transcendent, and absent, though this absence/presence is attested by the ethical encounter with the other. This solution does not satisfy Irigaray. Though she acknowledges the other as transcendent

– and here the influence of Levinas on her is obvious – this format will have other resonances for Irigaray. She introduces a change of emphasis in the depiction of transcendence. She is also concerned that 'respecting the other in the name of God means imposing my God upon him, not respecting him as other' (108). In one sense, this involves interposing a specific idea of God between oneself and the other that interferes with the dialogue that Irigaray deems requisite for a true relationship of equals (108). She is equally anxious that, if there is speech, it can occur only within the horizon of this intervening God's authority. For Irigaray, such authority issues from a past that is ordered in accordance with a patriarchal worldview that does not accept women's autonomy. For Irigaray, if the transcendent God were to have a voice, it would be a male one.

In Irigaray's alternative vision, transcendence will still refer to the irreducibility of the other: 'Transcendence unveils itself in the other who is here present to me, but irreducible to my rational perception' (93). The other stays a mystery, as it does in Levinas. The adjustment that Irigaray introduces is one where a person's conduct towards an other fosters a love of genuine reciprocity that permits the divine to be present in sexual love. This is an affirmation of all that is human. 'To recognise you – man – you, as transcendent to me, to uphold in nature and spirit the transcendence between us, women and men – wouldn't this be the way to attain another subjectivity, another alterity, another community, more real, concrete and human?' (1996: 144). At the same time, Irigaray also wishes to sing a paean to the wonders of the body as an incarnation of the divine. The divine is now experienced in the flesh as 'through his presence as nourishment, including nourishment of the senses' (Irigaray 1991b: 116). There is no such sensible transcendental, no coincidence of the carnal and spiritual, for Levinas. The respective ethical demeanours of men and women in relation to God or the divine, and their repercussions for a transformation of ethics, mark the great dividing line between the worldviews of Irigaray and Levinas.

Conclusion

Levinas's last word on the topic of the 'feminine' is found in an interview with Bracha Lichtenberg-Ettinger. In their discussion, Lichtenberg-Ettinger tries to elicit a reaction from Levinas on her own interpretation of the 'feminine' in his work. Levinas himself is reticent at first: 'best to make only a few allusions to the subject of the difference of the feminine' (Levinas 1997: 14). Lichtenberg-Ettinger presents her thesis that, in Levinas's work, 'feminine' difference is originary, and that it is constitutive of the ethical space itself, marked by a certain interiority. Levinas replies that he does not conceive of the feminine in exactly this way, and states: 'the feminine is a necessary complementary category for the masculine and has nothing to do with the exteriority of the Other. For women as for men, the Other is the essential source of a person's life' (16). Lichtenberg-

Ettinger presses on regardless, determined to find some core of wisdom for the 'feminine', because she believes that its resources for philosophy have not begun to be mined. Levinas, however, does not want to have anything to do with this. In his short, but succinct answers, Levinas presents his present position: 'The feminine is the future ... Woman is the category of the future. It is that human possibility which consists in saying that another human life is more important than my own ... that the Other comes before' (20). His final summation is an extraordinary utterance: 'The feminine is that difference, the feminine is that incredible, unheard of thing in the human by which it is affirmed that *without me the world has meaning*' (22). Here the 'feminine' and women are identified with utter renunciation – in a way that reiterates his depiction of maternity, rather than his earlier views of the 'feminine' as the evocation of alterity.

Everything that Levinas himself has said, and all that has been said about him in this chapter, comes to a climax in this statement. The exorbitance of his message is as deliberate as ever. The language is exact and exacting. His conflation of the 'feminine' and woman continues. There is the intimation, however, that he is now aware, particularly in his reluctance to address the 'feminine' according to Lichtenberg-Ettinger's interpretation, that this term can also have a general application to every human being in an ethical relation to the Other. Yet he seems reluctant, in this particular setting, to further clarify the shifts in his meaning, or to correct ambiguities.

It needs to be admitted that Levinas may not be guilty, as charged by Beauvoir and Irigaray, of designating woman as the other of men, if this is taken in a simplistic fashion. Similarly to Levinas, Irigaray is herself also somewhat indiscriminate in her own switching between the 'feminine' and woman, for her own idealised purposes. Nevertheless, Irigaray's criticism of Levinas has been telling. It has made apparent that Levinas, by his use of the word 'feminine', whether deliberately or not, conveys a composite of certain physical and emotional qualities considered suitable for women since time immemorial. Contemporary feminists have faulted this automatic association, understanding that these qualities are basically culturally and historically relative. To employ them uncritically indicates a presumptuous, if not patronising attitude towards women. This is because rarely, if ever, have women been consulted by male writers (from biblical times onwards) in prescriptions of ideal feminine behaviour. Such generalisations also fail to account for the diversity of women from those races, classes and forms of religions that are not encompassed by the mainstream mind-set. Women's variations are completely disregarded in universal descriptions that erase the ability of those who are excluded to affirm their respective distinctiveness. Thus the indiscriminate usage of the term 'feminine' in this day and age is dangerous. It is symptomatic of a lack of sensitivity on the part of male users towards the changed awareness and aspirations of women. While these deficiencies may not be sufficient to discredit Levinas's entire undertaking, they point to a blind spot in his conception of otherness. Thus, although Levinas cannot be taken to task for not being up to date on the most recently debated issues of sex and gender, his work is symptomatic of the neglect by many male scholars of the subtle theoretical discussions and distinctions by women available on this subject.[21]

Levinas's mixture of conservative religious values with a radical interrogation of traditional western ethics is a potent but confusing one. It has made it awkward for feminists to speak to his work. Secular feminists, such as Elizabeth Grosz and Tina Chanter, concentrate on the dynamics of alterity as exteriority, and on its excessive demands. For Grosz, alterity, in its 'feminine' mode of difference, confounds the logic of identity. Its asymmetrical relation promotes a destabilisation of ingrained preconceptions. Grosz perceives this as a contribution toward 'a (feminist) questioning of sexual difference, and the possibilities of communication and exchange between different races' (Grosz 1987: 26). Chanter, quoted in an epigraph at the beginning of this chapter (53), views Levinas's work as challenging 'the logic of metaphysics with a radicality hitherto unprecedented' (1988: 209). She holds a similar view to Grosz of the introduction of new perspectives of otherness, but she registers her reservations about his use of the 'feminine' (213). Finally, Chanter regards Levinas's work as providing the impetus for Irigaray's own contestation of Levinas in her construct of sexual difference. These recent assessments respond to the epigraph of Beauvoir where she suggests that, in regard to Levinas's work, the tired old dialectic of sameness (male) and otherness (female) remains dominant.

In the end, the question that looms is whether Levinas has made a contribution to scholarship in the area of women and religion. There is no clear-cut answer. Despite Levinas's idealisation of women, his treatment of *eros* as excess, in the key of the 'feminine', has only served to accentuate the suspicion of female sexuality as contributing to the downfall of men. But perhaps it is now time to take Levinas at his word – literally – and undertake an application of his programme. Thus, if it is a woman who is regarded by a man as the other, then, according to Levinas's rubrics, surely it will be she who puts the male, and all that he stands for, into question. She no longer represents a hostile difference, whose perceived autonomy must be subdued, nor need she be the quintessential paragon of a deferential piety and goodness. He, as subject, is open to her, to the manifold possibilities that may emerge in an open-ended and non-ideological process of relating. This indeed is revolutionary: the boundaries of what has been regarded as traditionally 'masculine' and 'feminine', in so far as they are cultural artefacts, will certainly dissolve. Each partner is now affirmed in their separateness and their completeness. The words of merger or incorporation are no longer relevant in such relationships. Levinas's programme, from this perspective, can be seen as a reform of any ethics of subordination that has operated in a way that demeaned the other. This system has functioned with reference not just to women but to all of diverse races, classes and religions whose inferiority was automatically assumed by a dominant elite. In this regard, Levinas's vision of ethical primacy is a salutary development that recasts an ethics of assimilation into one of respect and responsibility for others in all their heterogeneous singularity.

Yet a slight discomfort becomes apparent if one takes another perspective. What of a situation where it is a woman who is the subject, and a man is the other who makes a claim on her? Can a woman break easily and painlessly from those centuries of enculturation when mentally, emotionally and physically she has been at the disposal of men? Given that most women until quite recently have been conditioned to defer to the wishes of the other, how is it possible to accept that Levinas brings a more nuanced differentiation to this situation? It would seem to me to be a dangerous and even compromising counsel to enjoin a woman to be unreservedly responsible to a man as the other without a careful analysis of the context involved. There are major problems embedded in the social fabric that prevent an easy application of Levinas's programme. To call for the ethical in the absence of any social or political reform is to highlight the utopian or messianic nature of Levinas's proposals. Even worse, from a woman's viewpoint, it could seem that an ethics that supported responsibility as passivity could easily be understood as a glorification of victimisation.

Yet Levinas is not utterly without redemption. He envisions a time when 'The justice which will rule the relations between men amounts to the presence of God among them. The differences between masculine and feminine are blurred in this messianic age' (1990a: 35). Unfortunately, we are not yet living in a messianic age, and, as yet, neither men or women have entered into a kingdom which encourages the blurring of distinctions (whether physically, figuratively or spiritually). In the end, Irigaray's question persists: Where do women stand today in relation to God or the divine? Levinas's work has been a cautionary reminder that men still, even in their best efforts, tend to exclude women from what they consider the symbolic highest status, or the abode of the divine. At the same time, as Irigaray has brought to our attention, women are all too often judged by the ideal of the male gender (1991b: 112). A critical evaluation of Levinas's work, and of Irigaray's response to it, suggests innovative ways of reconsidering divinity as manifest in the mundane world, and ethics as grounded in loving human relationships. Maybe their diverse recommendations for a new ethics mark a new beginning in demolishing those clay effigies we keep constructing in our own image, and in whose name we oppress and annihilate others. In this way, Irigaray's work can have salutary implications for such an ethics, despite her manifest heterosexist bias.

CHAPTER 4

Love and the labour of the negative: Irigaray and Hegel

For woman, therefore, the universal comes down to practical labor within the horizon of the universal delimited by man. Deprived of a relationship to the singularity of love, woman is also deprived of the possibility of a universal for herself. Love, for her, amounts to a duty – not a right – establishing her role within humankind where she appears as man's servant. (Irigaray 1996: 22)

One cannot help reflecting that in the same year that Hegel published this affirmation of man's capacity to transcend sexual desire in the pursuit of the ethics of Universality, his own illegitimate son was born. (O'Brien 1996: 204)[1]

Love, even carnal love, is therefore cultivated and made divine. The act of love becomes the transubstantiation of the self and his or her lover into a spiritual body ... Love is redemption of the flesh through the transfiguration of desire for the other (as an object?) into desire with the other. (Irigaray 1996: 139)

Introduction

Throughout the work of Luce Irigaray, the thought of Hegel has resonated with recurring intensity that reaches its culmination in her work I Love to You (1996), with her vindication of a new version of heterosexuality. From her early reflections on the situation of Antigone and the master/slave relation to her final revision of the dynamics of the Hegelian dialectic, and its movements of negativity and recognition, especially with reference to desire, Irigaray engages with Hegel.[2] She rejects his increasingly conservative and ultimately inconsistent treatment of women,[3] which subordinated them 'to destiny, without allowing them any access to mind, or consciousness of self and for self' (Irigaray 1993b: 130).[4] In contrast to Hegel, where negativity (as the necessary second movement of the dialectic, which involves engagement with an other) functions to integrate that other in the interests of a final mode of supreme self-consciousness or universality,[5] Irigaray seeks to transform radically this triumphalist procedure. Her intention is to rescue differentiation or negativity from its employment as a device that introduces alienation in the service of a higher autonomous unity, which Hegel identified with Geist/Spirit.

In this alternative modality of differentiation, negativity is not eradicated but reformulated by Irigaray, so that recognition is understood as a positive affirmation of an other, rather than an appropriation. Then, according to Irigaray, women, as no longer abstract and disembodied ciphers in a system not of their own devising, can become both initiators and partners in a revised model of relationship that incorporates a positive mode of sexual difference. This affirmation does not come at the cost of negating the other. Women attain the universal in their own right, but not in a dominant manner. One of the ways that Irigaray proposes to remedy the current situation is that 'at every opportunity, we ourselves take the negative upon ourselves. This would amount to allowing the other his/her liberty, and sex' (1993a: 120; translation emended).

This postulate of 'taking the negative upon oneself' – which will be investigated more fully later in the chapter – involves certain tasks, specific to each gender. Given the nature of Hegel's curtailment of women, both theoretically and physically, it is not problematic to appreciate Irigaray's call for liberty for women. But what of the call for allowing the other his or her 'sex'? Obviously this is not a literal call for mindless sexual indulgence or even an impassioned plea for a positive re-evaluation of sex in response to rationality's apparent dismissal of the body and its pleasures. It is rather the result of an appeal for the appreciation of a distinct sexual difference between men and women – not simply one that rests on a biological division according to sex, but a form of gendered differentiation that will have specific ethical, legal, linguistic, social and religious implications.[6] Irigaray postulates that the problem of sexual difference is probably the most significant philosophical issue of our era, and that it could provide 'salvation' if it was addressed with due attention (5).

Irigaray's proposal of sexual difference is not simply a confirmation of women's irreducibility and resistance to preordained categories (though it involves this). It is rather an acknowledgement that women themselves will no longer conform to definitions of femininity that do not respect a woman's integrity and her responsibility for her own becoming. Each woman should seek the 'perfection of her gender' (1993b: 64). For Irigaray, this is equivalent to the attainment of a form of universality. Women, as no longer the dominated other, will also attain a revised form of universality in their own right, a prerogative Hegel denied them (Mills 1996: 84).

> Being born a woman requires a culture particular to this sex and this gender.... She should not comply with a model of identity imposed on her by anyone, neither her parents, her lover, her children, the State, religion or culture in general.... She should, quite the contrary, gather herself within herself in order to accomplish her gender's perfection for herself, for the man she loves, for her children, but equally for civil society, for the world of culture, for a definition of the universal corresponding to reality. (Irigaray 1996: 27)

This task that Irigaray endorses, with its innovative repercussions for women and the notion of universality, is a complex one. This is because Irigaray, in interrogating the symbolic order, posits women no longer as a subsumed other but as constituting a distinct and separate sphere. Her claim is that a woman, as a representative of this separate sphere of gender, will break the male gender's social and symbolic monopoly. Irigaray, however, is not a separatist. In fact, it is her move endorsing a felicitous meeting of female and male genders that marks a distinct development in her work. Indeed, since *An Ethics of Sexual Difference*, she has been preoccupied with establishing a right order of relationship, of a sexual ethics, between men and women. It is this emphasis on an ethics of relationship between a woman and a man that becomes the focal point of much of Irigaray's later work:

If sexual difference is to be overcome is it not imperative first of all to find a sexual ethics? If one day we are to be one must we not now be *two*? Otherwise we fall back into some formal and empty (*male*) *one*, back into hierarchies we are familiar with, or into a nostalgia for returning back into the womb where the other is nothing but an encompassing source of food and shelter. (1993b: 179)

For Irigaray, ethics will involve moving beyond the undifferentiated state of the couple as it exists within Hegel's privatised domestic realm. She affirms that in its place, 'we need to establish an ethics *of the couple*, a place, a bond, where the two halves of the natural and spiritual world can be and change' (Irigaray 1993a: 132). And though the ethical ideal that Irigaray promotes is a love relationship between women and men, it is not to be confused with a facile fusion of romantic sensibilities. For Irigaray such hackneyed conventions simply feed into an absorption that obliterates necessary distinctions. Irigaray's understanding of love then presupposes a movement away from Hegel's definition of desire and love, which excluded women from full participation in its realisation. Rebuking Hegel, Irigaray writes, 'Love, as Hegel writes of it, is therefore not possible on the part of a woman.... In other words, a woman's love is defined as familial and civil duty. She has no right to singular love nor to love for herself' (1996: 21–2).[7] Irigaray's depiction of love does not indicate a return to the ethical of Hegelian proprieties which reinforced women's reproductive rights and duties. Irigaray wishes to dissociate love from any regimen of reproduction. For Irigaray, the child is no longer the required outcome of the union of love, as it was for Hegel. The relationship of love itself, attained by separate gendered tasks of the 'labour the negative', or, later, the 'labour of love', alone marks the culmination of the process as recognition.[8] Only if this process is engendered, does Irigaray believe that the spirit can unfold properly in the world and that humankind can today be 'saved' or spiritualised. 'The process whereby gender might become perfect is lacking in Hegel, and indeed in ourselves. If gender were to develop individually, collectively, and historically, it could mark *the place where spirit entered human nature*, the point in time when the infinite passed into the finite, given that each individual of a gender is finite and potentially infinite in his or her relation to gender' (1993a: 139).

This is no neutered Geist/Spirit unfolding its purpose in History.⁹ It is an intimate and passionate involvement, animated by desire that is no longer only in the service of consciousness. It is thus a form of desire that is no longer enslaved in the dynamics of need and demand in a phallic economy. Desire is now to be informed by a disciplining of the instincts that will permit the development of love and a disclosure of spirit. Irigaray, however, is no less exultant than Hegel in her own claims for the work of spirit in History, though her vision differs markedly.

> We need to realize History – or at least continue it – as the salvation of humanity comprised of men and women. That is our task. In accomplishing it, we are working for History's development by bringing about more justice, truth and humanity in the world. This is the task for our time.... It is a task for everyone. No one is beyond it, and it makes no one naturally a master or slave, poor or rich. (Irigaray 1996: 29–30)

In all these rewritings of Hegel, the principal intention of Irigaray is to renegotiate Hegel's understanding of universality, reformulating the dialectic in terms of sexual difference. The realisation of Spirit in the world will have implications different from those of Hegel. Irigaray's work, none the less, is not without complications. Despite her disclaimers that the modifications in male and female roles lead to open-ended forms of identity and relationships, inevitable questions arise regarding Irigaray's emphasis on a heterosexual bond, as well as on the conduct that she will endorse for women. The issue that arises is whether Irigaray, in her effort to transform the Hegelian dialectic, unnecessarily employs her own version of universalising strategies that has restrictive consequences for her vision of innovative relations between men and women.

Women, civil identity and the figure of Antigone

For Irigaray there are two fundamentally separate but related tasks that must be accomplished if women are to achieve a form of universality in their own right. One is that of obtaining rights according to civil laws that protect their social needs. This will help establish the basis for women to acquire an objective form of female identity. Irigaray acknowledges this need for civic identity by stating: 'for ... social justice to be possible, women must obtain a civil identity ... otherwise these rights will never be gained exhaustively, once and for all' (1994: 63). In contrast, the other task of cultivating a 'feminine' identity is of a more subjective import. Women need to accomplish a culture that is particular to their gender. For Irigaray, 'it is important for the woman to realize [this] without renouncing her natural identity' (1996: 27). It is the figure of Antigone who features in Irigaray's work as a multivalent indicator of the changes that need to occur not just in the polis but in the cosmos and the natural world. Irigaray first engages with Hegel's work in the essay 'The Eternal Irony of Community' (1985a: 214–26; French version, 1975). This is a response to Hegel's domestication of women.[10] Later, in *Sexes and Genealogies*, Irigaray introduces sexual difference into the process of mediation in 'The Universal as Mediation' (1993b: 125–49). Finally, in *I Love to You* (1996), Irigaray completes her sustained involvement with the work of Hegel that began in 1981 (12).

Irigaray's reflections on Antigone in Hegel's work are not focused on a refutation of Hegel's interpretation as simply a distortion of Sophocles (as they are in Mills 1996), nor are they a direct confrontation with his specific pronouncements on Antigone (as in Chanter 1995: 115). She discerns that the figure of Antigone in the literature is an equivocal one, and that most interpretations have been slanted by a 'masculine' viewpoint (1993b: 121). Her initial interrogations involve a sophisticated mimetic double play of the Hegelian rendition of Antigone in *Phenomenology of Spirit* (Hegel 1977). In disclosing Hegel's biased assumptions, Irigaray reveals his 'amazing vicious circle' (Irigaray 1985a: 223) of quasi-logical manoeuvres that both exclude women and render them powerless, if they attempt to redress their allotted situation.

Irigaray's admits that her own interpretations reflect an equivocal attitude, similar to those found in many readings of Antigone. In *Speculum*, Antigone can be read as a woman who is defiant towards the male system of values as represented by Creon's social dictates: 'the law of the city, of its sovereign, of the man of the family' (1985a: 218). From this perspective, Antigone is praised for her defence of the familial, private values. Antigone is 'Faithful to her task of respecting and loving the home, careful not to pollute the hearth flame' (1993b: 111). From another perspective, Antigone is viewed by Irigaray as a victim for this act of fidelity in burying her brother, and in vindicating his honour (which itself rests on martial values of the male world) (110). Irigaray continues by describing Antigone as thus performing 'the dark side of that task' (111). This association of women with the earth and death marks their connection with the repressions of men that women have always unconsciously mediated.[11] Irigaray declares: 'She [Antigone] must protect him both from all base and irrational individuality and from the forces of abstract matter, which are now more powerful than he. Shielding him from the dishonoring operation of unconscious desires and natural negativeness ... she places this kinsman back in *womb of the earth* and thus unites him with undying, elemental individuality' (1985a: 215).

The Hegelian dialectic, articulated in such power struggles as Creon's with Antigone, is thus erected on a denial. In such a context, the association of women with the sensible and the natural world is not a positive one. For Irigaray, both in Hegel and western culture, 'she [woman] is never anything but the still undifferentiated opaqueness of sensible' (224). Yet the situation is not hopeless, for though Hegel's depiction of Antigone might appear to reduce her to the situation of a slave, 'both silenced and reduced to nothingness' (224–5), Irigaray understands her also as signifying the subversive potential of slaves to 'whisper their revolt against their masters secretly' (218). Thus, as Irigaray's own work develops from a critical to a more constructive stance, her depiction of Antigone becomes more complex.

In *An Ethics of Sexual Difference*, Antigone is described as 'neither master nor slave. And this upsets the order of the dialectic' (1993a: 119). None the less, Antigone's experience becomes the basis for a cautionary tale: 'If we are not to live Antigone's fate, the world of women must successfully create an ethical order and establish the conditions necessary for women's action' (108). Then, In *Thinking the Difference*, there is a further development where Antigone is portrayed as indicating the civic and political mediations that Irigaray now finds necessary for women to undertake – explicitly the task of obtaining civil rights specific to women. 'It seems to me to be worthwhile reconsidering the content of the civil law today, in the light of the truth about Antigone' (Irigaray 1994: 70).[12] In this guise, Antigone becomes a reminder of the need for women to take their rightful place in the public world, but not, as Irigaray warns, without careful consideration of the actual context – which is not always ordered in women's interests. 'Her [Antigone's] example is always worth reflecting upon as a historical figure, and as an identity or identification for many girls and women living today. For this reflection, we must abstract Antigone from the seductive, reductive discourses and listen to what she has to say about government of the polis, its orders and its laws' (70).

Such a statement is also a prelude to Irigaray's declaration that women's recent admission to the public forum has not been without its difficulties. She decries the unilateral promotion of equality, fearing that this is just another reduction of women to the level of sameness – that is, identification with the male standards and privileges that feature in a democratic society. 'The rights women have gained in the last few years are for the most part rights that enable them to slip into men's skin, to take on the so-called male identity. These rights do not solve the problems of their rights and duties as women towards themselves, their children, other women, men and society' (79). Irigaray is not against equal rights, but she believes that equivalent relations between the sexes can be established only if there are special collective civil and legal rights to protect women's specific sexual identity.[13] These rights will establish the political and civil status that Hegel had denied Antigone and, by inference, all women. When asked to identify these rights, Irigaray has defined the principal ones as follows:

Women's rights must be redefined so that women can tailor the rights they have gained in the name of equality to their own identity as women.... enshrining these rights in the law, ... is the best way for women to hold on to rights already gained, have them enforced, and gain others more specifically suited to female identity ... [such as] the right to physical and moral inviolability (which means a woman's own right to virginity of body and mind), the right to motherhood free of civil and religious tutelage, women's right to their own specific culture. (xv–xvi)[14]

Irigaray make clear that she wishes women not only to assume the responsibility of adult citizens but to reinforce these rights by also undertaking the necessary tasks of subjective discernment and reclamation of their identity which are no longer imposed by alien directives. This would mark the attainment of subjectivity or, as Irigaray names it, 'the perfection of their gender'. Irigaray issues specific instructions for this task: 'It is up to them to protect their virginity, their motherhood, their bit of nature, their house, their images, languages, god(s) or goddess(es). It is therefore up to them to become subjects capable of sublimating their sexual drives, cultivating their sexuality, giving it rhythm, temporality, stakes' (81).

A culture of women

As an integral element in the process of women achieving their own culture, Irigaray believes that the relation of women to nature must be reconstituted, so as to allow for the restoration of a different cultural understanding of maternity and virginity. Again, it is Antigone who serves as a model for the ideals to be established so that women can achieve full subjectivity. 'She [Antigone] reminds us that the earthly order is not a pure social power, that it must be founded upon the economy of the cosmic order, upon respect for the procreation of human beings, on attention to maternal ancestry, to its gods, its rights, its organization' (70). Thus far, in Irigaray's view, because of men's repressions and consequent disrespect for the natural world, women have borne the brunt of what she describes as an 'insufficiently thought out relation between biology and culture' (1993c: 46). Irigaray acknowledges that, in some respects, Hegel was conscious of this fault, yet he believed that 'natural immediacy' requires subjugation if Spirit, as universality in both the rational and the political realms, is to be attained: 'Hegel in particular was aware of this ethical failure in our relation to the natural world and to genders and their genealogies. Antigone is sacrificed because she respects the blood and the gods of her mother and therefore performs the rites over her dead brother. Hegel has written that the whole subsequent development of the spirit was mortgaged against this original sacrifice' (1993a: 194).[15]

Irigaray does not view this development with the same equanimity as Hegel because, as she understands it, what he terms 'natural immediacy' has nothing to do with her ideal of a natural harmony. In Irigaray's estimation, patriarchy imposes an artificial ethical structure because 'natural immediacy', as in Hegel, is associated with unmediated passions or drives. 'Hegel adds that the love between man and woman remains in a state of natural immediacy and is not capable, as such, of assuring the passage to culture' (2001: 82). This uncultivated state that is traditionally restrained by imposed civic and religious regulations, and ordered to the perpetuation of the species, does not allow, in Irigaray's opinion, for a positive relation to nature. Irigaray proposes Antigone as model of a needed positive connection to the elemental forces and rhythms of the natural world. Romantic as this may sound, Irigaray is no Rousseau-like sentimentalist when it comes to human nature. Her 'revisionary' programme, influenced by psychoanalytic thought, springs from a realistic assessment of the destructive havoc wreaked by unrestrained expression of the instinctual drives, both primary and partial, and the need for a conscious discipline.[16] Irigaray gives an eloquent description of the preparation she herself undertook as part of this process of conscious sublimation that she posits as indispensable for a new mode of the labour of the negative.

> In my case it was more a question of inverting myself.... I carried out an inversion of the femininity imposed on me in order to try and define the female corresponding to my gender.... I wanted to begin to define what a woman is, thus myself as a woman – and not only a woman but a freely belonging to the female gender or generic – by carrying out a particular process of limitation or negation relative to my natural immediacy.... Hence I attempted to sketch a spirituality in the feminine, and in so doing, of course, I curbed my own needs and desires, my natural immediacy ... [and I called] into question the spirituality imposed on me in the culture appropriate to the male. (1996: 64)

This is Irigaray's account of the task of 'taking the negative on oneself'. It is an interior asceticism that ensures a new form of spirituality. It is one where the desires of natural immediacy are redirected rather than unconsciously projected on the other. Such a process takes on very different significations from Hegel's dialectic movement towards a disembodied triumph of an artificial ideal that entails 'The mastery of consciousness (historically male), over nature and humankind' (Irigaray 1996: 13). Irigaray believes that women who undertake this task will no longer see themselves as objects of male desires, nor as driven by their own uncontrollable passions, which has been attributed to their identification with natural immediacy. In this way, Irigaray suggests, the transition from nature to culture can be achieved without denial and repression, evident in both the Hegelian and the Freudian models. The question is whether this movement, with its positive and creative consequences, can be quite so easily accomplished as Irigaray envisions.[17]

As an antidote to 'natural immediacy', Irigaray also wishes to re-enforce her own belief in a positive relation that women have with nature – their natural identity. Irigaray wants women to re-own an intimate (and spiritual) connection to a harmonious cosmos, and to the cycles and rhythms of the natural world, as part of their achievement of a cultural identity. Irigaray's own thesis is that, in the natural world, women do have a 'natural identity' in that they are born female.[18] The terms 'natural identity', 'natural world' and 'natural reality' or 'real' are all extremely problematic and easily misconstrued. Irigaray's views on this matter derive from the fact that nature has two genders – not one. As she states: 'The natural, aside from the diversity of its incarnations or ways of appearing is at least two: male and female' (1996: 37).[19] This notion of two distinct genders, so basic to Irigaray's programme, is postulated as an 'immediate given' and 'a real and irreducible component of the universal' (47). Irigaray elucidates the significance of this natural identity for a distinct ontological difference for women. '[T]here is no more "natural immediacy". I am a sexed ontological and ontic being, hence assigned to a gender ... each gender must define and retain mediations appropriate to it' (107).[20]

Unfortunately, the culture into which women have been born was not supportive of a such a female ontological identity. According to Irigaray, the task of women today is: 'a matter of demanding a culture, of wanting and elaborating a spirituality, a subjectivity and an alterity appropriate to this gender: the female' (107). Irigaray posits two interrelated recommendations as the appropriate mediations that she believes are necessary for women's own attainment of a separate culture – one that will make possible the perfection of their gender. One is a re-evaluation of the mother/daughter relationship; the other is a restoration of the notion of virginity. From a psychoanalytic viewpoint, the reworking of the mother/daughter relationship involves a dismissal of Freud's oedipal theory.[21] Irigaray observes that the Freudian-Lacanian model has relevance only for a patriarchal culture. Daughters must no longer reject their mothers, and seek a substitute for the penis that both they and their mothers lack, in marriage with the birth of a child (ideally a male). Irigaray describes this regrettable situation in Hegelian terms: 'The girl's only reason for being is to become a wife and mother. In this respect, her mother represents this abstract role for her, as she does to the mother' (1996: 26). For Irigaray, there are no loving relations between mothers and daughters as long as they are caught in this repetition of roles, and do not acknowledge each other as individuals in their own right. To remedy this state of affairs, Irigaray recommends a refiguration of the mother/daughter relation whereby each woman consciously separates from her mother and thus does not have to unconsciously 'reproduce' motherhood.[22] There remains a difficulty for a daughter in learning to separate constructively from her mother. Irigaray notes: 'She [the daughter] must become a woman like her mother and, at the same time, be able to differentiate herself from her. But her mother is the same as she. She cannot reduce or manipulate her as an *object* in the way a little boy or man does' (1994: 18). Cornell provides a clear explanation of Irigaray's intentions:

> The daughter recognizes the cost to the mother/daughter relationship of the feminine being reduced to the maternal function.... The problem is less a fusional relationship between women, particularly mothers and daughters, as much as the imaginary projection of Woman which does not allow women to fashion their own lives. We need to reinterpret and, more importantly, to *reaffirm* the feminine as other than their [men's] projection. (1991: 76–7)

Motherhood is then not an automatic reflex but a conscious decision. To effect the cultural mediations necessary for a reconceptualisation of motherhood to occur, Irigaray, following Freud, appeals to mythological narratives. She posits a prehistoric gynocracy whose demise is variously depicted in Greek mythology. To illustrate this, Irigaray selects a version of the Demeter and Persephone myth as being paradigmatic of the shift that took place when patriarchy disrupted a gynocratic idyll. Demeter and Persephone epitomise the time when, in this gynocracy, the mother/daughter couple flourished, forming 'a natural and social model' that was also 'the guardian of fertility of nature' (1994: 12). This state was supplanted by patriarchy.

> The abduction of the daughter of the great Goddess serves to establish the power of male gods and the structure of patriarchal society. But this abduction is a rape, a marriage with the consent of neither the daughter nor the mother, an appropriation of the daughter's virginity by the God of the underworld [Hades] ... a descent for her (them) into the invisible, oblivion, loss of identity and spiritual barrenness. (111)[23]

According to Irigaray, the resultant spiritual barrenness in the mother/daughter relationship is still evident today. In its original positive manifestation, however, the relationship was fostered in a culture that worshipped the body and natural elements. Thus the mother/daughter couple inhabited a spiritual dimension, embodying a divine relationship. As she states in 'The Universal as Mediation': 'The mother–daughter couple is also divine' (1993b: 132).[24] As a remedy for today's compromised circumstances, Irigaray proposes that women, both mothers and daughters, have to reclaim their spiritual ancestry as part of the process of affirming their gender difference and subjectivity. Irigaray is resolute in her assertion that 'without the possibility that God might be made flesh as a woman, through the mother and daughter, and in their relationships, no real constructive help can be offered to a woman. If the divine is absent in woman and among women, there can be no possibility of changing, converting her primary affects' (1993a: 71).

To assist the establishment of such relationships today, Irigaray recommends that female lines of descent or genealogies be set up as an antidote to the male genealogies that have dominated in a patriarchal world.[25] She also recommends that pictures of mothers and daughters be placed in public places.[26] As I described the process in Chapter 1, Irigaray does not, however, support a literal revival of a goddess religion, but she recommends cultivating the values of tranquillity and harmony that she associates with this benevolent world. It is these values, reminiscent of uterine plenitude, that Irigaray understands as formative for a contemporary female spirituality. 'This woman I am has to realize the female as universal in the self and for the self as far as she is able during the period of History in which she finds herself and given the familial, cultural, or political contingencies she has to overcome' (1996: 144–5). The efficacy of such values today, while not without precedent in other spiritually oriented feminist movements such as that of the G/goddess, can be extremely problematic. This is because while Irigaray is not espousing timeless ideals of an essentialist variety, she is endorsing actual qualities from a supposed bygone era as a prerequisite for contemporary women to achieve spirituality.

The redemption of virginity from its characterisation within a patriarchal system is also a necessary undertaking. This is because Irigaray believes that 'patriarchy is founded upon the theft and violation of the daughter's virginity and the use of her virginity for commerce between men, including religious commerce' (1994: 111). The corrective task for this offence also inevitably has spiritual implications, because, for Irigaray, virginity represents a woman's autonomy – both physical and spiritual. '[B]ecoming a virgin is synonymous with a woman's conquest of the spiritual' (1993c: 117). Thus, the autonomy of virginity, together with a renegotiated mother/daughter bond and a conscious redirection of her unconscious impulses, are, from Irigaray's perspective, the most indispensable requirement for women intent on an integral identity. These attainments will augment their civil autonomy. None the less, Irigaray's quest for a just society cannot be divided from the spiritual dimension of her programme. Irigaray describes what she ultimately intends as a society where both civil and spiritual requirements of women are met: 'Justice would mean woman's being virgin and mother for herself, these properties of her nature founding her spiritual becoming, her rights and duties, instead of her being reduced to an elementary naturalism in which virginity is equated with the presence of the hymen, and maternity with the fact of actually haven given birth' (1996: 136).

This whole process of the attainment of objective and subjective identity is delineated by Irigaray according to a dialectical negotiation that mirrors Hegel's model, if not his content. It moves from a generic unity of biological or natural definition, by way of particular cultural differentiations (protected by the civil code), to the attainment of a distinct (gendered) individuality. This unique identity, as in Hegel, involves a complex interaction of the component parts that effects a refined mode of universality. But for Irigaray, there is a change from the negative and repressive Hegelian implications for women. As Irigaray states: 'The universal [universality] – if this term can be used here – consists in the fulfilment of life and not in submission to death, as Hegel would have it' (24). In so far as this universality also entails the achievement of consciousness, there is a spiritual dimension involved. In Irigaray's model, however, there is no totalisation or identification with Geist. For Irigaray, spirituality is not thus equated with the estrangements of a disembodied ideal or an illusion of absolute transcendence. Instead, the spiritual aspect is promoted as involving an enlivening energy that animates and regenerates, but neither suppresses nor exhausts existence.

Irigaray supports a spirituality that is open-ended in its modality of becoming. In one sense, Irigaray's understanding of the term 'spirituality' involves a combination of both the metaphysics of Hegel and the ontology of Heidegger that, at first glance, would not seem necessarily compatible.[27] But this does not seem to bother Irigaray. Although she does not comment directly on this amalgamation, it emerges in *I Love to You*, where Irigaray combines women's sexual difference as an ontic and ontological dimension (where it is the mother who the forgotten originary source of *physis*/matter),[28] with women's attainment of universality according to a reformulation of Hegel's dialectic. Irigaray's intention, however, is not to construct a comprehensive or consistent system in the mould of 'male' philosophy. Instead, her intention is both to demonstrate the omission of women from the objective world and to restore their indispensable and distinct 'feminine' mode of becoming. In so doing, Irigaray chooses only those aspects of philosophical thought that are of most significance for her own anti-systematic approach.[29]

Equality and difference

In her insistence on the fact that simple equality under the law is not enough for women to attain their own autonomy, Irigaray does state views somewhat similar to those of Simone de Beauvoir, especially as the latter is interpreted in a recent work by Debra Berghoffen: 'For though Beauvoir clearly believes that without economic and political equality women will be deprived of their status as subjects, her discussion of passion, the body, and the gift indicate that by themselves, revised economic and political arrangements will not transform patriarchy' (Berghoffen 1997: 201). There is also a similarity in the fact that both Irigaray and Beauvoir use the term 'transcendence' with reference to their conviction of the new status of universality to which women should aspire. Another correlation is that Irigaray and Beauvoir both refer to the Hegelian model of the master/slave dialectic in describing the situation of women. But there the similarity ends. (It is worth noting, however, that, technically speaking, because of their restriction to the domestic dimension by Hegel, women themselves did not even qualify for inclusion in this dynamic public contest of master and slave.)[30]

Beauvoir's analysis of women as other, delegated to the position of slave with a distinctly negative designation as non-male, demonstrates the need for women to reject such a construct. Her solution for women is one of defying this otherness that she describes as associated with immanence, inferiority and the claims of motherhood. Instead, they should assert their transcendence not just by their mastery of biology but by challenging man's control of culture.[31] For Irigaray, however, this remedy is tantamount to becoming a male. She refutes Beauvoir's famous dictum: 'one is not born, but rather becomes, a woman' (Beauvoir 1975: 249). Irigaray recasts this statement as: 'It's not as Simone de Beauvoir said … but rather: I am born a woman, but I must still become this woman that I am by nature' (1996: 107). In this way, Irigaray demarcates a division between an egalitarian feminism and one of difference.[32]

For Irigaray, as a proponent of a gender difference, there are both rights to be achieved and distinctive feminine cultural characteristics to be cultivated. Perhaps this opinion is the major obstacle that many women thinkers have with Irigaray. The focus on sexual difference with its specific 'feminine' characteristics again brings to the forefront the issue of essentialism which, as I observed earlier in this chapter, was the centre of debate about Irigaray's early work. Though her recommendations, according to Naomi Schor, may be a more a form of universalism, rather than an ahistorical or ontological mode of essentialism,[33] Irigaray's use of the term 'natural', and her conditions for achieving a spiritual universality – albeit a modification of Hegel's transcendence – complicate, rather than resolve, the issue. It has lead to extremely diverse evaluations of her work, which will be discussed in Chapters 5 and 7.

The return of the couple

It is only once a woman has attained her own identity that, for Irigaray, she is sufficiently prepared to enter into a relationship with the opposite gender. In Irigaray's depiction of the relationship between the two sexes, there is the insistence on two distinct gendered universals (1996: 106), and the task of each to realise, both separately and together, the fullness of life that is expressed in the currency of universality. These interrelated activities are what Irigaray proposes as a constituent of the 'labour of love': 'I thus differentiate myself within myself through the facts of my being a particular individual and of my belonging to a gender. This process enables me to make a pact with a person of the other gender without the mediation of the object' (145).[34] Irigaray posits that such a labour, undertaken separately by a woman and man, encourages love, that is both bodily and spiritual, to flourish. Together, they create the world. 'Woman and man remain two in love. Watching over and creating the universe is their primary task, and it remains so' (1996: 138).[35] In this task, each partner retains their subjectivity and thus discovers their particular aspect of the universal. 'The particularity of this universal is that it is divided into two' (50).

This depiction of a heterosexual relationship by Irigaray supersedes what has been the traditional rendition of love, principally the 'instinctual or drive-related attraction in natural immediacy' (147).[36] In contrast, it is love enacted – with attentiveness, with generosity, with a form of intransitivity – that Irigaray denotes by the phrase 'I love to you' (102). This non-dominant partnership provides the basis of Irigaray's passionate refutation and reformulation of Hegel's idea of Spirit as a singular achievement. In fact, Irigaray will introduce a triple dialectic at the core of this exercise. 'In *Speculum*, I wrote that to re-establish a political ethics a dual dialectic is necessary, one for the male subject and another for the female subject [1985a: 223–4]. Today I would say that a triple dialectic is necessary: one for the male subject, one for the female subject, and one for their relationship as a couple or in a community' (1994: 39).

Within this framework, the role of negativity in the dynamics of recognition, as it appears in Hegel, is also reworked. Negativity remains, but instead of being a confrontational element, it implies a stage of self-analysis and critical appropriation. For both women and men the main task involved is the 'mastery and culture of energy rather than its instinctual expenditure' (1996: 138).[37] As Irigaray states: 'the negative can mean access to the other of sexual difference and thereby become happiness without being annihilating in the process' (13). She then adds: 'Hegel knew nothing of negative like that' (13). It is here that the negative takes on a new connotation. The negative marks an admission of one's lack of mastery, of an acknowledgement that the other can never be a possession or under control. Thus: 'There will be no definitive "negation of negation". Man being irreducible to woman and woman to man, there no longer exists any *absolute* spirit nor *one* finality of being' (107).

This new appreciation of the labour of love gives access to an affirmative recognition of the other that enhances life, rather than imposing a sacrifice or death on women by precluding their access to self-determination. Recognition, as no longer dependent on a mastery or assimilation of otherness in the name of a greater unity, is given a more positive designation. This involves an acknowledgement of one's limitations and of the transcendence of the other. In Irigaray's reformulation, the notion of recognition is no then longer simply an abstract principle, but becomes a living interchange 'With this recognition, I mark you, I mark myself with incompleteness, with the negative. Neither you nor I are the whole nor the same, the principle of totalization' (105).

It is this admission, on the part of each partner in the relationship, that allows Irigaray to extol the nature of love that is thus generated. 'Love, even carnal love, is therefore cultivated and made divine' (1996: 139). The act of love becomes a transfiguration of the self and his or her lover into a spiritual state (like that of mother and daughter). Such an ideal of divine love, identified with spirit, is the culmination of Irigaray's rehabilitation of Hegel's neutral idea of Spirit and its ethical prescriptions – so alien to carnal love – particularly as it is depicted in Hegel's *Elements of the Philosophy of Right* (1991: 199–203). Irigaray eulogises: 'The wedding between man and woman realizes the reign of spirit. Without it, there is no spirit. Any universal corresponding to a single gender or claiming to be neuter sins against spirit. And to sin against spirit is absolute' (1996: 147).

Irigaray's engendered revision supplants the former ritualised rivalry of Hegel, by permitting both parties separate access to self-consciousness. Hegel was often taken to task for his arcane abstractions in this regard, particularly with reference to the reconciliation of subjective and objective spirit. Irigaray has no patience for these abstruse meanderings, for she does not see them connected in any intimate way with issues of flesh-and-blood human beings. Irigaray situates an ultimate realisation of spirit as embodied in the actual physical embrace of male and female. She views this as introducing a new meaning of transcendence: 'Transcendence is thus no longer ecstasy, leaving the self behind toward an inaccessible total other, beyond a sensibility beyond earth' (104).[38] Rather, transcendence is an entasy – a realisation in the here and now.

Heterosexism and its exclusions

In establishing this new heterosexual ontology of love and spirit, Irigaray excludes same-sex relationships, particularly those of women, from participation in the realisation of spirit. While she acknowledges that same-sex relationships do liberate people from the necessity to procreate that has dominated the paternal rule, they do not foster her approved form of sexual ethics and its outcome (1993b: 143).[39] Indeed, in the Prologue to I Love to You (1996: 5), Irigaray depicts same-sex relations between women as being an indulgence in natural immediacy. She regards them as a distraction from the tasks needed to reform the discriminatory structures that distort male and female relations. She is quite adamant in her declaration: 'These women are still in a state of natural immediacy or unhappy consciousness, the traditional lot of the female gender. Consequently, they confuse their unmediated will with the model of law or the way to happiness for all women – indeed, for all women and men' (3).

Irigaray's appraisal is that lesbian relationships do little to contribute to the dismantling of present social structures and belief systems (5). She asserts that, for a woman, an encounter with otherness should be with a male (as is portrayed in her model of the labour of love).[40] This is because Irigaray maintains that until there is specific institutional and symbolic reform, a woman needs an encounter with the other of sexual difference to attain the universal for herself. 'In other words, engaging with a person of my own gender is threatened with superficiality, dissolution, with an unethical sensibility as long as there are no just institutions appropriate to it' (145–6). There are supporters, such as Peng Cheah and Elizabeth Grosz, who acknowledge that Irigaray has always been heterosexist in her approach, but that other readings – such as a lesbian one – of her work are possible (1998b: 28–32).[41] Such is the harsh tone of Irigaray's anti-lesbian language, however, that at times her work borders on homophobia.

As a consequence, Irigaray's quest for a 'felicity within history' (the subtitle of I Love to You) would appear to be compromised by her restrictive model of relationship to the 'fecundity of the couple'. Her depiction of this new community in I Love to You, which is a rejoinder to Hegel's idea of community that she criticised in her essay 'The Eternal Irony of the Community' (1995a: 214–26), contains its own determinate ideals. Thus, though the dialectic will no longer be configured according to patriarchal mechanisms of power, it will operate for Irigaray along the lines of a necessary separation of the male and female sexes. Specific gendered values will be recommended. As a result, even though a totally different dynamic of the dialectic takes place for both women and men, the dialectic's movement of spirit in the world, as in Hegel, is not without constraints.

Conclusion

While it is easy to concur with Irigaray's observation that without sexual difference there would be no life on earth, it is not so simple a matter to agree with her assertion that a gendered difference is an essential element for the realisation of spirit. Firstly, if each sex undertakes its own self-differentiation in Irigaray's reworking of the dialectic, there would no longer be a need for an encounter with otherness. Secondly, if each sex is freed from its duty to procreate, it does not appear that the dominant sex-specific genital categorisation should still exert control in such a decisive way. Ironically, however, this liberation from physical regeneration appears to be the basis of a reaffirmation of traditional gender roles. Irigaray is inflexible on this point, and such rigidity would seem to mar her otherwise powerful refutation of traditional feminine categorisations. Again, as I noted in Chapter 1, Irigaray would seem to be advocating two inconsistent agendas. One is the dismantling, in the name of infinite possibility, of the univocal arrangements that have pervaded western traditions in the name of gender. At the same time, there is the endorsement of definite sex-specific qualities and a structure of relationship that is to be observed.[42] There is a tension between Irigaray's static idealization of the couple and the fluidity that she wishes to maintain as intrinsic to the participants' boundless connections. Such a mixed message has led to intriguing differences in interpretation.

Perhaps one of the ways that Irigaray's work thus far could be appreciated is that it is inextricably caught up in the paradox that Joan W. Scott detects at the heart of the modernist feminist project. In Scott's view, the neutral individual who is the subject of rights cannot but be at odds with any distinctive type of female or 'feminine' difference she may want to support. Scott believes that this paradox is insoluble – and that the inevitable conflicts of feminism exemplify the preferences of different feminist factions seeking a single – though impossible – solution (1996: 17–18; 174–5). The implicit recommendation of Scott's provocative thesis is that feminists should learn to live with this contradiction. They should also take advantage of the opportunities it provides for double-duty experimentation. In one way, though probably not in quite the way Scott intended, Irigaray could be said to be doing exactly this. Yet there would need to be further qualifications made, in so far as Irigaray seems to be curtailing the extent of the experimentation for feminists. For the moment – as this topic of paradox will be revisited in the Conclusion of the book – two observations can be made. One is that Irigaray delimits the terms of reference of sexual identity.

For Irigaray, one's sexuality is not arbitrary. As a result, though she has contested the phallus as prerogative of male power, Irigaray is not supportive of a move to let the phallus become a free-floating signifier in the manner of Judith Butler.[43] Thus, Irigaray's conception of the gender that constitutes sexual difference is quite narrow. As Cornell observes:

Irigaray conceives of the individual as either man or woman, and argues that each individual lives a natural reality that corresponds to his or her sexual difference. She goes on to call for a law capable of recognizing lived sexual difference as a universal. In so doing, however, she restricts definitions of personhood by remaining in a system of difference made up of two, and only two, kinds – male and female. (1998: 200)

Further, this notion of difference is restricted in another way. This is that Irigaray's model is insufficiently sensitive to other problems of difference, such as race, that pervade a multinational or multicultural setting.[44] Although Cornell does not state explicitly that Irigaray's traditionalist model of the two sexes is reactionary, it is obvious that, by grounding her proposal on gendered ontological foundations, Irigaray's tactics render her work vulnerable to a conservative reclamation of compulsory heterosexuality.[45]

On the positive side, Irigaray's strategy can be appreciated for its determination to right the wrongs perpetuated by instrumental dualisms that have operated in the service of a male hierarchy. In defence of her idealisations of women's gender, Irigaray no doubt believes that it is only by insisting on specific forms of mediation for women – with distinct spheres in language, law and other material structures – that they will attain the symbolic status and respect that society has long denied them. While women are not compelled to agree or practise Irigaray's preferences, both her sentiments and moral weight lend support to the principle that, in this epoch at least, women need to privilege both gender as the difference that matters, and heterosexuality as its preferred mode of sexual expression. Such a stance is controversial at best.

None the less the magnitude of the task that Irigaray has undertaken must be appreciated. In Irigaray's view, throughout history, women have been sacrificed. From Antigone's silencing, entombed by the male's addiction to war and conquest; to the sexual slave, deprived of the right to life and liberty; to finally the wife and mother, starved of life-blood as her substance is consumed by reproductive and marital duties – the scenario is similar. Hegel's interpretations in his various works have provided graphic evidence for Irigaray's repudiation of women's traditional fate. She wishes to rescue women 'from the sacrifice of sexed identity to a universal defined by man with death as its master' (1996: 26). Irigaray endorses the necessity for each woman to come into her own. She also advocates that this flourishing should not be simply a subjective exercise but one that would contest established institutions and values, including those of religion.

It remains difficult, however, to appreciate the reason why Irigaray retains the Hegelian system – even in its revised form. It is not as if Hegel's dialectic, especially with its fascination for the contrivances of *Geist*, has wide appeal or application today. It may well be, however, that in Irigaray's view his totalising manoeuvres epitomise both the material and spiritual machinations that have conspired to prevent women from accomplishing their full potential as human beings. Irigaray does indeed want women to be able to undertake the risk of consciousness and realise a form of universality, though with far different applications from those envisaged by Hegel. This is particularly so with regard to the supreme manifestation of *Geist*, or spirit, which had both potent philosophical and religious associations for Hegel. While the Absolute Spirit or Consciousness that figures as the consummation of the *Phenomenology of Spirit*, is not necessarily identical with the transcendent God of Christianity, it none the less intimates a spirit at work in the world that fosters the reconciliation of subjectivity and objectivity, of self and other. The *deus ex machina* of Absolute Consciousness, as both an artificial and an abstract contrivance, is invoked by Hegel as a heuristic principle to justify the social, ethical and religious determinations that he deemed indispensable for humankind. It is with this disembodied, all-encompassing and conflictual model which limits human desire that Irigaray effectively takes issue.

While Hegel vindicated the freedom and rationality of modern man, Irigaray disputes and disrupts the inevitable distortions of desire by her appeal to carnal love. While Hegel extols the virtues of family life and recommends the restriction of women to secondary status, Irigaray rhapsodises about the spiritual transformation that a truly autonomous and self-possessed woman can effect in male/female relationships. Irigaray's spirit, in contrast to Hegel's, is solely one of this world. The infinite is now manifest in the finite not because God has become incarnate but because both male and female, in their sexualised embodiment, disclose their inherent divinity, as well as celebrate their infinite capacity for love. It is this affirmation of the sexual as having a spiritual dimension that is probably Irigary's most important contribution to the study of women in philosophy and religion. This is mainly because of its symbolic implications. The female body is no longer representative of all that is shameful and corrupting in the sins of the flesh.

Irigaray's spiritual vision is indeed an impassioned plea for a revolution in the traditional mode of interaction between of the sexes. The question persists, however, as to whether Irigaray's own ethically based solution depends overmuch on her insistence of a bilateral structure of sexual difference. In her criticism of Hegel, Irigaray's rejection of patriarchal formulas of identity, originally proposed as a hitherto unexpressed mode of sexual difference, transmutes in the course of her work. It changes from an emphasis on infinite variety into a formal separation of the sexes, which, as in Hegel, leads to regulative pronouncements regarding their proper roles and mode of relations. Could it be said that Hegelian megalomania remains insidious, even perverse, in its attractions? By succumbing to its enchantment, Irigaray could be said to confine, if not compromise, the ideal of women's spiritual self-realisation and social transformation that lies at the heart of her project.

CHAPTER 5

Homo- and heterogeneous zones: Irigaray and Mary Daly

> By serving in this way as mediation from within the [masculine] symbol, the feminine would have no access to sharing, exchanging or coining symbols.... [but] as mediators, women can have within themselves and among themselves a *same*, [they can have] an *Other* only if they move out of the existing systems of exchange. (Irigaray 1993a [1984]: 114)[1]

> The method of liberation – *castration* – *exorcism*, then, is a becoming process of 'the Other' – women – in which we hear and speak our own words.... Women will free traditions, thought and customs only by hearing each other and thus making it possible to speak our word. (Daly 1974: 10–11)

> Is not God the name and the place that holds for us the promise of a new chapter in history and that also denies this can happen? Still invisible? Still to be discovered? To be incarnated? Archi-ancient and forever future. (Irigaray 1993b [1987]: 72)

> The Way Out of the mazes of fallacious faith, false hope, and dead love begins with a Leap of Living Faith.... Leaping beyond these processions of possession, Lusty women experience Archaic Time. By Archaic I do not mean merely ancient. The word is derived from the Greek *arche*, meaning 'first principle or origin'. Archaic time is Original Time – beyond the stifling grasp of archetypal molds. (Daly 1985b: xvi–xvii)[2]

Introduction

Luce Irigaray and Mary Daly are contemporaneous figures who both allude to a future-perfect attainment of women. This future/past involves a form of recuperation and anticipation, of an *Archi*/Archaic time whose movement of becoming is unceasing. For both thinkers, this movement involves a refiguration of the status of otherness to which women have been consigned by what both specify as the patriarchal tradition. The future perfect tense also reclaims their own absent o/Other, according to a new constellation of ontology and transcendence. This reversal, or transvaluation of otherness, signals an attainment of a social independence and personal fulfilment for women in ways that reject a male God figure and his legitimation of women's inferiority (Daly 1974: 19–22; Irigaray 1985a [1974]: 330–1), as well as the sacrificial demands of patriarchal religions (Daly 1974: 2–3; Irigaray1993b [1987]: 190).

There are many other similarities that can be detected in the works of Daly and Irigaray, e.g., their extravagance, even flamboyance, of style; their innovative word usage; their dismissal of any easy equality; their advocacy of a passionate existence; their rejection of woman as simply a mirror that reflects to men their own idealised image. In addition, they both appeal to angels, and manifest a concern for the natural world and women's relation to it. Finally, they both present imaginative evocations of an alternative mode of existence for women, including an amended mother/daughter relationship. But it is in the ultimate depiction of this new reality that comparisons cease. Thus, Daly will advocate that women, in ending their unconscious conscription into the ranks of patriarchy, claim an original wholeness and become consciously sufficient unto themselves (though she rejects both the terms 'homosexuality' and 'heterosexuality' as patriarchal classifications (1974: 124–6)).[3] In contrast, Irigaray, while concerned with reforming women's affiliations in her early work, finally supports a revolution of the male/female bond, in a renegotiated form of heterosexual relationship. This will reject the male economy of sameness, or *hommesexuality* as Irigaray divertingly names it. The mode of divinity that presides over these distinct operations will inevitably be construed in ways that challenge traditional man-made models, but that, at the same time, illustrate the diverse strategies of each woman.

For both Daly and Irigaray, God is no longer a noun, an object of masculine projections, stagnating in transcendent categories, nor is he aligned with the metaphysical category of Being.[4] God becomes a mode of dynamic energy, suffusing and vitalising life. Although both thinkers conceive of this God in a verbal form of 'becoming', rather than as an abstract concept of 'Being', their descriptions differ somewhat as to the actual nature of this source of an indwelling force, which Daly terms lust (1984: 3), and Irigaray desire or love (1993a: 65).

Common ground

Daly, with her years of Aristotelian and Thomistic study, engages in a dazzling display of words, both flaunting and flouting the scholastic tradition that formed her (1992: 58–63; 69–75).[5] In her naming of God as a verb, Daly acknowledges that, particularly in existential philosophy, with its emphasis on existence rather than essence, there are certain precedents for her repudiation of the reified figures of conventional ontology. She acknowledges these influences, but moves beyond them, in her affirmation of divine existence.

> This Verb – the Verb of Verbs – is intransitive.... When Sartre wrote that 'man fundamentally is the desire to be God,' he was saying that the most radical passion of human life is to be a God who does not and cannot exist. The ontological hope of which I am speaking is neither this self-deification nor the simplistic reified images often lurking behind such terms as 'Creator,' 'Lord,' 'Judge,' that Sartre rightly rejects. (1974: 34)

In response to existentialism, Daly suggests a new awareness of God that the atheistic Sartre could not have even begun to conceive of, so adamant was he in his rejection of all religion. Daly is also critical of the recommendations of Karl Jaspers and the more traditional, religiously inclined views of other existentialist fellow travellers, such as Rudolf Bultmann and Paul Tillich (20–1; 44–5). This is because they do not appreciate the exclusionary gendered nature of their own reflections. To counter their formulations, Daly proposes a remedial communal and participatory understanding of God as an intransitive verb – as 'Be-ing' – that can be discerned especially by women in their rebellion against a male-ordered model. 'Women now who are experiencing the shock of nonbeing and the surge of self-affirmation against this are inclined to perceive transcendence as the Verb in which we participate – live, move and have our being' (34). For Daly, participating in Be-ing involves becoming (38). Borrowing certain ideas from Paul Tillich's work *The Courage to Be* (1952), Daly states: 'This becoming who we really are requires existential courage to confront the experience of nothingness' (1974: 23). Daly also proclaims that, in embracing Be-ing, women not only empower themselves but also inaugurate a new moment in history. 'Women conscious of the vocation to raise up this half of humanity to the stature of acting subjects in history constitute an ontological locus of history. In the very process of becoming actual persons ... women are bearers of history' (35). Daly's declaration of a new era echoes the proclamation that Irigaray makes when she grants women a separate ontological status, and states that, if women acknowledge their own irreducible significance, an unrealised dimension of spirit, and thus of History, could become manifest (Irigaray 1996: 56–7).

In a similar vein, in their revisions of western philosophy and theology, Daly and Irigaray will repudiate the work of Nietzsche. Irigaray will state that it is not the time to mourn for the death of God promulgated by Nietzsche, nor to wait for a salvific deity to come, but to realise a form of God incarnate in love (1993a: 129). Daly herself accomplishes a skilful overturning of the scheme of the master of reversals and his figure of the Antichrist. In a sense Daly administers to Nietzsche a dose of his own medicine. Her disruptive intervention in portraying women as the Antichrist, as beyond good and evil, embodies Nietzsche's own worst fears of female dominance. 'The Antichrist dreaded by the patriarchs may be the surge of consciousness, the spiritual awakening [of women], that can bring us beyond Christolatry into a fuller stage of conscious participation in the living God' (1974: 96). This development heralds an iconoclastic 'Second Coming' which, instead of conjuring up spectres of beasts and ogres 'slouching towards Bethlehem', designates women, in their overcoming of traditional sexual and conceptual stereotypes, as the new revelation (95–7). For Daly, this Second Coming amounts to an installation of a new, divinely sanctioned order that initially confirms both female and male as made in the image of God.[6] In the original version of this new order in *Beyond God the Father*, Daly conceived of the process entailed as 'a qualitative leap toward psychic androgyny' (97). This image was, however, soon repudiated. In her next work, Gyn/Ecology (1978: xi), Daly abandoned androgyny. In Pure Lust she acknowledges that this concept is completely inadequate, 'conveying something like the images of Ronald and Nancy Reagan scotch-taped together' (1984: 341). Although men are not totally banished,[7] Daly reiterates that the notion of Be-ing, in its premier mode, is principally evident today in the becoming of women whereby 'The becoming of women in sisterhood is the countercultural phenomenon par excellence which can indicate the future course of human spiritual evolution' (1974: 11). In this belief, Daly is in accord with Irigaray, who declared in Sexes and Genealogies: 'To become means fulfilling wholeness of what we are capable of being. Obviously, this road never ends' (1993b [1987]: 61). Both thinkers exhort women to explore the infinite vista of possibilities that stretches before them in previously inaccessible ways.

Daly is also in agreement with Irigaray on the passionate nature of this undertaking. Indeed, Daly's book Pure Lust (1984) is a paean to the wild and wilful embracing of life by women in quest of Be-ing. Lust is appreciated as a primal life force and is a reformulation of the classical notion of potency (potentia). For Daly lust is no longer an impersonal concept but an animate power imbued with the vibrancy of women striving to express their own experiences. It is not constrained by the alienating abstractions that dictated classical oppositional modes of reasoning.

Primarily, then, Pure Lust Names the high humor, hope and cosmic accord/harmony of those women who choose to escape, to follow our hearts' deepest desire and bound out of the State of Bondage, Wanderlusting and Wonderlusting with the elements, connecting with auras of animals and plants, moving in planetary communion with the farthest stars. This Lust is in its essence astral. It is pure Passion: unadulterated, absolute, simple sheer striving for abundance of be-ing. It is unlimited, unlimiting desire/fire. (1984: 3)

With this unabashed indulgence in a virtuosic display of language, Daly begins to chart her own course, transvaluing words and traversing worlds, as she refashions modes of becoming in accordance with her own limitless experimentation that takes on cosmic proportions, as it does for Irigaray (1993b: 60).[8] While Daly will credit Aristotle and Thomas Aquinas, her erstwhile mentors, for not rigidly separating soul from body, and mind from matter, as did Descartes, she regards their model of reasoning as inert and non-evolutionary (1984: 338), and thus inappropriate for her revised view of the world. In her new cosmos, there will be a revised 'physical space-time [conceived] by and for women' (1985a: xx).

Irigaray is equally inordinate, if not ostentatious in her assertions, and equally insistent on the intense nature of her aspirations for women to be able to express their desires. In her own transvaluation, Irigaray initially honours desire as the impetus for change that can never be contained. As such, the interval, posited also as a primordial spacing, is the abode of desire. 'Desire occupies or designates the place of the interval. Giving it a permanent definition would amount to suppressing it as desire. Desire demands a sense of attraction: a change in the interval, the displacement of the subject or of the object in their relations of nearness or distance' (1993a: 8). For Irigaray, it is desire that thus does away with rigid binaries, in the same way that lust does for Daly. Again, in her own countermanding of tradition, Irigaray is as revolutionary as Daly in her physical and metaphysical innovations of time and space. 'The transition to a new age requires a change in our perception and conception of *space-time*, the *inhabiting of places*, and of *containers*, or *envelopes of identity*.... Each age inscribes a limit to this trinitary configuration: *matter, form, interval* or *power* [puissance: potentiality], *act, intermediary* – *interval*' (1993a: 7–8).

Desire and lust are thus positively construed to confound the conceptual foundations of western philosophical or theological thought. Interestingly, both Daly and Irigaray invoke angels as facilitators of the momentous changes needed. Angels represent this positive force that occupies the interval and reanimates the dualisms that have hardened into exclusive divisions. As Daly observes: 'The word *angel* originally means emissary, messenger. An angel is a spiritual being of great intelligence. Claiming that speaking Radiant Words has Angelic power is Naming/re-claiming primal force. It is overcoming the false dichotomy between spirit and matter, proclaiming Lust for that Integrity of be-ing from which we have been separated and which we have half-forgotten, but never lost' (1984: 19). For Irigaray, the angel is not simply an instigator but an unconditioned mode of mediation, inhabiting the interval and dismantling the past while initiating a new future. 'The angel is that which unceasingly *passes through the envelope(s)* or *container(s)*, goes from one side to the other, reworking every deadline, changing every decision, thwarting all repetition. Angels destroy the monstrous, that which hampers the possibility of a new age; they come to herald the arrival of a new birth, a new morning' (1993a [1984]: 15).

Angels function as mediators, as emblems of change, bringing to bear new dimensions and connections between word and world.

Metaphors and metamorphosis

This coincidence of angels as intermediaries signals that both Daly and Irigaray, in their undertaking to dismantle much of the traditional conceptual superstructure of western Christianity, will still select and appropriate particular features that contribute to their own ontological framework. For Daly the most appropriate tool to do this is metaphor. She relies on metaphor in an act of defiance against a hidebound tradition that had relegated metaphor to a rhetorical ornament of speech, devoid of any substantive contribution. It is also a rejection of the classical doctrine of analogy of being (*analogia entis*) which spurned metaphor. The predications of analogy, expounded in Aquinas's theology, took human characteristics and raised them to the highest degree of perfection, e.g., God was omnipotent. Daly regards this manoeuvre as simply reifying human qualities that do not have anything to say about God. In contrast, for Daly, metaphor is a vibrant new mode of revelation. Women and words alike are summoned to constant transformation or metamorphosis. 'Be-Witching metaphors transmute the shapes of consciousness and behaviour, that is, they change the context of perception. They do this by jarring images, stirring memories, accentuating contradictions, upsetting unconscious traditional assumptions' (1984: 405). Such a process will involve metamorphoses, and it is metaphors that serve Daly as agents of innovation. Daly views symbols as part of the theological tradition that have deprived metaphors of their power. 'Symbols, at least as they are used in patriarchy, are commonly flattened-out, frozen metaphors that have been captured, reduced and reversed into one-dimensionality' (405–6).

In the place of sterile symbols, Daly employs her dextrous manipulation of metaphors. She admits that they still include an ontological quality attributed to symbols – 'they participate in that to which they point' (25).[9] At the same time, however, they also introduce a transfiguring logic, represented by the labrys – the two-sided axe of the legendary Amazons. 'Metaphors function to Name change, and therefore they elicit change. When, for example, I write of women using double-edged words as *Labryses* to cut through mazes of man-made mystification, the word *Labrys* is not a static symbol; rather, it is associated with transforming action. Thus the very arduousness of the task of naming and calling forth Elemental be-ing requires metaphors' (25). The doubled-edged sword of the mythical Amazons thus operates as Daly's own primary 'metaphor', representing her own double-dealing way with words that will, for her, change the world.[10]

Irigaray's usage of metaphor is not as immediately obvious as Daly's, though her own figurative or mimetic style cuts both ways – both subversively and affirmatively. The reason for the lack of the prominence of metaphor in Irigaray is that she is battling with a somewhat restrictive use of metaphor – Lacan's influential distinction between metonymy and metaphor.[11] As many commentators have remarked, Lacan's employment of the terms metaphor and metonymy are eccentric and even inconsistent at different stages in his work. As David Macey notes: 'Although the metaphor-condensation and metonymy-displacement equations rapidly become an integral part of Lacanian linguistics or *lingusterie*, they rest upon highly unstable definitions' (1988: 157).[12] It is this very intricacy of the metaphoric/metonymic interplay both in Lacan and in Irigaray's response that make it extremely difficult to pinpoint the exact nature of the status of metaphor in Irigaray.

In Lacan's adaptation of Freud by way of Saussure and Jakobsen (Lacan 1977: 146–78), there was obviously an interpolation of a chain of signifiers (verbal terms of reference) which eventually solidified into a posited separate (though interactive) relation between metaphor and metonymy. Metaphor became associated with a process of substitution on a vertical axis whereby there is a resolution of the oedipal complex and the child rejects the mother and identifies with the phallus. For Lacan, this marks the entry into the symbolic world of the father and the repression of the mother. In contrast, metonymy, on a horizontal axis, involves a constant process of succession of one term by another. This form of semiotic displacement in language demarcates theoretically for Lacan the interminable operation of a negative sense of desire (for the repressed unattainable maternal). It would appear that in Lacan the fixed paternal metaphor of the phallus sets in motion an endless metonymic chain of words or objects as potential, yet unsatisfactory, surrogates. In this structuring of metonymy and metaphor, Lacan appears simply to be manipulating language to serve his own purposes. There is no doubt that Irigaray is suspicious of metaphor in this phallic mode (1985b: 60; 67). Her wariness of Lacan's use of metaphor has since led to its dismissal by many feminists as being a tool of the fathers to keep them in their defective place. It remains questionable, however, whether Irigaray herself dispenses totally with metaphor, though initially she sees it as a masculine manoeuvre. In her analysis of Freud, she states: 'Therefore the girl shuns or is cast out of a *primary metaphorization* of her desire as a woman, and she becomes inscribed into the phallic metaphors of the small male. And if she is no male, because she sees – he says, they say – that she doesn't have one, she will strive to become him, to mimic him, to seduce him in order to get one' (1985a: 84).

Irigaray does not accept this metaphorisation of the girl within a masculine system (346), which does not allow women to appreciate or express their desires (or allow men to understand the source of their repression). As I proposed in Chapter 1, in *This Sex Which Is Not One* (1985b), Irigaray introduces her controversial image of the two lips as an alternative to the privileging of a phallic symbolic system. This proposal is often regarded as merely the female counterpart of the phallus, i.e., another metaphor. Far from being a compensatory measure, Irigaray's female-inspired mediation is a rebuttal of Lacan's system in a way that contests his metaphoric/metonymic division while exploring a more permeable syntax (132). Diana Fuss gives another possible interpretation of this ploy of Irigaray: 'What is important about Irigaray's conception of this particular figure is that the "two lips" operate as a metaphor for metonymy; through this collapse of boundaries, Irigaray gestures toward the deconstruction of the classic metaphor/metonymy binaries. In fact, Irigaray's work persistently attempts to effect a historical displacement of metaphor's dominance over metonymy' (1990: 66). As a result of this sophisticated process of constant displacement, women, no longer subject to a unitary system and its dualist divisions, will proclaim, for the first time, a new heterogeneous awareness of their own becoming. Such a move, however, introduces its own forms of metaphoric diversions.

Comparative studies

Both Daly and Irigaray, from similar motivations and for distinct tactical purposes, can thus be said to exploit the resources of metaphoric mutability for their projects. Daly's work can be contrasted with that of the early Irigaray who questions the basis of traditional representational standards and its discursive practices which she understands as totally controlled by patriarchal rule. Daly does not worry unduly about undertaking such a systematic overhaul. She believes that her wayward indulgence in words and her use of metaphor will unproblematically change the world for women. In Daly's view, it is metaphor's neglect by mainstream philosophy's theoretical language that provides sufficient recommendation for its use as her weapon of choice. In contrast, according to Irigaray, women have never had an opportunity to represent themselves. It is thus the time to realise that it is not just words but the system and its exclusions that have failed them. Women need first to find their voice, and then the words to express their desires. Meaghan Morris has depicted Daly's and Irigaray's comparable yet distinct approaches to the process of self-designation.

If Mary Daly explicitly pursues a policy of subverting the signs of the patriarchal code, Luce Irigaray is rather concerned with dismantling discourses. Like Daly she mimics the procedures of her opponents, in order to pull them apart. But unlike Daly, she is concerned with the discursive (as well as the semantic) modes of phallocratic knowledge; the focus of her own writing is on the conditions of possibility for women's *speak-ing* (their bodies, their desires, their oppressions, their differences) and not on producing a model of realized female speech. (1988: 49)

In this account, Morris is referring only to the destabilising work of *This Sex Which Is Not One* (1985b). In her later work, as I depicted it in Chapter 1, Irigaray focuses on women being able to establish their own process of becoming, which she appreciates as divine. She will honour a vibrant mode of synergy which holds both spirit and matter in balance (1993b). Though she promotes the bonding of women, in her recent work, specifically in *I Love to You* (1996), Irigaray initiates a new appreciation of God, or the divine, who is revealed through the flesh, in a heterosexual relationship, not just arid conceptualisations. In this regard, Irigaray differs from Daly. On Daly's part, the 'potted love' of traditional romance (1984: 210–11) is replaced by an advocacy of women-identified bonds of 'Sisterhood' or 'Be-Friending'. Such female-centred relationships take precedence. Indeed, for Daly, these relationships in their various gradations provide women with support and sharing in all aspects of life. For Daly, it is this female bonding that will be transformative for both word and world. Daly is specific in her recommendations for what she terms 'Be-Friending'.

Most essential is the fact that Be-Friending is woven of the fibres of women's lives. A Wild woman's participation in Be-Friending is conveyed not only by words, but also in a myriad other ways. Gestures, witty comments, facial expressions, glances, a certain light in the eye, caresses, styles of clothing, ways of walking, choices of occupation, of environment – these are a few of the signals of a woman's participation in Be-Friending. (385)

While this Be-friending is inclusive of lesbian relationships, Daly does not develop an explicit erotic component in any way – except by extolling lust in a universal fashion. Irigaray, in her early work, does encourage women to establish new affiliations so that they can begin to reappropriate relationships to their own selves and to other women – from which a masculine economy has banished them (1984: 373–86). In her chapter 'When our Lips Speak Together' (205–18), Irigaray celebrates the beginnings of a fluid and open female bonds. This text has often been celebrated as an endorsement of lesbian relationships, yet, in a basic sense, it is an exhortation to women to learn to love and respect each other, though not necessarily sexually, despite the explicit sexual image of the 'two lips'. For Irigaray, it is only by acquiescing to a multivalent and non-determinate option that women will bring about the requisite revolution.

We can do without models, standards, or examples. Let's never give ourselves orders, commands, or prohibitions.... If one of us sits in judgment, our existence comes to an end. And what I love in you, in myself, in us no longer takes place: the birth that never is accomplished, the body never created once and for all, the form never definitely completed, the face always still to be formed. The lips never opened or closed on a truth. (217)

For both Daly and Irigaray, it is only on the basis of women forming such close alliances, that they can attain the fulfilment of their gender on their own terms. In describing this accomplishment, it is fascinating that both Daly and Irigaray support the mode of becoming as suitable manner of existing for women and appeal to goddesses to provide exemplars of life-affirming behaviour. Daly and Irigaray both cite Merlin Stone's provocative book *When God Was a Woman* (1976), in their evocation of a pre-patriarchal era when goddesses were revered. Daly portrays goddesses as having 'elemental spirits' or potency (1984: 183) which were later attributed, in a sanitised form, to the Virgin Mary in ways that have since tokenised women (102–16). Though she invokes the Goddess, Daly does not condone a simplistic mode of replacement therapy. In keeping with her notion that ideas of God need ultimately to be designated by a verb, Be-ing, Daly remains wary of any anthropomorphisms, even those of the Goddess, though she acknowledges their salutary effects: 'Goddess images are truthful and encouraging, but reified/objectified images of "The Goddess" can be mere substitutes for "God," failing to convey that Be-ing is a Verb, and that She is many verbs' (1978: xii). Daly thus coins the term 'Archimage' to refer to the 'Metaphor of Metaphors', the Goddess.[13] With this term Daly provides a caution that any symbolic fixation, even that of an Archimage, could impede encounters with the ultimately inexhaustible dimensions of Be-ing. None the less, metaphors, according to Daly, provide a means for women to recuperate their identity (or original, pre-patriarchal Self (1984: 98)). In a sense, Goddesses are metaphors for 'elemental powers', which affirm women's sense of being connected to the earth.[14] In her emphasis on elements or Elemental life, Daly also testifies to a concern with the matter of life that has been forgotten or been mistreated by the tools of an abstract intellectualism (reason). She specifically cites nuclear weapons as one of the outcomes of such abstraction from the natural world (125–7).

Irigaray also appeals to goddesses, and, while like Daly, she is not an apologist for actual goddess worship, she does affirm pre-patriarchal goddesses as repositories of life-promoting values that are beneficial for today's women. One of the values commended by Irigaray is an empathy with the natural world – 'a connection to natural rhythms and formations' (1993a: 139).[15] Irigaray focuses on the neglect of natural life, specifically the four base elements of earth, air, fire and water. In a 'Chance for Life', Irigaray, in a manner similar to Daly, describes how the human link to nature and the elements has been elided by an emphasis on various types of 'technical imperialism' in the service of reason. As she reflects on the disaster of Chernobyl and its horrendous aftermath, Irigaray states: 'We need some regulation that matches the rhythms of nature: we need to cultivate this affiliation and not to destroy it in order to impose a double nature that has been split off from our bodies and their elementary environment' (1993b [1987]: 200–1). It is appeals such as these, where women are associated with the goodness and bountifulness of nature, and men with technology gone awry (both in a somewhat uncritical and uncomplicated way), that underlie the basic charges of essentialism brought against Daly and Irigaray.

Where Daly and Irigaray will differ will be on the issues of the ultimate grounding of their philosophic positions and the final dynamic of a relationship that witnesses to a new world order. It is Irigaray who steps into new territory when she suggests that once women attain their own identity as divine – 'the perfection of their gender' – they can progress to another aspect of the divine. This is because Irigaray has come to believe that there can be a new collaborative relationship between men and women, where women participate as full partners. Irigaray begins to develop this understanding in detail in *An Ethics of Sexual Difference* (1993a), stating that a couple can experience the divine in and through an intimate carnal connection. Words of love are not simply reflections of inner states or experience, they express the genesis of growth, of a transfiguration, that takes place. Daly is much more reticent when it comes to things corporal. Her style is more one of 'ludic cerebration' (Daly 1975: 49), where words themselves indicate metamorphoses, often in both an uproarious and an outrageous fashion. Her modernist temperament relies more on an empathetic verbal exuberance than on any carnal intimacy.

This is not to say that Daly is just on a mind trip, for her encouragement of women is aimed at fomenting rebellion so that they will act in devious or deviant ways. The lust that she recommends is a life-affirming energy that suffuses all of existence. She is concerned not so much with either reforming or responding to theorists such as Freud in the subversive mimetic mode of Irigaray as with consigning them to the scrapbook of antiquated ideas. Daly does not deny the unconscious, but she views both the Freudian and Jungian methods of interpretation and application as working hand in hand with traditional religion to enforce a damaging patriarchal social system. Instead of untamed libido, Daly posits a primal energy that can help women mobilise an evolutionary awareness that reveals their own 'Real presence' (1984: 147–501).[16]

Perhaps it would be true to say that Mary Daly is having a love affair with words. The Word/word becomes incarnate within each woman who stays in touch with the life-source of primal energy that Daly names 'Metabeing' (26). This is indeed a form of first philosophy – ontology – which is not simply a clever variation of scholastic hierarchical thought. It involves a metamorphosis, an operation that relies on 'biophilic intuition',[17] rather than on logical deductions and abstract analogical derivations. Within this ontology, Daly appears to presume that there is a distinct mode of an 'always/already' female awareness, stifled by patriarchal norms, that can be liberated. This is the Real Presence or 'deep Original Self in women, the living spirit/matter, the psyche who participates in Be-ing' (238). Daly's appeal to metaphor as the vehicle of expression for the 'Original Self' or 'Real Presence' has not been without its critics. Activists, in particular, question the effectiveness of metaphor as a instrument of rebellion. Her assumption of an 'Original Self' is also labelled as essentialism.

At the same time, Irigaray's later position depends on an understanding of both woman herself and the heterosexual couple as having separate ontological dimensions. This ontological modality is evident in her postulate of the divine as a mode of experiencing the world that both women individually and women and men in relationship can realise. Her ontology, however, is not derived from the Aristotle–Aquinas lineage (as is Daly's), but from Heidegger. Irigaray adapts 'Being' as a modality of the divine that is indwelling, and that refuses to acknowledge old partitions of the transcendent and immanent of nature and culture. Nature/culture, body/spirit, female/male are no longer polarities but mutually informing modes of experiencing the world.[18]

Towards a new ontology

While Daly's pyrotechnical display of word power presumes the resources of a metaphysical worldview, she generally does not emphasise this metaphysical frame of reference, leaving the impression that words are asked to carry a heavy, if not overladen, burden. What needs to be appreciated is that, for Daly, words do have metaphysical implications, operating according to an intimate relationship with an ontological conception of Be-ing as the place where meaning is conceived and grows.

From the beginning, Daly is forthright in her pronouncements. In her 'Feminist PostChristian Introduction' to the second edition of *The Church and the Second Sex* (1975) – originally published in 1968 – Daly identifies herself as a 'postchristian radical feminist'. In this later introduction, she undertakes a criticism of her own earlier work, particularly her (misguided) attempt to rescue Aquinas's ontology (123). It is in *Beyond God the Father* (1974) that she begins to develop her own vision. Rather than maintaining the classical form of ontology with a static noun to describe Being, Daly, in her presentation of 'the universal presence of the Verb who is Be-ing', uses the term 'ontophany' to refer to the genuine manifestations of a dynamic Be-ing in which all participate (34–5). In a comparable way, Daly will modify other metaphysical terms, giving them her own idiosyncratic twist. Thus, although she will dismiss the traditional concept of final causality as referring to a life ordered towards a supernatural incentive, she substitutes her own 'Telic Focusing Principle' (1984: 342). This principle is attuned to a lived reality in this world. For Daly, this postulate helps women to focus on their connections to each other; to their elemental past; to their yet to be realised earthly future. Daly exalts these connections, promoting them as part of a 'biophilic' belonging or participation in Be-ing, rather than excluded by the 'necrophilic' categories of traditional metaphysics of Being (1978: 39). Daly will also reject ontological Being as One or Absolute by introducing 'Metabeing', a pluriform term, which names 'the realms of active participation [by lusty women] in the Powers of Be-ing' (1984: 26).

Daly is aware that with such terms as 'Metabeing' and 'Archimage' she introduces the old problem of the one and many. This is perhaps the area where Daly strays least from classical metaphysics, despite her radical revisions. This is because, while she acknowledges the diversity of women, it is with the term 'Metabeing' that Daly demonstrates her intention to name a 'Cosmic Commonality' of women (27). Daly acknowledges that while there is an extremely rich, complex variety among women, and within each individual, there is something above, beyond, and beneath all this diversity. She names this entity as Cosmic Commonality – a tapestry of connected threads that women are constantly weaving. The weaving of this tapestry is the realisation of a dream which, Daly acknowledges, was named by Adrienne Rich as 'The Dream of a Common Language' (Daly 1984: 27). It would thus seem that identification with this Commonality supersedes any individual commitment to one's own identify, and to other affiliations, such as those of race, class, people.

Daly requires this sole commitment because of her decision to position women as constituting a totally separate community from men. Daly wishes women to be unified in their opposition. As a result, while Daly may not actually employ the word 'essence' with its actual metaphysical connotation of substance, the hypotheses of Metabeing and Cosmic Commonality attest to an elemental identity shared by women, and functions in a virtually identical fashion. In the remainder of her work, Daly remains unapologetic about such claims and has not attempted to refute the ascription of 'essentialism' to her work. It is Daly's adaptation of such Aristotelian ideas, and her employment of first causes and telic principles, as well as her abstract expressions, that have alienated many feminists. Meaghan Morris records a response to a talk of Daly's:

> I speak as a member of the third world women's group and also as a former Catholic. Your talk is at best bad poetry and at worst anti-feminist. I say bad poetry not because I have a notion of good poetry based on certain aesthetic criteria but because your language is derived from western philosophy and from the following discourses in particular: Catholicism, 18th century Romanticism, Existentialism – all of which are incompatible with feminism. (1988: 27)[19]

In her more recent work, Daly has moved away from such terms with their metaphysical baggage, while still remaining wayward in her wordplay. This is especially evident in her work *Quintessence*, which she none the less places in a direct line philosophical of succession to *Pure Lust* (1998: 15). She will still refer to the movement of women's liberation as an ontological one, and, in this way, Be-ing remains at the centre of her work. The crucial question for Daly is whether, despite her prodigious efforts at reform, her work remains within a western metaphysical worldview that is dualist in its presuppositions. The further concern is whether this worldview, with its appeal to a separate community of women, only serves to reduplicate, if not exacerbate, the divide between men and women that brought about the situation that Daly so deplores.

Irigaray's early work explored the implications of a deconstructive posture, stating: 'no such thing as woman', in the sense that women have no specific identity, let alone an ontological dimension of their own. Thus she used deconstructive devices to disrupt male impositions, such as 'femininity' and compulsory maternity (1985b: 84). For Irigaray, the tragedy is that the masculine modality of Being or God, which has regulated the symbolic structures and discourse of western societies, is not even mindful of the erasure of women that has taken place as a result of its monopoly (1985a: 295–6). Irigaray takes Heidegger's questioning of such ontotheological pretensions seriously, and will use it to aid her own investigations of the foundation of western thought. Yet even though she credits Heidegger with formulating the right critical question, 'what we [do] really mean by this expression "Being"?' (Heidegger 1962: 31), Irigaray will also find fault with Heidegger for his 'forgetting of women' (Irigaray 1999a: 31–2).[20]

For Heidegger, the truth of existence is not a formula to be deduced. Heidegger believed that 'both realism and idealism have – with equal thoroughness – missed the meaning of the Greek conception of truth' (1962: 57). Truth, as the meaning of existence, could be discerned only by placing all investigations against a backdrop of what Heidegger termed 'a universal and primordial horizon' (31). For Heidegger, the authentic mode of being, or 'Being-true', has a significance of disclosure (263). This is indicative of an approach which allows knowing to occur as an 'unconcealing', rather than as a proof, or an imposition from an external point of reference. (Heidegger's seemingly obscure language comes from the fact that he is trying to express ideas as yet 'unthought' within western reason or *logos*, and which defy its dualist mechanisms.)[21]

Irigaray's work displays Heidegger's influence in her attempt to rebuild the edifice of traditional western ontology. Similarly to Heidegger, she is critical of Plato, declaring: 'Here then, man does not have the plenitude of Being within him, but a whole range of theoretical tools (geometrical, mathematical, discursive, dialogic), a whole technique of philosophy and even of artistic practice, [that] are being worked out to form a *matrix of appropriation* for man' (1985a: 151). Yet Irigaray is troubled that even Heidegger, in developing his own ontology of the unthought dimension of being, has overlooked the status of the mother, as the primordial matter or *physis* of life, or archaic Being. In her book *The Forgetting of Air*, Irigaray describes this rupture: 'But he remains within its architectonics: the *logos*. Seeking the cause of the loss in the forgetting of this architectonics, though it is the architectonics itself that accounts for the loss.... the loss and the oblivion proceed from an *architechne*: from the meta-physical *logos*' (1999a: 87).

Irigaray initially understood her task as one of unsettling this architectonics. To this end, she adopted Derrida's strategy of differential disturbance as mimicry. In time, Irigaray came to realise that the differentiating tactics of deconstruction, though salutary in exposing the effects of female erasure, were not sufficient to establish any mode of self-representation for women. It also was not conducive to the expression of a women's desires within the patriarchal 'syntax of social organization' (1985b: 132). Another approach was needed. Irigaray's resultant concentration on sexual difference led in two directions, both with ontological applications. One was of an 'feminine' nature, where women would explore a dimension of their gendered identity in accordance with a 'becoming divine'. The other reference was to a relationship where sexual difference found divine expression in a heterosexual embrace. In both of these ontological orientations, marked by distinct sexual difference, it would seem that Irigaray has unfortunately reiterated a binary separation of the sexes that, ironically, can only help to reinforce resistance to more nuanced understandings of the interaction of sex and gender.

The problem of essentialism

The ontological premises of both Daly and Irigaray, and their proclamations of women's relation to the natural world – with their cosmic resonances and goddess-like affinities – render their work problematic for many feminists. In the discussion in Chapter 1 on the question of essentialism in the work of Irigaray, I observed that, in this controversy, much depends on the understanding of the term 'essentialism' employed. This observation is now in need of further amplification. Judith Butler describes this problem:

> What's available to description is the realm of appearance, not the realm of essence, unless you have a certain kind of phenomenological description that is disclosive in the Heideggerian sense. But it's still very interesting that essentialism has been collapsed with categories that describe adequately when, in fact, what an essence is, is something that is always escaping the domain of appearance. The other way in which the notion of essence is used in the history of philosophy is that if something is essential, it is that without which we cannot do, it is essential, it is a precondition, it's a necessary precondition without which one cannot move.... So it's extremely important that people think a little bit more critically about what they are saying when they are talking about essences, and I have probably been as guilty or more guilty than anybody else in not thinking quite clearly enough. (Butler in Cheah and Grosz 1998b: 22)

In this context, it is worthwhile to consider the changing perspectives in feminist studies with regard to the term 'essentialism'. Such perceptions were not current at the time the original charges were levelled at Irigaray's early work. In a 1990 article, in an endeavour to move beyond a simplistic division between biological sex and enculturated gender, Teresa de Lauretis bemoaned the use of 'essentialism' as a term of critique to discredit positions that did not coincide with the writer's position. For De Lauretis, this was too easy a rejection that, in its categorical distinctions, simply replicated the dualisms that much feminist scholarship wished to avoid. As if in response, Gayatri Chakravorty Spivak, in another 1990 publication, acknowledged that, in her own work, she deliberately employs what she terms 'strategic essentialism' because she regards some form of essentialising as inevitable. She recognises, however, that context is important. 'Since the moment of essentializing, universalizing, saying yes to the onto-phenomenological question, is irreducible, let us at least situate it at the moment, let us become vigilant about our own practice and use it as much as we can rather than make the totally counter-productive gesture of repudiating it' (Spivak 1990: 11).

In this move beyond the 'holier-than-thou' position that De Lauretis criticised, Spivak implies that no one is innocent and that self-implication is unavoidable. This has practical as well as theoretical consequences. There can be no assumption that specific conditions, however pertinent, can be made into a universally representative situation. In this way, no one is excused from examining the limitations of any such strategic tactic. The implication for Spivak is that self-awareness is all – with regard to both the advantages and the unavoidable omissions that are always involved in taking a position. Still, this refinement does not seem to have halted the indiscriminate use of the term 'essentialism'.

Kathy Ferguson, in her book *The Man Question* (1993), attempts to bring some order to bear on the variety of ways that the term 'essentialism' has been employed. She distinguishes between three types of essentialism that are not necessarily mutually exclusive and that do, in fact, often overlap. She describes 'essentialism per se' as a form of essentialism where definite traits are attributed to 'women's physiology or a larger order of things' (81). Another type of 'essentialism' can be attributed to a form of universalisation where one's position is taken as a norm. A third type is 'categorical universalisation', which involves singular or partial characteristics being lifted from the multifaceted context of life experience and treated as exemplary (82). Ferguson is extremely careful not to absolutise any of these definitions. She illustrates their predictable interaction in an analysis of three flexible categories of feminist thought that she names, respectively, praxis (59–96), cosmic (97–120) and linguistic feminism (121–52). Such divisions are provided as a provisional guideline for clarification, rather than as a final blueprint.

In Ferguson's discussion of 'essentialism per se', she presents a description of cosmic feminists which, without mentioning Mary Daly, none the less displays a striking resemblance to her work.

Cosmic feminists tend to invoke premodern forms of faith in an order already inherent in nature.... The appreciation of the non-discursive is strong, but the realm of the non-discursive is read as having a consistent and available meaning, one that can absorb all apparent disruptions and mysteries into an inherent order of things. Difference – the concrete differences among/within women and men, and the elusive differences residing in the margins of any unified field of meaning – are easily lost in affirmations that subdue discrepancies by enveloping them. (1993: 110–11)[22]

At the same time, however, Ferguson will exclude Irigaray from inclusion in cosmic feminism, connecting her work more with the mode of essentialism she names 'categorical universalization', which seems to Ferguson an appropriate description for Irigaray's early work.[23]

Unlike many cosmic feminists, Irigaray does not seem to posit a natural or spiritual essence prior to culture that characterizes all women ... she wants to be able to speak of women as a coherent category in contrast to men. Her mistake, then, is not one of essentialism per se. Instead she loses sight of the provisionality of her categories and lets the unifying power of her figures speech take over the text. (147)

A consultation of Ferguson's bibliography reveals that she makes this remark with reference only to *Speculum* and *This Sex Which Is Not One* – Irigaray's early works, which appeared in English in the mid-1980s. As noted in Chapter 1, there were a number of charges of what could be regarded as 'essentialism per se', made against this early work. In that chapter, I noted that Elizabeth Grosz argued against any such essentialist impulse, appreciating Irigaray's work at this stage from a constructivist, as well as from a deconstructive, stance. 'Her concepts of the body and corporeality refer only to a body that is structured, inscribed, constituted and given meaning *socially* and *historically* – a body that exists as such only through its sociolinguistic construction' (1989: 112).[24] None the less, in her recent work, especially in *The Age of Breath* (1999b) and *Between East and West* (2002a), when she depicts women as more spiritual and closer to nature (than men), Irigaray seemingly refutes both her own early work and the words of her defenders. Perhaps critics such as Toril Moi did have a prescience of the direction in which Irigaray was headed, though at that early stage there was no reference to goddess-like ideals or affiliations with nature.

This alliance of women and nature could also be said to reflect a form of naive realism, not just essentialism. Daly and the recent Irigaray seem to be in agreement that not only do women have a special bond with nature but that there is a similarity to be found in the abuse that has been inflicted on both entities. This is an idea that has gained prominence in Goddess spirituality and elements of ecofeminist movements over the last twenty years. The classic book that is responsible for popularising this thesis is *The Death of Nature* (1980), by Carolyn Merchant – though she is a Marxist, and not a proponent of the goddess herself.[25] Starhawk (Miriam Samos), whose work *The Spiral Dance* (1979) was one of the most influential in stimulating the contemporary Goddess movement, understands the Goddess religion as intimately intertwined with 'Nature'. Merchant's influence is clearly demonstrated in Starhawk's 1982 work, *Dreaming the Dark*, as well as in Mary Daly's *Beyond God the Father* (1984), with both feminists connecting the goddess with a creative harmony in the natural world. However, Starhawk, in company with Daly and Irigaray, cannot be regarded as a literalist. She declares: 'Let us be clear when I say Goddess I am not talking about a being somewhere outside of this world, nor am I proposing a new belief system. I am talking about choosing an attitude: choosing to take this living world, the people and creatures on it, as the ultimate meaning and purpose of life, to see the world, the earth and our lives as sacred' (1992: 11). Starhawk illustrates this allegiance when she states: 'The goddess can be seen as the symbol, the normative image of immanence. She represents the divine embodied in nature, in human beings, in the flesh' (9).

Ferguson, in her discussion of cosmic feminism, is only too well aware of the pitfalls that await such a simplification in associating women with nature. 'Cosmic feminism lends itself to kitsch. Its emphasis on wholeness and completion and its promise of plenitude slide easily into categorical agreement with being [sic] ... These glib and superficial paeans to blissful merger with the cosmos are often sold in upscale specialty stores along with overpriced crystals and other occult accessories' (1993: 111).[26] It is because of this easy degeneration into slick commercialism or trite New Age slogans that the work of Daly and Irigaray in this particular area leaves an impression of disquiet, of a certain distrust that they have taken an easy way out in their attempt to exalt women. Nature is not necessarily benevolent, and it is misleading to pretend in a generalised fashion that women are the more beneficent of human creatures in their treatment of it. It is for this reason that qualifications, such as those of Kate Soper, are in order. Soper is concerned that positioning women as agents of spiritual recovery, because of their affinity with nature, could lead to a reactionary politics of woman as being attuned only to the world of feelings, and not of thinking. It also overlooks the complexities of the different modes of relationship that human beings can have with the natural world. For Soper, neither religion nor spirituality is an indispensable requirement for a solution to the contemporary estrangement from nature.

> It is not clear that by becoming more mysterious or religious about nature one necessarily overcomes the damaging forms of separation or loss of concern that have been the consequence of a secular and instrumental rationality ... The sense of rupture and distance that has been encouraged by secular rationality may be better overcome, not by worshipping this 'other' to humanity, but through a process of re-sensitization to our combined separation from it and our dependence upon it. We need, in other words, to feel something of the anxiety and pain we experience in our relations with other human beings in virtue of the necessity of death, loss and separation. (1995: 277)

In their essentialising of women in relation to nature, Daly and Irigaray seem oblivious to the problematic character of their universalising gestures. At worst, their work presumes a core identity in women, a natural self, in which all women share. This is unfortunate because such a stance takes their position as members of wealthy western societies for granted, and does not problematise their own perspectives of privilege, however much they may deplore the excesses of their culture. In a telling statement, Ferguson takes cosmic feminism to task especially in its tendency to posit 'a kernel of selfhood' which presumes that those who are 'marked by color, class, passion' can also easily assume this cosmic mode of identity once 'the veil of colonization is lifted' (1993: 119). As a result, the charge of racism can also be levelled at both Daly and Irigaray, given their benign neglect of minority women within their own culture, let alone in others.

Racism

Both Daly and Irigaray have indeed been labelled as racist and exclusivist. While both do pay lip service to diversity, there is no detailed defence in their work as to why sexual difference takes precedence over other differences. In their respective delineations of sexual difference, the concentration is on a gendered mode of sexual difference, to the near exclusion of questions of race, class and ethnic variations, even those of other religions, and this has alienated certain groups of women. There is a telling admonition in the form of a letter from Audre Lorde that chastised Daly for her lack of awareness regarding race, specifically in her work Gyn/Ecology.

> As an african-american women in white patriarchy, I am used to having my archetypal experience distorted and trivialized but it is terribly painful to feel it being done by a woman whose knowledge so much matches my own. As women-identified women, we

cannot afford to repeat these same old destructive, wasteful errors of recognition.... To imply, however, that all women suffer the same oppression simply because we are women, is to lose sight of the many varied tools of patriarchy. It is to ignore how those tools are used by women without awareness against each other.... What you excluded from *Gyn/Ecology* dismissed my heritage and the heritage of all other non-european women, and denied the real connections that exist between all of us. (1981: 95)

Daly did not respond personally to Lorde, but in her next book, *Pure Lust*, there was an acknowledgement of the many important differences between women. Daly confirms the existence of 'ethnic, national, class and racial difference' (1984: 26), and the resultant necessity for women to place their need for individual telic becoming in perspective. Nevertheless, though her work describes a dynamic interweaving of diversity, Daly describes a particular form of connectedness, 'Be-longing' – which posits a oneness of all women – as taking precedence. 'The Lusty longing for ontological participation is an intrinsic aspect of Be-Longing. It is a longing to live in connectedness that already is, but is not yet Realized' (Daly 1984: 354). Ellen Armour, in her book *Deconstruction, Feminist Theology, and the Problem of Difference*, questions the adequacy of this response. She observes: 'In *Pure Lust* ... Daly was careful to include positive references to women of colour and to attend to racism as a force that oppresses women. *Outercourse* [1992] appears to follow strategy.... However, Daly gets no further than other white feminist theorists in doing what I am arguing needs to be done if white feminist theory is to truly move beyond racism: namely, interrogating whiteness as a racial mark' (1997: 111).

Armour's interrogation suggests that something more than a perfunctory nod in the direction of diversity is needed. Any discussion of racial diversity must take into account the fact that subjectivity, as it has been traditionally formulated in western thinking, is 'constitutively raced (as white)' as much as it is 'gendered (as male)' (1997: 115). Armour stresses that, to counter this situation, it is incumbent on women theorists to examine carefully their situatedness and their own presuppositions, as well as the implications of their unconscious assumptions of privilege toward women of colour. Armour also castigates Irigaray for her concentration on sexual difference. While granting that Irigaray's early work was helpful and non-essentialist in its deconstructive procedures, Armour is disturbed by Irigaray's move when she 'proposes replacing male imagery for the divine with female imagery' (1999: 181). In so doing, Armour believes Irigaray both betrays her earlier commitment to the infinity or multiplicity of women and makes the same racist mistakes that have haunted 'whitefeminist theology' (180).

It is in this connection that Irigaray proves less than helpful when, in *I Love to You*, she states categorically:

Sexual difference is an immediate natural given and it is a real and irreducible component of the universal. The whole of humankind is composed of men and women and nothing else. The problem of race is, in fact, a secondary problem – except from a geographical point of view? – which means we cannot see the wood for the trees, and the same goes for other cultural diversities – religious, economic and political ones.

Sexual difference probably represents the most universal question we can address. (1996: 47)

There are those that would argue that Irigaray can be read in a pluralist way, and her work can be applied to issues of difference other than sexual difference (Oliver 1995; Ziarek 2001),[27] but it is of paramount importance to recognise, as Patricia Huntington does, that 'Irigaray's dyadic conception of the patriarchal symbolic order, as organized around a simple dyadic masculine-feminine hierarchy, continues to depict the perspective of white middle-class women as normative or universal' (1998: 262). In Irigaray's opinion, sexual difference may indeed be the most important question that can be addressed from her own specific reference point – both intellectual and geographical – but this does not automatically imply that it necessarily takes priority over other forms of difference that are all too evident in other countries and cultures. It is their insensitivity to the question of race in particular that marks Daly's and Irigaray's work with an ethnocentric orientation that does not examine its own inherent biases. Other conspicuous differences, such as those of class and ethnicity, have also alerted many scholars to the fact that that sexual difference also cannot be studied in isolation from the entangled realities of gender, race and class differences with their attendant economic, legal and political provisos. Drucilla Cornell describes this situation eloquently: 'We cannot even begin to understand gender unless we understand how gender is "colored" and how "color" is in turn engendered, in the psychosexual dynamics of desire.... if we are to adequately understand racism we must also understand its sexualization in and through a phallic logic which reinforces race as much as it does gender' (1993: 131).

It is with reference to this wider and more sensitive domain of differences that both Daly and Irigaray are at fault. Their attitudes reflect their own presuppositions. They both lack self-reflection of the multiple biases that are a component of every person's cultural formation and the intellectual outlook. It would be inaccurate, however, to label their positions simplistically with the term 'essentialism'. This is because, as has become evident in this chapter, 'essentialism' can too easily be employed as a catch-all phrase that puts an abrupt end to further investigation. 'Essentialism' is an imprecise charge because, as Ferguson's guidelines have demonstrated, this word can be employed with certain accuracy to apply to three types of essentialism – normative, categorical and 'essentialism per se' with its cosmic resonances. In their claims and directives, both Daly's and Irigaray's approaches could be identified at different times with each of these types of essentialism. This is because they assume universal definitions that reflect their own preoccupations and pre-empt other women's own self-determinations.

Before closing these reflections on the work of Daly and Irigaray, I would like to add a further qualification to Ferguson's definition of 'essentialism per se' which she associates mainly with cosmic feminism. In a further very general phrase, she describes this essentialism as connected to 'the larger order of things'. As a further qualification, I want to introduce, in this context, the term 'ontological feminism'. I also want, however, to distinguish it from the way in which it was employed by Braidotti and Cavarero. This is because I understand 'ontological essentialism' to indicate a deliberate attempt to apply eternal ways of being or becoming as specific to women. Such an ontological orientation does attempt to locate a primordial and timeless identity of women, of either the Aristotelian or the Heideggerian variety. Thus, as I stated in Chapter 1, when Irigaray recommends certain 'feminine' qualities, such as goodness and care, to be cultivated as ideals worthy of imitation by women, I do not understand this as ontological essential. However, I do discern in Daly's invocation of women's 'elemental qualities', and 'elemental identity', which are in need of restoration, a mode of ontological essentialism. I also detect this in recent work by Irigaray, such as *Between East and West* (2002), when she describes women as innately more spiritual than men, and more innately attuned nature and to eastern religions. (This form of essentialism will be discussed in more detail in the following two chapters.)

Conclusion

Daly and Irigaray have been resolute and courageous women in their outspoken promotion of the cause of women. As such, they have provided inspiration for many. They have been leaders in an area of feminism that has been called 'difference feminism' in its articulation of women's unequivocal distinctive identity. Their analyses of patriarchy and its 'phallacies' are extraordinarily alike in many ways, but their final conclusions could not be more incompatible. Whereas Daly continues to entice women into an outercourse of further realms of realisation of their elemental selves, Irigaray sanctions a spiritual intercourse where both women and men achieve divine status.

Daly's work remains radical throughout in its defiance, even derision, of an irredeemable patriarchal worldview. Her call to action has mobilised many radical feminist protestors to boycott traditional religious practices and institutions. In its exclusiveness, however, Daly's approach leaves the actual structures unaltered. Her words may incite anger, but they also induce an antagonistic standoff that precludes subversive tactics from within. In the end, though women may feel empowered, they remain isolated in their separate ontological realm. There they can be very enterprising in their metaphoric metamorphosing, while the mainstream religions, particularly in their recent fundamentalist regressions, continue to restrict women. Such isolation, unfortunately prevents strong countermeasures against a backlash that threatens many of the gains made by the feminist movement in the 1970s, in social and not just religious matters.

Irigaray's early work could also be considered to be radical as Daly's in its condemnation of patriarchy, particularly in its philosophical and theological manifestations. In her reparative project, however, her recommendations change from being revolutionary to reactionary in their formulaic assignations of the 'feminine' and of heterosexuality. In the end, while they are extraordinarily articulate in their condemnation of traditional religion, neither Daly nor Irigaray has been especially successful in implementing a transformation in society and its symbolic structures. While they both have provided visions that still inspire many women, the effectiveness of their ideas, specifically with regard to religion, in its broadest sense, remains debatable.

CHAPTER 6

Irigaray's eastern excursion

Introduction

The work of imagination, in various guises, both psychoanalytical and philosophic, is at the heart of Irigaray's project. Intricately interconnected with her appreciation of women's bodies and minds, the imagination is at once constrained by patriarchal precedents, yet an agent of challenge and transformation. In Chapter 1, I described how, in *Speculum* (1983), the Lacanian psychoanalytic theory of the imaginary and the symbolic are not so much confronted as undermined in ways that provide space for envisioning alternative creative configurations. It is from *Sexes and Genealogies* (1993b) onward that Irigaray adopts a more dynamic notion of the imagination, with its own generative capacity. It is this innovative notion of imagination that she invokes when proposing the idea of women becoming divine. Irigaray's appeal to an active imagination, while it rereads the past, also envisages new explorations or expressions of being and acting for women. Her work in this area is both provocative and suggestive of ways that women can indeed change the world, or forge a new era of History (1996: 141).

In her most recent writings, *I Love to You* (1996), *The Age of Breath* (1999b) and *Between East and West* (2002a), Irigaray does not confine herself to subversive rereadings of the myths and images of women in ancient Greek culture, e.g., Antigone (1994: 67–87), or even reinterpreting the Annunciation of Mary (1996: 140–1), but she turns her creative musings towards what she terms 'Far-Eastern traditions' (1996: 137), specifically India. This chapter will be an exploration of this turn in Irigaray's work and the implications of this change, which also moves beyond simply the imaginative to a more spiritually apologetic mode of writing. It will also examine Irigaray's work in the light of recent discussions of Orientalism.

Imaginative explorations

In her essay 'Divine Women' (1993b: 57–72) Irigaray first advocated that women begin to explore ways of becoming divine, so as to counteract centuries of a God made in the image of men. To become divine for women implies a fulfilment by a woman of the potentialities of her being (116–17). For Irigaray, ontologically this involves a mode of becoming for women that is intimately related to a distinct mode of sexual difference between men and women (1996: 61–5). For women, this mode of sexual difference requires acknowledging a mode of the divine in accord with women's desires for identity and fulfilment. As I noted in Chapter 1, this does not, however, entail a return to literal worship of ancient goddess figures, rather it envisages re-establishing a society 'that reflects their values and their fertility' (1993b: 81).

In 'Divine Women', Irigaray also posits that the only task God asks of all humanity is that it become divine. This mutual task demands of all 'to become divine men and women, to become perfectly, to refuse to allow parts of ourselves to shrivel and die that have the potential for growth and fulfillment' (1993b: 69). Thus, males have not been automatically excluded from this process, but, for Irigaray, their participation would require that they no longer assume a mode of dominance. Instead, they would abide by a new mode of interaction between the sexes. This would involve a radical revision of previous forms of heterosexuality. Irigaray elaborates this new mode of relationship between men and women in *An Ethics of Sexual Difference* (1993a) and *I Love to You* (1996). This new sexual relationship, which was discussed in Chapters 2, 3 and 4, requires that each person cultivate their own instinctual drives and not impose unmediated desires on 'the other of sexual difference'. For Irigaray: 'The [new form of] negative in sexual difference means an acceptance of the limits of my gender and a recognition of the irreducibility of the other. It cannot be overcome, but it gives a positive access – neither instinctual nor drive-related – to the other' (13).

This self-reflective task of differentiation fosters love. It is, as Irigaray describes it, a spiritual undertaking that brings about the divinisation of both participants. Love thus becomes divine (1996: 139). Irigaray even proposes that, as a result of this development, 'The Third era of the West might, at least, be the era of the *couple*: of the spirit and the bride? After the coming of the Father that is inscribed in the Old Testament, after the coming of the Son in the New Testament, we would see the beginning of the era of the spirit and the bride' (1993a: 148). It needs to be noted, however, that Irigaray has not been particularly sympathetic to traditional western institutional religions. Irigaray's 'age of spirit', as will become apparent in the course of this chapter, will involve a very different understanding of spirituality and God from those of orthodox western religious interpretations. In this connection, Irigaray's use of the word 'spirituality' has much in common with that of New Age practitioners who employ the term to distinguish their orientation from that of traditional religion and its perceived restrictive regulations (Sutcliffe 2003: 9–13).[1]

Much of Irigaray's spiritual exploration, however, has thus far been theoretical. She has been somewhat at a loss to provide specific images from traditional western religions to illustrate the new form of divine relationship between man and woman she promotes. This is because, in Irigaray's view, western civilisation and religions have been dominated by the image of an omnipotent male God. Patriarchy, on Irigaray's account, has obliterated from its pantheon – except for the Virgin Mary in her popularised version – any traces of goddesses or a gynocratic culture. Yet, according to Irigaray, things have not always been this way. As discussed in Chapter 1, Irigaray postulates that 'A return to the origins of our [pre-Christian] culture shows that this was not always the case, that there was an era in which it was the woman who initiated love. At that time woman was a goddess and not servant, and she watched over the carnal and spiritual dimension of love' (1996: 135).

In the change of emphasis since *Sexes and Genealogies* (1993b), Irigaray has also begun to manifest an interest in Asian culture as providing exemplifications of a distinct form of relationship to other people and the cosmos: 'Thus in certain Asian countries, ritual and individual prayer consists in bodily exercise that is either personal or collective: yoga, tai chi, karate, song, dance, the tea ceremony, flower arranging. There is no sacrifice of the other, and yet there is a much richer spirituality as well as a more fertile eroticism' (77). Irigaray continues with this form of 'Oriental' idealisation in her quest for images that would be suitable for the new era of spirit that she envisages with figures of male and female lovers who are both sexual and spiritual: 'Only certain Oriental traditions speak of the energizing, aesthetic, and religious fecundity of the sexual act: the two sexes give each other the seed of life and eternity, the growing generation of and between them both' (14).[2]

It is India and its pantheon of gods and goddesses that has a special attraction for Irigaray. As she states, 'In India, for example, and at the beginnings of our Greek culture – for to some extent this era still exists in India – sexuality was cultural, sacred' (1994: 11). Specifically, it is the notion of the relationship of the gods and goddesses that attracts her: 'In India, men and women are gods together, and together they create the world, including its cosmic dimension' (1993a: 29). Irigaray intimates that there are elements of this spiritual dimension that are still extant today, though she is aware that they may not be consistent with former precedents, particularly with regard to the demands of sexual difference: 'Even the teachers of yoga trained in India forget the importance of sexual difference in the culture that they pass on' (2002a: 10).

Irigaray is specifically interested in two interrelated aspects of Indian or Hindu culture and their importance for providing data on the subject of a female divine, and of a divine couple. One aspect is the tantric yoga where women are revered in the act of sexual union, the other is the existence and legacy of a gynocentric society. These two themes interweave in her work in ways that are difficult to separate out – but for purposes of this chapter I will examine the background of each separately, and the way in which Irigaray links them together.

Yoga and Tantrism

Irigaray, like Eliade (Eliade 1958: 254–67, 343–8), integrates the appreciation of gynocratic ideals with the practices of yoga and Tantrism. The basic presupposition of this development is that traces or remnants of pre-Aryan, gynocentric cultures are at the basis of yoga and Tantrism in India. There are indeed many scholars today who admit to the effects of indigenous influences, by way of a long undocumented process of infiltration into the orthodox brahmanic tradition of Hinduism, and that 'Hinduism' as a tradition has been much more heterodox than the brahmanically centred scholarship allowed. (Roy 1995) In support of her claims, Irigaray, on her own admission, is not so much concerned with traditional scholarly procedures which she now considers as 'obsolete' (2002a: 6), and no longer appropriate for her approach. She prefers instead to follow the 'eastern' ways of transmission by masters or gurus who have instructed her in yoga, and to elucidate her own selected readings (6).[3]

Thus, in both *I Love to You* (1996) and *Between East and West* (2002a), Irigaray continually makes reference to yoga, which has become a personal discipline for her. She relates, 'Through practicing breathing, through educating my perceptions, through concerning myself continually with cultivating the life of my body, through reading current and ancient texts of the yoga tradition and tantric texts, I learned what I knew: the body is the site of the incarnation of the divine and I have to treat it as such' (62). It is obvious that Irigaray's practice of yoga is not just for her personal well-being – it is a spiritual undertaking. This personal practice strongly influences Irigaray's discussion of both yoga and Tantrism, which is conducted against a Hindu background. Irigaray understands yoga as intimately connected with Tantrism, where the body is educated to become both spiritual and more carnally sensitive at the same time (1996: 24). In this connection, Irigaray is again influenced by Eliade – this time by his reading of yoga, and his romanticised view of women, along the lines of 'the eternal feminine' (Eliade 1969: 178–9). Eliade focuses on the divine feminine power, referred to as *Shakti*,[4] but always in the context of wife or mother – never depicting woman as the initiator of the relationship.[5] In appropriating Eliade, Irigaray appreciates the image of a male and female in sexual union as a revered symbol of enlightenment in Tantrism. She also understands it as an exemplar of fecundity, both natural and spiritual (2002a: 60). What is of central importance for Irigaray, in contrast to Eliade, whose work was preoccupied with the status of the male initiate, is the fact that Tantrism favours a disclosure of 'The worship of a Goddess (worship of her body and her sex) by man' (Irigaray 1996: 137).

In this tantric discipline of spiritual transformation, Irigaray recognises that the breath is of utmost importance. The role of breath, as associated with the life source and the mother, featured in Irigaray's previous work. In *An Ethics of Sexual Difference*, Irigaray observes, with critical reference to Heidegger, that 'To forget Being is to forget the air, this first fluid given us gratis and free of interest in the mother's blood' (1993a: 127). She also refers to this forgotten alliance in 'Belief Itself' where she recognises the mother as the substrate of all life (1993b: 46). For Irigaray, air, as natural sustenance, is related to both breath and spirit. In her later works, the composite of air/breath/spirit represent the generative life-force, and is given a vital role in the movement from a simply carnal to a spiritual union (1996: 148–9). She describes the movement involved: 'Becoming spiritual amounts to transforming our elementary vital breath little by little into a more subtle breath in the service of the heart, of thought, of speech and not only in the service of physiological survival' (2002a: 76). In this way the body itself will be transformed. It thus becomes a vehicle for the divine and an exemplar of the sensible transcendental.

> In these traditions, the body is cultivated to become both more spiritual and more carnal at the same time. A range of movements and nutritional practices, attentiveness to breath in respiration, respect for the rhythms of day and night, for the seasons and years as the calendar of the flesh, for the world and for History, the training of the senses for accurate, rewarding and concentrated perception – all these gradually bring the body to rebirth. (1996: 24)

In Irigaray's depiction, the male (*yogi*) and female (*yogini*), by controlling the breath and stabilising concentration, can proceed in the practice of kundalini yoga where a process of directing energy through the seven *chakras*[6] aids the attainment of Enlightenment (*moksha*), or the realisation of Self (*jivan mukhti*) which, within Hinduism, are two of the most recognised descriptions of this ultimate state. The final product can be symbolised in various ways. Most often it is represented as the union of the god Shiva with an embodied aspect of feminine power, *shakti*, in a goddess form. This union also represents the fact that duality of consciousness, which operates at the level of conditioned reality, is thereby overcome. For Irigaray, however, it is not necessarily an ultimate overcoming of dualities that is of primary importance, nor is it the union with *shakti*, if it remains simply a abstract form of an ideal feminine (2002a: 63). For Irigaray, the union must be one of both a spiritual and a corporal nature.

Yoga, as a discipline, also has an ancient lineage in India, with some scholars dating it back to images found on clay seals at Mohenjo-daro, a pre-Vedic third millennium BCE site. It featured in the *Upanishads* and was systematised as a discipline in the *Yoga Sutra* of Patanjali (ca. second to third century CE).[7] In the introduction to her translation of the *Sutra*, Barbara Stoller Miller states: 'At the heart of all meditative practice in Asia is what Indians call *yoga*, the system that "yokes" one's consciousness to a spiritually liberating discipline. In his *Yoga Sutra* the ancient Indian philosopher Patanjali presents us with the possibility of complete psychological transformation through the discipline of yoga' (1995: ix).[8]

In time, however, yoga became associated with another indigenous legacy, that of Tantrism. Tantrism is a much revered, though often exoticised, form of religious practice. Its origins may well also go back to pre-Vedic times and there is speculation as to an early relationship between yoga and Tantra. George Feuerstein explains: 'Tantra, or Tantrism, is an exceptionally ramified and complex esoteric tradition of Indic origin. It made its appearance round 500 CE, though some proponents claim a far longer history.... As a full-fledged movement or cultural style extending over both Hinduism and Buddhism, however, Tantra seems to have originated around the middle of the first millennium CE' (1998: ix–x). Tantra has many different traditions or schools in both Buddhism and Hinduism, but it appears to be the Hindu variety that most interests Irigaray. Georges Varenne alludes to actual tantric texts in Hinduism which can be dated from about 1000 CE. 'These texts have been given the name *Tantras* (books), which is why we speak of Tantrism when referring to this branch of Hinduism. At other times the term Shaktism is referred to denote the same current of thought, because the Sanskrit word *shakti* (power, force) is the one that best evokes the goddess's true nature: divine energy emanating from brahman, the concrete manifestation of her power of creation' (1976: 144).

Tantra, and its relation to yoga, however, has never been a unified or authoritative body of knowledge, and its history is subject to different interpretations. There have been multiple goddesses and gods and various types of adepts. There have also been many schools (in Buddhism as well as Hinduism) with complex formulas and practices that are of either an externalised or an internalised nature. All of these are concerned in one way or another with the transformation of the body into a spiritual vessel.[9] The majority of books on Hindu Tantrism in English have been discreet regarding the exact function of *shakti*, regarding it mainly as the female principle of energy, or describing the union of a goddess, such as Parvati, with the god Shiva as being merely a symbolic depiction of the overcoming of duality. More recently, however, there have been lurid western appropriations that reduce the whole tantric exercise to one of erotic pleasure.

> It is ... not surprising that so many Neo-Tantrics in the West look upon Tantra as a sexual discipline promising pleasure beyond all expectation, mostly in the form of prolonged or multiple orgasms. Neo-Tantrics seek to emulate the divine couple but typically forgot that the union between Shiva and Shakti is transcendental and therefore also asexual. The fruit of their union – and hence the goal of Tantra Yoga – is not bodily orgasm, however overwhelming, but perpetual bliss far beyond anything the human nervous system is capable of producing. (Feuerstein 1998: 80)

Irigaray would agree with Feuerstein's criticisms of Neo-Tantrism, particularly in her attitude that the practice of love must be not simply sexual but spiritual (2001: 59). Irigaray, however, would not condone enlightenment as genderless, or an out-of-body mystical experience. It is the affirmation of the human body itself as divine and as a means of spiritual enlightenment that she has been seeking all along, as well as the appropriate images to portray it. Body and spirit must coalesce.

Gynocratic cultures

In *Je, Tu, Nous*, Irigaray develops her understanding of gynocratic culture: 'Gynocratic traditions – which should not be restricted to matriarchy but should include eras when women reigned as women – predate patriarchy but don't go back to the time of cave living, nor to the early palaeolithic period, nor to certain forms of animal behaviour as is interpreted and understood in supposedly knowledgeable circles' (1993c: 24). In *Between East and West* (2002a), Irigaray identifies this approach as also sympathetic to pre-Aryan gynocratic elements that she believes survive in contemporary Hinduism (29). Nevertheless, Irigaray does not appear to have undertaken extensive original textual research in support of her thesis, though she does name the *Upanishads* as important (2002c: 200). In her writings, she basically appeals to secondary sources such Bachofen (Irigaray 1993c: 24) and Eliade (Irigaray 2002a: 65) to support her claims for this gynocentric period and legacy in India (1993c: 90). As described in Chapter 1, Bachofen, a problematic nineteenth-century scholar, wrote a treatise, *Mother Right* (1967), on the existence of a primordial matriarchal culture. Eliade, in turn, proposes that 'Mother religion ... once reigned over a huge Aegean-African-Asian area and from the beginning of time was the major form of devotion among India's many autochthonous populations' (1969: 178). Irigaray accepts this model unquestioningly. Such a hypothesis, as I discussed in Chapter 1, is an especially controversial one, and a subject of intense debate in Anglo-American feminist thinking, especially in the disciplines of Archaeology, History and Religious Studies (Goodison and Morris 1998).

With the exception of one reference to Merlin Stone (Irigaray 1993c: 24), however, Irigaray does not cite any arguments that have engaged feminist scholars on the subject of the existence of gynocracies or matriarchies (Tringham and Conkey 1998: 22–45).[10] In addition, Irigaray does not take into consideration the questioning of both Bachofen and Eliade's approaches by women scholars, specifically concerning these male scholars' adulation of the conquering male warriors and their rightful suppression of the purported matriarchies (Christ 1991; Goodison and Morris 1998: 7–21). There is also no reference to any historical studies of the period concerned by prominent Indian women scholars (e.g., Bagchi 1995; Chakravarti 1989; Roy 1999). Finally, there is no mention of the work of post-colonial scholarship regarding the complexity involved in cultural misappropriations of traditional interpretations and cultural ideals of other peoples – especially with regard to women (e.g., Narayan 1997; Spivak 1990).[11] Thus, Irigaray's work would seem to be written without reference to issues that are prominent in contemporary feminist scholarship, to recent historical research of early India and to post-colonialist discussions. Her interests have become more spiritual and her writing more hortatory than discursive in nature.

In *I Love to You* (1996), Irigaray integrates selective ideas from tantric yoga and gynocracy into her own spiritual quest, which was evident, though not developed in any sustained way in certain earlier texts. As a result, Irigaray departs from her early radical rereadings of the western philosophical and religious traditions to explore and envisage a way that a person, and the world, can be changed by this new spiritual perspective. Irigaray is now more concerned with the dynamics of personal spiritual experience, rather than simply theoretical recommendations for 'the perfecting of our gender', as the means of fostering the integration of spirit and nature. Irigaray's perspective has changed from philosophical critique of the western tradition to a form of confessional advocacy that basically distances itself from a philosophical or theoretical study of religion. In one sense, it has been Irigaray's aim from her earliest work to expose the objectivist illusion that she believes underlies western conceptions of rationality – its repressions and its unconscious sexualised dichotomies. It is something else, however, to opt out of it totally. Her alternative imaginative forays have now led her to promote living according a spiritual path. This path respects nature and the body with its sexual differentiation, and is more conducive to achieving the changes Irigaray perceives as necessary for the (western) culture's and the cosmos's survival than promoting an intellectual philosophical orientation.

Irigaray's stance would seem to have a marked affinity with New Age religious developments in North America and parts of Europe. It is hard to gauge, however, if Irigaray has been influenced by this movement, because she does not refer to it in any way, and the movement is not particularly strong in France (Introvigne 2004).[12] From her writings it appears that Irigaray is following in the path of Hindu spiritual direction – though she does not name any particular school or guru. From a contemporary perspective, this path cannot be said to be particularly unique, as she is following in the footsteps of many westerners who, since the aftermath of the First World War, have sought consolation in eastern religions (Sutcliffe 2003: 201–8).

It is not as if Irigaray is unaware of the difficulties involved in the alteration of her orientation, nor of the problems that she faces in this enterprise of adapting eastern ideals and images. She does make several qualifications in the opening pages of *Between East and West* to the effect that she is conscious of the complexities that preclude any simplistic adaptation of other religions. It can no longer be simply a matter of extracting one pristine element from the living matrix of the religious ferment that comprises Hinduism, or any other eastern religion. Irigaray also admits that there is far more to be learnt in this area (2002a: 7). As she declares: 'the Eastern traditions themselves are multiple at present and the Asiatic aboriginal and Indo-European contributions live together there without real articulation between them' (2002a: 15). None the less, it appears that Irigaray's treatment of one dimension of Hinduism, tantric yoga, is somewhat idiosyncratic in its implications for a new spirituality. This appropriative tendency she shares with many other New Age adherents.

Irigaray also acknowledges that she is not ignorant of the atrocities that are perpetrated on women in the name of religion – a fact that was evident to her on her voyage to India (2002a: 65). As a consequence, she admits that there are two completely different attitudes in India: one where women are regarded as goddesses and one where men continue to exercise their unquestioned supremacy over women. Yet she continues this discussion by observing that it was during this voyage to India that she heard a master, T. Krishnamacharya, affirm the importance of the notion of sexual difference as a part of the culture of yoga (65). Though it is not stated explicitly, Irigaray's conclusion is that, if men and women learn to respect sexual difference, this practice of yoga, where women are respected as inherently spiritual in their bodily form, will be effective in changing the current social ills. Though I do believe that Irigaray means this in a sincere and profound way, her strategy seems more of a personal response. It is also highly debatable, given the evidence of the continuing mistreatment of women in India, where a majority are still living according to the traditional ideals of service to their husbands.

India today

Perhaps at this stage it is relevant to enquire about the number of contemporary women in Hinduism who are qualified or permitted to undertake the path of tantric yoga. This is because it seems that only a select number of women could devote themselves to such a discipline, as it appears that they have done in certain historical periods.[13] Another important matter to be evaluated concerns the actual consequences for women of the fact that in Hinduism itself, and not just in the tantric variety, they have been regarded as embodiments of the divine. The responses to these questions indicate a troublesome situation. For although *shakti* is honoured and feared as a divine principle, and women are revered as goddesses in ritual worship by both men and women, this does not necessarily translate into respectful treatment of women, within either Buddhism or Hinduism.

This anomaly has puzzled many Indian women scholars. As Leela Gulati asks: 'Why does the status of women remain so low when goddesses are considered as powerful as god?' (1995: 83). For Gulati there is no simple answer to this situation, but there is no doubt about the social restrictions placed on many Indian women. There are exceptions to this rule in the history of Hinduism, such as the medieval poet saints (Gupta 1992) and contemporary female ascetics, even of the tantric variety (Denton 2004), who have chosen to renounce traditional marriage and householder rules. The regulations derived from the *Dharma Shastras* (the sacred law codes) as propounded in the *Laws of Manu* (1969) – written somewhere between the second century BCE and the second century CE – have none the less provided the principal guidelines for women's conduct, though they have not been ubiquitous throughout India.[14] In the Brahmanic tradition, a woman's husband is regarded as her god — she is vowed to her husband's service (*pati vrata*) (Leslie 1991). Thus, whatever realisation of self a woman attains is regarded only as a reflection of the spiritual stature of her husband. It is this wider background of women in Hinduism that Irigaray does not mention in her study, and needs to be taken into serious consideration.

In making the inference from an idealised time of gynocracy and goddess worship, with its notions of both respect for women and social structures of an egalitarian nature, Irigaray herself is implying a strong link between notions of the divine and concomitant social values. Yet this connection is not a necessary one. Tracy Pintchman, in her essay 'Is the Hindu Goddess Tradition a Good Resource for Western Feminism?', will argue that 'there is no inherent correlation between any particular representation of divinity and social or political attitude toward women' (2000: 196). In fact, any such association needs to be investigated thoroughly for its presuppositions. In their criticism of the interpretation of the goddess figurines and the cultural implications of peace and harmony that are attributed to matriarchal societies, the feminist archaeologists Tringham and Conkey state that 'Phenomena such as the correlation between social change and symbolic change or between social and symbolic continuity must be questioned and problematized, not assumed' (1998: 24). In their own interpretations of goddess figurines, they refuse to establish any definite linkage, of a broad historical and geographical scope, that would relate goddesses with social and political structures.

In her book *Caste as Woman*, Vrinda Nabar does analyse the mythological heritage for evidence that the myths, particularly the grand epics, such as the *Mahābhārata* and *Rāmāyana* of medieval Hinduism, do reflect social practices of their time of their writing (1995: 150–4). She mentions two recent television productions of these epics which endorse this image of ideal wifehood today and that she believes, whether directly or not, has contributed to the devaluing of women.

We are fond, in India, of speaking of an ideal past when women were equal with men and no discrimination was visible. Such an unreal vision ignores the Sītas and Draupadīs [heroines of classic and beloved epic sagas] who are as much the postscripts of that allegedly idyllic age as are the male protagonists of our national epics. The myth denuded would reveal a pattern of unequal prescription.... Both Sīta and Draupadī herald an ongoing tradition of long-suffering women whose real heroism is overlaid with the message of devotion and service to their husbands, [and] a glorification of these qualities so that martyrdom is seen, in some cases, as preferable, desirable, virtuous, and even imperative. (22–3)

Nabar then discusses what she sees as the repercussions of these attitudes which exalt woman, as long as she stays within prescribed roles, in the contemporary context where dowry-deaths, abortion of female foetuses, widow mistreatment and *sati* still occur (Narasimhan 1990; Thapar 1995). The continued practice of dowry – though officially illegal – points to the fact that wife as object remains within the orbit of a crude system of gift-giving. This system is open to, if not encouraging to, an extreme exploitation of the 'goods' – be they material commodities, or the body of the wife (159–67). Often in these situations, women, such as the mother-in-law, collude in the abuse of another woman. Though Nabar praises the advances by Indian feminists who are working for social change (6–15), others are more pessimistic. They view these societal ills as stemming from such deeply ingrained psychological attitudes that even legal measures appear ineffective as a means of redressing crimes, or reforming social practice (Narasimhan 1992: 152). Irigaray does not even begin to address these issues.

Ironically, June Campbell, in *Traveller in Space: In Search of Female Identity in Tibetan Buddhism* (1996), uses the work of Irigaray as the basis of her criticism of the role of women within contemporary Tibetan tantric Buddhism. Agreeing with Irigaray's critique of the place of women in traditional religion, as articulated in *Speculum*, Campbell states:

> This seems particularly true in the Tibetan system where the potential of wholeness in the female form, quite clearly represented in some of the more archaic Tantric images, is somehow never realised in the social sphere. I have argued that this is because the association of emptiness with the female links the female body to a concept of the transcendental, which means that the female body is exploited by the male in his quest for his own typology, while she herself has no adequate means to realise her own. The transcendental therefore becomes, as Irigaray understands it, 'the arena of the (philosophical) subject split off from its ground'. (1996: 154)

Campbell draws attention to the fact that, while there is an emphasis in Tantric Buddhism on honouring the female principle, for which there may be evidence of an earlier period in pre-Vedic India, the subsequent history has not always been so positive (153–7). One development has been that the predominantly monastic movement gradually eroded the vital participation of women into more formalised meditative rituals. Even so, as Campbell graphically depicts in her own experience of exploitation, women themselves could still be sexually manipulated by monks.

The cultural representations at the heart of the oppression of women are also being contested today in more complex ways by post-colonialist feminist scholars, such as Chakravarti (1989) and Roy (1995), who question contemporary nationalist appeals to the glories of an Indian past and its emotional evocations of women as the guardians of the spiritual essence of the tradition – basically as a hedge against encroaching westernisation. Uma Narayan is particularly concerned about this reconstructed past, much of which is actually of recent date, and was the result of a collaborative effort on the part of British colonialist and Hindu nationalists. This is at present being exploited by the Hindutva right-wing movement (Narayan 1997: 25).[15] Irigaray does not undertake any interrogation of the legitimacy of this supposed tradition, especially of the way it could function as an ideology of repression for contemporary Hindu women. Nor does she ask herself whether her adoption of such aspects of the tradition might also have reactionary significations. Thus Irigaray may be introducing forms of cultural constraint to the west, disguised as exalted ideals of womanhood. Irigaray, in her concern for the spiritual aspects of tantric Hinduism, does not question the implications of incorporating constructs and conventions that are less than favourable for women. Tracy Pintchman worries that such appropriations are not necessarily a compliment to the culture from which they are borrowed, as they are too often for the benefit of the borrower alone (2000: 198–200). Irigaray again does not acknowledge this possible distortion, as she believes that her own experience and her vision of woman as mediator of the world of breath/spirit is a role that has beneficial universal dimensions.

Thus, in her most recent writings, Irigaray has made this remarkable and somewhat surprising move towards spirituality – though it is possible, in retrospect, to detect the beginnings of the change, starting with 'Divine Women' and 'Belief Itself' (1993b). Such a development needs to be put in the context of a remark made by Irigaray in an interview to the effect that 'I think when people have looked at my new books a little they're going to understand everything I've done leading up to them' (Hirsh and Olson 1995: 112). In the light of this statement, Irigaray would perhaps disagree with any description of her work as changing in direction, as, in this interview, she also describes her work as having three phases that have an overall continuity (96–7). She also remarks that she does not approve of her work being separated into unrelated parts (2002b: 200). I think, however, that there is a distinct difference in her most recent approach. In her early work Irigaray's voice was a critical and radical one, working to subvert entrenched western cultural structures and practices that had been detrimental to women. Yet in her adaptation of Indian mythology and spiritual practices, Irigaray does not subject them to the same type of critical analysis that she applied to the Christian and western myths and structures. In particular, the unquestioning promotion of a specific mode of the Hindu tradition, a form of tantric yoga, at the expense of Hinduism's multilayered mosaic of movements, is problematic.

In the same vein, Irigaray is reluctant to admit that the tantric tradition has a distinct antinomian aspect – known as the left-hand (or deviant) path. In following this path, the aspirant inverts all that is sacred. The representation of *shakti* in this aspect is a destructive goddess, Kali, who can be worshipped by sacrifices and by perverse graveyard rituals – definitely taboo territory (Kumar 1974: 151–5; 199). Kali can also manifest herself in angry and loathsome forms (Kanna 2002). From a scholarly perspective, Irigaray should be held to account for such omissions, but she has made it quite clear that she is not inclined to answer to the traditional academic enquiries concerning the transmission of knowledge. She insists that her quest has become one of a spiritual nature, where she respects the practices of spiritual masters. Irigaray also listens 'to the words and writings of those men and women who, in the last century especially, try their best to unite in themselves European traditions and those of the East' (2002a: 70). None the less, her selective reading of source material, as well as neglect of the work of contemporary Indian women scholars, leaves her work open to charges of indulging in her own imaginative fantasies of a glorious past and an idyllic future. This is because it has become evident that the more Irigaray moves in this idiosyncratic religious or spiritual direction, the more essentialist, in the traditional metaphysical sense of the word, she becomes. This essentialism involves a number of assumptions that need further examination.

Ontological essentialism

This movement toward an ontological essentialism is very evident in *The Age of Breath*, where Irigaray amplifies her basic reformative model of sexual difference and its spiritualisation, postulating that women are not only spiritual initiators but mediators between the different religious traditions, as for them 'neither dogmas nor rights, and even representations are [not necessary] to approach the divine' (1999: 18). In *Between East and West*, Irigaray also affirms that a woman who is 'faithful to herself' is 'close to Eastern cultures, close to the Buddha, who, moreover venerates the feminine spiritual' (2002a: 79). In addition, woman who, 'more spontaneously, keeps breath inside her' thus 'remains in greater harmony with the cosmos' (85). The principal distinction of women for Irigaray, however, is that it is woman who, similarly to the creator God, engenders life with breath (80). Woman is thus the harbinger of a new age of spirit. 'This passage to another epoch of the reign of spirit depends upon a cultivation of respiration, a cultivation of breathing in and by women. They are the ones who can share with the other, in particular with man, natural life and spiritual or divine life, if they are capable of transforming their vital breath into spiritual breath' (91).

Such declarations of the innate and spiritually superior dimension of women are disturbing because they are no longer simply recommendations of appropriate conduct as described in Chapter 1. Irigaray now asserts that women's way of being (as becoming) has definite properties that distinguish them from men, and render them more receptive to the natural world and eastern religions. I describe this position as 'ontological essentialism' for a number of reasons. Firstly, it names a foundational reality in women's lives that is in keeping with definition of metaphysical essentialism that indicates innate and permanent characteristics. Secondly, I want to indicate that, in her most recent work Irigaray has moved beyond the strategic mode of 'ontological essentialism' attributed to her by Braidotti, as we saw in Chapter 1. She has also gone beyond the general position that Ferguson termed 'cosmic essentialism', as cited in Chapter 5. It may well be that Irigaray has found the western tradition virtually bankrupt in her search for images conveying her new appreciations of the divine, and her turn to the east has fulfilled her imaginative expectations. Irigaray's new depiction of the divine 'feminine', however, promotes a form of the romantic idealisation of women as being inherently the more spiritual species of the human genus. This, I believe, amounts to an ontological essentialism. One redeeming feature of this programme, that distinguishes it from the conventional motif of the 'eternal feminine', however, is that women are now permitted to act as equals, even initiators, in an erotic encounter. Regrettably, this elevation of women would seem to come at the expense of their active participation in the philosophical or political realm. Spiritual superiority has too often been offered women as a compensation for their exclusion from participatory intervention in changing the material conditions that govern their lives. In addition, while an erotic and spiritual bond – pleasing as it is with its recognition of the body and the passions – may change ethics, it cannot of itself effect social and political reform. Thus, while this spiritual relationship may revolutionise the life of lovers, it fails to pay attention to women who are marginalised or oppressed by a society. Perhaps it also raises the question of what the less spiritually inclined rational males, and lesbian females – confined to 'natural immediacy' – will be doing the meantime.

Post-colonialism and Orientalism

It is in the context of this new spiritual dispensation that Irigaray reiterates her earlier observation that 'In the third age of the history of Judeo-Christianity, after the age of the world's redemption, thanks to Mary and to Jesus, the task of humanity will be to become itself divine breath' (1999: 13). Such a declaration arouses concern that Irigaray's explorations of Hinduism may have been only in the service of her 'revisioned' ideal for Christianity and its symbolic structures. This raises a number of contentious issues, especially the charge of Orientalism, which involves the appropriation of other cultures or religions, even if in idealised forms. Ronald Inden, a critic of Orientalism, has been particularly censorious not only of those who undertake reductive western analyses of India but also of those who romanticise Hinduism, among whom he lists Mircea Eliade, C. G. Jung and Joseph Campbell. As he elaborates: 'The adherents of the romantic view, best exemplified academically in the discourses of Christian liberalism and analytic psychology ... insist that India embodies a private realm of the imagination and the religious which modern, western man lacks but needs. They ... have a vested interest in seeing that the Orientalist view of India as "spiritual", "mysterious", and "exotic" is perpetuated' (1986: 442).

From Inden's perspective, Irigaray's recent work would certainly fall within his designation of romantic Orientalism. Another perspective, however, is presented in J. J. Clarke's Oriental Enlightenment (1997). Clarke analyses Edward Said's original depiction of *Orientalism* (1978). While Clarke acknowledges that Said is correct to emphasise specifically the imperialistic and ideological elements that were intrinsic to the western Orientalist and colonialist impulse, he believes that Said's original description remains dualistic, and does not fully acknowledge certain complexities involved in a dynamic interaction of 'East' and 'West' – terms that Clarke does not want to see as simplistically opposed monolithic entities.[16] Clarke's own particular focus, in contrast to that of the Islamic world of Said's study, is more on South and East Asia. I will briefly examine his work, particularly with regard to Hinduism, as a foil for further discussion of Irigaray's work.

It is worth noting that Clarke's approach does not fall within the traditional approach of theory and method in the study of religion. His work is a historical survey of western scholarly attitudes towards the 'East', particularly Hinduism. It ranges in its coverage from Romantic enthusiasm, as demonstrated variously by Schlegel, Schopenhauer, Nietzsche and Müller, to the devoted advocacy of many contemporary philosophers and students of religion. Clarke describes popular elements, such as esotericism and the occult, the work of Aldous Huxley and Hermann Hesse, the Zen Buddhism of the Beat Movement, the hippie movement of the 1960s and 1970s, and contemporary New Age variants. While he acknowledges that certain of these treatments of the East and its religious philosophy are not necessarily satisfactory, and may well be distortions of Hinduism or Buddhism, he does not necessarily see blatant evidence of the hegemonic tendencies of the colonialist enterprise. Instead, he detects a subtle 'deployment of the East as a means of intellectual and cultural criticism [of the west]' (1997: 107). Clarke himself does not undertake any extensive critical evaluation of any of these movements – he seems merely content to document their development. Central to Clarke's thesis is the fact that 'orientalism has for three centuries assumed a counter-cultural, counter-hegemonic role, and become in various ways a gadfly plaguing all kinds of orthodoxies (e.g., especially traditional religion and a rationalist approach) and an energizer of radical protest, and in doing so, it has often been in the business of not reinforcing Europe's established role and identity, but rather undermining it' (1997: 27).

It is in the light of Clarke's thesis that a further look at Irigaray's recent work can be taken. Irigaray definitely sees her work as constituting a serious rebuke to the Jewish and Christian heritage, as well as to the cultural and religious attitudes and behaviour towards women. Her adaptation of the spiritual symbolism of tantric yoga's ideas and practices is an attempt to introduce a transformative way of appreciating a new dynamic of male and female relationship. For Irigaray, this mode, in its carnal and spiritual interplay, has innovative significance for its participants and their culture. (While Clarke does not refer specifically to Irigaray, he acknowledges the present popularity of tantric yoga (99) and its contemporary secular western adaptations.) The question that arises from Clarke's work is whether his discernment of these conflicting interests of appropriation and reform provides sufficient grounds to counter the inheritance of imperialism that has been deemed characteristic of Orientalism in its colonialist guise. Clarke himself admits that there remains a paradox at work here, where issues of 'power and interest' are still intertwined, not just in the multifaceted interactions between cultures but within the ambit of the 'Eurocentric' world itself and its response to these issues (111).

The employment of the term 'Orientalism' may raise more problems than it solves. The issue today is that, despite its critical impact, 'Orientalism' still tends to function, even in certain scholarly discussions, as a catch-all phrase, questionable in its own dualisms and caught in a narrow focus of east/west binaries. It is from this limited perspective, however, that Irigaray certainly fits the description of an Orientalist. Recent discussions in post-colonialism, however, have problematised such a simplistic apprehension of Orientalism. As Ali Behdad observes: 'In "Orientalism Reconsidered," Edward Said views the interventionist nature of postcolonial practices as a function of their interdisciplinarity.... The problematics and politics of postcoloniality ... demand a counterdisciplinary mode of knowledge to rethink the relations and distinctions between ideology, history, culture and theory' (Behdad 2000: 73). From this more nuanced post-colonial perspective, Irigaray's work appears as an instance of the inevitable problems, such as generalisations, omissions, impositions and selectivity that have basically occurred whenever attempts by western thinkers have thus far been made at religious integration and comparison. In the coming years, there will be an urgent need to unravel the multivalent interweavings and mutually implicated aspects of inter- and intracultural exchanges in religion, specifically taking into consideration the voices of contemporary post-colonial scholarship (e.g., Afzal-Khan and Seshadri-Crooks 2000). Such theoretical issues, however, will no longer be Irigaray's concern, and the result may be that her work will continue to indulge in gratuitous platitudes on the subject of other cultures.

Conclusion

So where does this leave the work of Irigaray? She asserts that she has left behind the established traditions of scholarly research and appraisal. Nevertheless, there do remain grounds by which her work can be assessed for its contribution for contemporary discussions on the topic of women and religion. From a post-colonial perspective – which would seem to be a required component in any consideration of cultural 'borrowing' – it appears that Irigaray's work is completely oblivious to the contemporary debate. As a result, while Irigaray's work does disclose elements of both trends that Clarke documents – a form of idealised recuperation at the same time as a critical attitude and a transformative intention to change western mores – her work participates in the paradox that Clarke discerns in Orientalism, ambivalent in its aims and implications. I believe that such a deficiency illustrates the problematic of appealing to other religions' solutions – particularly of an imagistic nature – if careful attention is not paid also to the social, historical and political contexts from which these ideas are being extracted.

There is a further comment that can be made on Irigaray's appeal to Indian goddesses. This is that her approach is not original. Rita Gross had proposed such a move in her 1978 essay 'Hindu Female Deities as a Resource for the Contemporary Rediscovery of the Goddess'. Gross's work did not recommend wholesale adoption, but suggested that 'Some Hindu goddesses provide something that is unavailable in the West's repertoire of images – strong-willed, creative, and powerful females who are auspicious and beneficial' (Gross 2000: 107). Gross's provocative proposal sparked much reflection at that time among Anglo-American women scholars. This has resulted in a number of books and essays that provide informed deliberations about the legitimacy of the insights to be gained by such appropriation. (See especially Hawley and Wulff (1996), King (1997) and Hiltebeitel and Erndl (2000)). Again, Irigaray shows no awareness that such literature exists.

A final problem is Irigaray's leap from the postulation of a gynocracy and goddesses to women's spiritual superiority. This is indicated in her unsubstantiated observations that women are closer to nature, to mythic (poetic or imaginative) thinking, and even to the Buddha (who is on record as being extremely hesitant to allow women to become nuns). Such designations are problematic for a number or reasons. Firstly, they strengthen the male/rational/history and female/imaginative/myth dichotomy. Secondly, they tend to correspond with contemporary reactionary forces that seek to remove women from the public world in order to restrict/uphold them as the unsullied guardians of society's or a nation's morality. In this way Irigaray's programme could simply reinforce rather than reform the existing polarities between men and women.

Irigaray has invested her creative energies in repudiating the Freudian and Lacanian prescriptions for women, and in subsequently substituting her own. Her rewriting of the oedipal script reclaims a positive mother and child relation that focuses on the relational bond, via the umbilical cord, of the embryo and placenta. It depicts a loving mother that is in harmony with nature and the cosmos. Children (particularly daughters) born to women who are thus attuned to the rhythms of the cosmos inherit a similar spiritual disposition. These modes do not involve a traumatic and necessary separation, nor do they result in repression. Yet everything depends upon a primordial spiritual eminence of women. As I presented the issues in Chapter 1, Irigaray posits a revised idyllic ontogenetic (personal) process, and a phylogenetic (species) mythology to counteract Freud's version of the necrophilic, paternal inheritance of religion in *Totem and Taboo* (1918). As a result of Irigaray's imaginative rewriting of Freud's script, sexual difference becomes reified in a way that privileges women and their 'feminine' spirituality and identifies them with affirmative ontological ideals. In such a construct, a form of natural law which asserts that whatever is in existence, i.e., sexual difference, is natural, and therefore right, is all too apparent. At the same time, a form of the naturalistic fallacy which views the female being as inherently good is promoted. Both these assumptions coincide in a fascinating, if eclectic mixture. Irigaray fails to realise that, in restoring women to their rightful place in the cosmic order, she endows them with a somewhat dubious mythical legacy and also issues proclamations as to their appropriate behaviour. She does not seem to realise that, in doing this, she risks being just as categorical as the traditional religions she contests.

CHAPTER 7

Conclusion: a world of difference

In this concluding chapter of the book, my intention is to evaluate the impact of the principal elements of Irigaray's work that are concerned with women and religion. Before I do this, however, I will undertake a survey of the way that Irigaray has influenced certain women philosophers, both religious and secular, and their responses to her work. Irigaray's work, particularly those explorations concerned with sexual difference, has been the subject of diverse reactions – both complimentary and unsympathetic. Her early work inspired a number of women scholars to drastically reappraise the western philosophical heritage from its beginnings. In Religious Studies, it also prompted women to develop their own critical analyses and creative experimentations, especially in reaction to the traditional formulas of philosophy of religion. The different works of Pamela Anderson (1998), Amy Hollywood (1998), Pamela Huntington (1998) and Grace Jantzen (1999) all exhibit the influence of Irigaray's initiative, but certain of their responses have varied, as they have become aware of the changing emphasis in the three stages of Irigaray's development.

In *A Feminist Philosophy of Religion*, Anderson does not consider Irigaray as a theologian but a thinker who provokes a radical reassessment of its philosophical foundations. Anderson appreciates Irigaray's criticism as one that will both enable her to challenge rationality's formal truisms and generate an exploration of alternative imaginary strategies. Anderson insists that 'The very structure of the philosophical imaginary must be queried in its employment of imagery which, in turn, constitutes the unity of reason and philosophy itself' (1998: 9). Through her own questioning, Anderson reaches the conclusion that reason itself is pervaded by certain forms of 'male' imagery. In response, Anderson proposes not substituting 'female' imagery, but introducing a new philosophical imaginary that reflects the input of both women and men.[1] Anderson understands the immediate task as one of transforming the abstract reductions that have functioned as truth claims surrounding the notion of belief in philosophy of religion. Anderson wants to expand the range of reason to include the contributions of both imaginative and rational procedures, but she is not sufficiently explicit as to the way, apart from the introduction of mythological motifs, this model is to be implemented. Nor is it clear as to how truth will be articulated. Her programme is thus more diagnostic in nature. Anderson certainly does acknowledge that further constructive work needs to be undertaken: 'Philosophical analyses of and feminist concerns with a combination of reason and desire, as expressed in the yearning for truth, need to come to the top of the agenda in contemporary philosophy of religion' (241), but further elaboration is beyond the scope of her enterprise. None the less, as a first foray by a woman into the bastion of rationality, as defended by the ranks of analytic philosophers in religion, Anderson's work marks a definite breakthrough.

Amy Hollywood, in 'Deconstructing Belief: Irigaray and the Philosophy of Religion', amplifies the need to revise the notion of belief in a way that totally subverts conventional definitions, especially as they have been associated with truth claims. Hollywood concentrates on Irigaray's dismantling of Freud's interpretation of the baby Ernst's game of 'fort-da', in her essay 'Belief Itself' (1993b).[2] Irigaray here demonstrates that while Freud's description of his grandson's behaviour ostensibly explains the child's conquest of his fears of abandonment by his mother, something of more tragic proportions is at stake. This 'mastery of the mother' both by Ernst himself and by Freud's commentary, is symptomatic for Irigaray of the original denial or repression of the mother's primal role in the child's life. As Irigaray observes:

Thus the body that gives life never enters language. Ernst, the son, believes perhaps that, in his first language game, he holds his mother. [But] she has no place there. She subsists before language as the woman who gives her flesh and her blood, and beyond language as she who is stripped of a matrix/womb, a veil, an enclosure or a clearing in which she might live according to the horizon of her games, symbolizations, representations. (46)

This sacrifice of woman to the 'rule of the father(s)' prompts Irigaray to reflect on the nature of religion that is built on such a foundation of denial. 'How are the spirit and mind to be woven of the threads of remoteness, belief, paralysis, denial, and negation of life?' (47). Hollywood elaborates on this question, indicating that, for Irigaray, belief itself is constructed on the basis of a disappearing act that substitutes an idealised father idol for a repressed mother figure. It is in this way that control over chaos is maintained. Hollywood depicts the implications of this renunciation: 'The constitution of the normative subject of western philosophy and theology then, whose elucidation is the necessary preliminary to any account of sexual difference, is dependent on an act of faith (in the absent mother's presence), which is itself an act both of mastery (the child holds the string) and concealment (he makes the toy absent in order to control its return)' (1998: 222). A significant consequence of such a delineation of the nature belief is that, from Irigaray's perspective, all abstract truth claims can be viewed as further defences to exclude the maternal from consciousness.

From this perspective, both Anderson's and Hollywood's work initiate a revision of philosophy of religion because truth claims are now recognised as providing protective mechanisms rather than as assuring certainty.

Grace Jantzen, in *Becoming Divine*, will take this insight further by stating that all such definitive preoccupations are part of a necrophilic tendency. '[A]greeing to construct the philosophy of religion around meticulously sophisticated and rigorous arguments about the coherence and truth of religious beliefs is only to reinforce the patriarchal necrophilia rather than to challenge it and or to learn to think otherwise' (1999: 21–2). Jantzen prefers to follow Irigaray in that, instead of seeking deadening theoretical closure at the expense of imagination and life, she will nominate the task of becoming divine as the main task for contemporary human beings. For Jantzen, this approach affirms life, and is linked with the term, associated with Hannah Arendt, of 'natality'.[3] Arendt herself did not associate natality literally with childbirth or maternity. For Arendt, in contrast to Heidegger's appreciation of human existence as one that is death-bound, natality imbues existence with a creative impulse, as an ever-present capacity for new beginnings. Jantzen enlarges on this depiction of natality: 'freedom, understood as the possibility of beginning which is rooted in our own beginning, is always material, embodied: there is no disembodied natality.... Thus the freedom of natality is not the putative freedom of a disembodied mind, a mind made as free as possible from bodily shackles, as Plato would have it, but rather a freedom that emerges from and takes place within bodily existence' (145). This transformative approach also stresses an embeddedness in the life world and the interconnection of all (human) beings.[4] It thus establishes a foundation for empathy and for respect of the other (150). Given this connection with all other human beings, an imaginary of natality would not be conducive to misogyny. One of the ways that Jantzen suggests such natality can be cultivated is by undertaking further imaginary explorations of divine possibilities in this life. Jantzen's own imaginative vision thus resonates with that of Irigaray, but she is not prescriptive of specific directions it should take.

None of these thinkers deals at any length with the issue of sexual difference, though Hollywood registers her disapproval of its centrality (1998: 232–3). I believe that the reason for the lack of engaged criticism on this topic is that, although all three women thinkers refer to *An Ethics of Sexual Difference* (1993a), their concern is more one of developing Irigaray's early ideas to revise traditional concepts of belief and divinity. At this juncture, Irigaray had not yet become as intransigent on the issue of sexual difference as she did in her later work. These primary responses can thus be accepted as the result of Irigaray's inspiration. It is perhaps this early creative phase of Irigaray's work that has had the most dramatic and profound effects on women scholars in religion.

Patricia Huntington, in *Ecstatic Subjects, Utopia, and Recognition*, is another who comments on the implications of the ideas of the early Irigaray on philosophy of religion. Huntington, however, also expresses concern about Irigaray's use of the 'feminine' and sexual difference. Similarly to Jantzen, Huntington agrees with Irigaray's advocacy of women envisioning imaginary possibilities that will transform their 'sensible, incarnate, embodied and reified natural desires' (1998: 127). Huntington also commends Irigaray's introduction of the interval that displaces dichotomies of an oppositional relationship. She quotes Irigaray with approval: 'The link uniting or reuniting masculine and feminine must be both horizontal and vertical, terrestrial and celestial. As Heidegger, among others, has written, this link must forge an alliance between the divine and the mortal, in which a sexual encounter would be a celebration, and not a disguised or polemic form of the master–slave relationship' (Irigaray 1993a: 17; quoted in Huntington 1998: 155). Huntington herself will appeal to Drucilla Cornell's *Beyond Accommodation* (1991: 168–79) to support her interpretation of Irigaray as encouraging non-essentialising poetic modes of possibility for women. Enlarging on the ideas of Cornell (whose work cites only *Speculum* and *This Sex Which Is Not One*), Huntington depicts Irigaray's position as incorporating a critical dimension – a deconstructive double-play – that prevents it from endorsing a uniform type of 'Woman' (138–40). Yet Huntington also appears apprehensive of the risk of essentialism that such a strategy runs, with its evocations of divine possibilities for women. She warns that 'Irigaray must delimit her invocation of new goddesses' (138).

It is Huntington herself, however, who provides a provisional justification for Irigaray by turning to Heidegger and drawing certain parallels between his and Irigaray's 'poetic' or imaginary interventions. For Huntington, this comparison depends on accepting the later Heidegger's notion of *poiesis* as referring to a form of ontological transformation of existence, that is, of the way that we inhabit the world (186). The crucial term for Heidegger in this new ontology is *Gelassenheit* or, as it is often translated, 'letting be' (189). This phrase indicates a way of being that does not subscribe to western rationality's preference for absolutist principles with its binary divisions, especially those of metaphysics. Huntington then indicates that the basis of Heidegger's new orientation is an affirmative recuperation of the term '*fantasia*', which is posited as at once both creative and critical.[5] Heidegger himself distinguishes this version of *fantasia* from delusion or 'fantasizing rooted in the abstract, speculative mind' (186). Huntington thus discerns similarities between Heidegger's use of this critical or creative imagination and Irigaray's strategic use of imagination, both in her mimetic dismantling of the delusions of western reason and in her evocation of creative possibilities. Huntington declares: 'I would claim that Irigaray, reflecting Heideggerian influence, differentiates between (a) fantasies which lapse into fetishising the real and (b) those which open productive pathways' (137). As a result of making this comparison between Irigaray and Heidegger, Huntington will further state: 'In Heidegger's language, she [Irigaray] lets divinities be' (278).

While I am sympathetic to Huntington's attempt to exonerate the early Irigaray, by way of Heidegger, from charges of essentialism, it has become evident during the course of the discussions in this book that, in the end, Irigaray actually does not allow divinities to be. Instead, she appropriates them to her own designs of what she considers to be a suitable demeanour for women. Nevertheless, I think that Huntington is correct in indicating the influence of Heidegger on Irigaray. In Chapter 1 of this book, when Irigaray's use of the word 'imaginary' was explored, certain significant understandings of imagination, particularly that of Merleau-Ponty, were indicated as having an impact on her work. Merleau-Ponty's own deliberations, however, were a refinement of Heidegger's own reclamation of Kant's productive imagination. Richard Kearney, in his chapter on the ontological imagination in the *Poetics of Imagining*, concisely describes this development in Heidegger's work: 'Imagination is part of the "unthought" (*ungedacht*) dimension of existence which escapes the objectifying classifications of metaphysical thought. Like *Dasein*, transcendental imagination belongs to the prereflective and usually ignored realm of the lived experience' (1998: 53). There is not an exact correspondence, however, between Irigaray and Heidegger. In Chapter 5, I observed that Irigaray demonstrated Heidegger's ignorance of woman as the primal 'unthought' dimension of western philosophy, rather than Being – as Heidegger supposed. It is for this reason that Irigaray modifies, with Merleau-Ponty's assistance, Heidegger's appreciation of imagination and its latent capabilities. A creative form of imagination, which is not just delusion, can instigate conscious imaginative play that will have practical applications for women. It is this aspect of Irigaray's use of the imagination that Huntington refers to when she describes Irigaray's use of 'imaginary' as delineating not simply a psycho-sexual fantasy (a 'male' imaginary of misrecognition) but rather a conscious, creative dynamic for women (163–7).

Yet even Huntington herself will detect that something is amiss in Irigaray's further pronouncements. Huntington's own critical eye will fall on Irigaray's depiction of sexual difference, and her focus in the final chapters of her own book is on what she terms Irigaray's 'monistic' or unitary approach (248). This monistic approach is evident for Huntington in Irigaray's proposition that 'gender provides the paradigmatic source of all other kinds of oppression' (xxx). Because gender takes precedence as offering a solution to contemporary societal ills, Huntington views it as having reductionistic consequences.[6] Huntington will then fault Irigaray on two counts. One is that this concentration on gender could introduce a solipsistic worldview, which simply reinforces the logic of identity that Irigaray presumes to avoid. A more telling observation is that Irigaray's assumptions preclude 'any examination of those specific conflicts among women – conflicts in perspective, in economic and political relations to one another, in symbolic position, and in strategies for social change – that permeate all the way down to the core attitudes and to the basis for the respective positions they hold' (1998: 265).

More precisely, for Huntington, Irigaray fails to pay attention to the material conditions of women's lives. The final result is that Irigaray's preoccupation with gender leads to a neglect of questions of difference in relation to race, class, history or other cultural biases. By thus taking western culture's (or a Eurocentric) perspective as the standard, Irigaray makes claims for the universal corrective potential of sexual difference. According to Huntington, this monism, conflated with a utopian idealism, interferes with the effectiveness of Irigaray's programme. Huntington comes close to recognising that, in Irigaray's work, an ontological separation of men and women, when combined with an essentialising conviction of gender-specific properties, leads to distinct and static identities (252–3). She is prevented from doing this, however, because of her admiration of Cornell's positive reading of the early Irigaray. (This is something Cornell will later come to negate.) Huntington appreciates that Cornell, in *Beyond Accommodation*, interprets Irigaray as having a utopian impulse that is not normative in its expectations. Cornell herself extends this impulse to incorporate the multiple intersections of difference – including those of race and class – in women's lives. (26). None the less, Huntington seems to remain suspicious that Irigaray is not quite as expansive as Cornell, but she does not develop this observation further (260–8).

Both Cornell and Huntington come to Irigaray's defence because they have discerned an original, if not ingenious mind (and body-consciousness) at work in her early writings. They are in good company, e.g., Braidotti and Grosz. In contrast, there are other scholars who, while fully aware of Irigaray's problematic approach, have appropriated her work in a deliberately selective way. Similarly to Cornell, they have intervened so as move in productive directions not addressed by Irigaray. The literature is too vast to discuss here in its entirety. Thus, in concluding this survey, I will restrict myself to the current work of a number of feminist scholars in order to provide an overview of the developments in the more recent scholarship on Irigaray.

In her book *Witnessing: Beyond Recognition* (2001), Kelly Oliver commends Irigaray's depiction of recognition, in its positive relational mode, as a constructive change from previous oppositional formulas. She appreciates Irigaray's emphasis on sexual difference as part of a strategic move towards the inclusion of other differences, such as race and class (2001: 209). Oliver understands sexual difference as the beginning of a movement towards multiplicity. This is a generous reading by Oliver, but it is not entirely obvious that this is what Irigaray intends. It is true that Irigaray referred in her early work to women as multiple in the sense of an 'indeterminate plural' (1993b: 69). This was intended to refer to the infinite and open possibilities of women's subjectivity, in contrast to the multiples of 'one + one + one' that Irigaray deemed as a 'delusive ['masculine'] resolution' of the problem of the one and the many. It was also a deconstructive device whereby the difference of woman subverted the logic of identity. From

An Ethics of Sexual Difference (1993a) onwards, however, the notion of women's difference takes on other nuances, with specific civic and cultural repercussions for women's subjectivity, as the status of sexual difference is negotiated. Irigaray maintains the necessity of both a biological and a cultural sexual difference between man and woman. For Irigaray, it is this new logic of two, as expressed in sexual difference, that takes precedence over multiplicity. She proposes that this couple can interact in infinite, not merely binary, ways. This dyad of the couple – the two – is the sole agent of disruption of the monopoly of the one. Irigaray has not, however, relinquished her fear of multiplicity, or the 'many', in the strict technical sense of the term, as a variation of the one (Cheah and Grosz 1998a: 6). As she declares: 'I do not believe that to question the universal subject starting from the multiple is sufficient, because the multiple can always be equivalent to a multiple or sub-multiple of *one*. The explicit or implicit measure remains the *one*, more or less real, imaginary or simply mathematical. The critique of the universal subject cannot be limited to the substitution of the multiple for the one' (Irigaray in Pluháček and Bostic 1996: 343).

It is not only Oliver who wishes to expand the possibilities of difference to which Irigaray's ideas can be applied. Ellen Armour, who also defends Irigaray's early work against essentialism, declares: 'Irigaray is not always claiming ... that she has gotten behind phallocentric discourse to the *real* woman or to her *true* language; rather, she is breaking open phallocentric discourse in such a way that the possibility of new ordering of that discourse ... might be possible' (1999: 127). Armour, like Huntington and Cornell, interprets this discourse as located within a deconstructive framework. In this context, it is 'difference, rather than sameness, and plurality rather than unity' that is posited (127). Armour does concede that, in Irigaray's early differential play, there is a possibility for introducing the difference of race in order to encourage 'a different mode of relationality among differing women' (134). However, she acknowledges that this differing/deferring strategy is forgotten in Irigaray's later more 'theological' work – and so the chance to investigate the plurality of differences, such as the problem of race, is squandered. As a result, Armour finally finds Irigaray's tactics to be inadequate (if not oblivious) to the task of undermining the exclusionary nature of the 'white solipsism' (134) that she believes has prevailed in much early feminist work of Anglo-American scholarship. Armour's conclusion is thus applicable not just to Irigaray but to all white feminists whose focus on gender erases race. 'Rather than leaving race to trace itself invisibly through whitefeminist texts, whitefeminists need to attend to the way race and woman always already intertwine through our own subjectivities and history. Since whitefeminism appears to be the product of the history of race, it needs to investigate the conditions of its own production' (167).

In her book *A Politics of Impossible Difference*, Penelope Deutscher will also argue for the deconstructive mode of impossibility or possibility as applicable to sexual difference in Irigaray's work. She surveys a number of variations on this paradoxical theme. For Deutscher, '"sexual difference" ... refers to an excluded possibility, some kind of femininity (open in content) that has never become culturally coherent or possible' (2002: 29). Thus, after *An Ethics of Sexual Difference* (1993a), when Irigaray does introduce the idea of a 'sexual difference as a possibility', this should not, according to Deutscher, be associated with any ontological reference, as questions about its existence remain hypothetical (Deutscher 2002: 108). Deutscher is thus somewhat dismayed when Irigaray, in her works following *An Ethics of Sexual Difference*, does seem to concentrate on identity of a gendered variety rather than on a continual mobility between the possibility and impossibility of identity (190). This is because Deutscher also wants to maintain that, if there is to be any identity in Irigaray, it will be of a 'religious' variety, in a Derridean messianic mode that is 'yet to come' — an as yet unrealised possibility (2002: 104–6). Thus, while Deutscher appears aware of Irigaray's tendencies towards defining a definite mode of identity rather than an indeterminate mode, she wants to hold Irigaray philosophically to an ideal of impossibility. She admits as much in her final rhetorical summation: 'One assumes that Irigaray sometimes falls short of the best deployment of her own best concept. But why suppose that the concept of impossible sexual difference that one might value as coherent and operative can be abstracted from, and can exist independently of, the moments of paralysis to which, in Irigaray's work, it seems regularly attached?' (2002: 190) Deutscher's concluding judgement of this development is a both a cautionary and a realistic one, if ultimately one of disappointment. She states: 'The intermittent paralysis in Irigaray's work may serve as a crucial reminder that self-undermining, rigidity, and appeals to identity inevitably haunt such politics' (190).

Eva Płonowska Ziarek also addresses the impossibility of sexual difference in *An Ethics of Dissensus: Postmodernity, Feminism, and the Politics of Radical Democracy* (2001). Ziarek bases her position on a key quotation from Irigaray to the effect that acknowledgement of sexual difference fosters the respect for 'differences everywhere' (Irigaray in Hirsh and Olson: 1995: 110). Her interpretation of this statement expands the range of difference from its basic confinement to the sexual. Ziarek includes homosexuality, in virtual defiance of Irigaray's own assertions on the topic, as one of these differences. To support her stance, Ziarek draws on a statement by Cheah and Grosz who express the opinion that 'neither respect for the other sex nor fidelity to one's sex necessarily implies an obligatory desire for the other sex' (1998a: 13). (Grosz herself has previously acknowledged that Irigaray has always been heterosexual by personal preference but she believes that her work lends itself to other interpretations, such as a lesbian reading (1994: 335–50).) I am not sure, given Irigaray's increasingly vehement proclamations in favour of heterosexuality (1996: 3; 145–6; 2002b: 134–5), that this interpretation, though a plausible one, is faithful to Irigaray's intentions.

Ziarek's position, aligning Irigaray's notion of sexual difference with 'a negation of any particularity positing itself as a universal' (2001: 153), could initially appear to be a development of the Derridean differential element in Irigaray's early work, supplemented by the Levinasian idea of the irreducible difference of the other. But Ziarek takes this idea even further, so as to articulate her own version of an ethics of difference within a politics of a radical democracy (2001: 9). She states that Irigaray's adaptation of Hegel's labour of the negative will undermine 'any identity – (individual or collective) based on wholeness' (2001: 153). Such an interpretation, however, is again at odds with Irigaray's own intention in her work on Hegel where, as I have argued in Chapter 4, the labour of the negative is employed within a distinct sexual identity, including specific gendered characteristics. None the less, Ziarek is quite deliberate in her move because she wishes to situate 'sexual difference in the context of the inaugural, disruptive temporality of history rather than conflating it with the constituted gender identity' (2001: 157). In making this move, Ziarek appeals to the thought of Cornelius Castoriadis and his hypothesis of a radical imaginary which opens up other possible future alternatives in the political sphere (2001: 155–7).

I appreciate Ziarek's intent to acknowledge the inevitable conflicts and resistance (dissensus) related to any social enactments of gender, race, class and ethnicity – elements that are noticeably absent from Irigaray's work. Ziarek thus draws attention to the conflict or death wish, which is something that Irigaray is reluctant to recognise in human, or particularly women's, relationships. I none the less think that Ziarek's reading overlooks the central aspect of Irigaray's position on sexual difference. This is that, for Irigaray, it is not a Derridean undecidability, nor an aspect of a politically radical imaginary that ultimately sustains her depiction of sexual difference. Ziarek, however, intentionally chooses to promote such a political agenda to the exclusion of Irigaray's reformulation of Hegelian spiritual transcendence and of a Heideggerian ontology in the key of woman. Fundamentally, Ziarek disagrees with the actualisation of sexual difference that becomes the rationale of Irigaray's later work.

It is in an interview with Hirsh and Olson that Irigaray makes the observation that Ziarek, as well as Cheah and Grosz, single out as the basis of their incorporation of other forms of difference that can be derived from Irigaray's ideas. For the record, I would like to cite this quotation in full so as to place it in its full context:

Yes, there's an irreducible difference between man and woman. It's not the same kind of mystery that exists between woman and woman or between man and man. It's not similar.... I think that it's because I situate it there that I'm able to respect the differences everywhere: differences between the other races, differences between generations and so on. And I'm not able to put that limit anywhere but there, because it's real. I'm not able to place it in the same way with another woman, where it's much less real, because we [she and I] are not at the same crossroads of nature and culture. (Irigaray in Hirsh and Olson 1995: 110)

Conclusion

While this statement of Irigaray may not preclude application to other differences, such as homosexuality and race, it definitely does not accord them equal priority. It is very much in keeping with Irigaray's statement in *I Love to You* that 'the problem of race is, in fact, a secondary problem – except from a geographical point of view' (1996: 47). Thus while thinkers such as Oliver, Armour, Ziarek and Cheah and Grosz, as well as Deutscher, are all intent on enlisting Irigaray's ideas regarding difference in the service of political ideals, her own heterosexism cannot be evaded.

Perhaps it is also important at this juncture to consider the significance of Irigaray's use of the term 'impossible'. In the prologue to *I Love to You*, Irigaray states that 'I am, therefore, a political militant for the impossible, which is not to say a utopian. Rather, I want what is yet to be as the only possibility of a future' (1996: 10). This statement was made by Irigaray in the context of a public dialogue with an Italian politician, Renzo Imbeni. Irigaray's description of this encounter demonstrates her belief that the dynamics of recognition that took place with this man provides a vivid illustration of the cultural revolution she wants to bring about (8). She acknowledges the difference between them, in that he supports an 'extant possible', whereas she is supporting what is, as yet, an unrealised social impossibility. As her description of the meeting continues, Irigaray clarifies her terms of reference. She expresses her regret about both the misinterpretation of her work and the reluctance of people to put her words into practice. Thus, it appears that she is not proposing the impossible but charging society to make possible, as a political reality, the position she is representing – one that hitherto may indeed have seemed unachievable. 'Rather than regressing to the simple authority of a religion – which one? – or blindly submitting to the rule of money, capital and methods of production that are competitive and irresponsible, we can pursue an oeuvre of justice and culture by elaborating a real civil culture of persons and of the subjective and objective relations between them' (1996: 14).

As Peng Cheah has noted: 'it is true that Irigaray is not utopian. She wants change to actually happen' (Cheah and Grosz 1998b: 32). There is no Derridean undecidability or impossibility here. It is, however, the further steps that Irigaray takes in *I Love to You* that prove problematic for all the above-mentioned commentators on Irigaray's work. This is mainly because of the spiritual and ontological deliberations that are attached to Irigaray's recommendations for making her social and personal vision a reality. In my analysis of Irigaray's most recent work in Chapter 6, we saw that she affirms what I call an 'ontological essentialism' by invoking women's innate spirituality, and their inherent closeness to nature. She also appreciates that women initiate men into a relationship of love that becomes a divine partnership. It is this aspect of Irigaray's work that most feminist commentators don't want to touch. I have no quarrel with the way that Ziarek and Deutscher do try to interpret aspects of Irigaray's proposals so as to construct a productive agenda of reform. It could be termed 'a salvage operation' that intends to rescue a viable political programme from Irigaray's work rather than accept her spiritual commitment. Yet I believe that, if the intention is to appreciate fully Irigaray's undertaking, it is the spiritual dimension of her work, with its possibility for a realisation in this world, that needs to be addressed.[7] As I have contended in the introduction to this book, Irigaray cannot be considered as religious in any conventional way, but the spiritual and ontological dimensions of her work, though incipient in the early work, take on an increasing, if not pre-eminent significance. Cheah is well aware where this change became apparent: 'It seems to me that there [in *An Ethics of Sexual Difference*], Irigaray's idea of sexual difference changes dramatically, and it is formulated as a generative interval that exists between the two sexes. She calls sexual difference a sensible transcendental. This reformation is partly grounded in a rereading of Heidegger in which the copula of Being, that which gives being, is rewritten as the fecundity of the couple' (Cheah and Grosz 1998b: 27). Yet it is not only, as Judith Butler observes, that a 'presumptive heterosexuality' emerges with this move (Butler in Cheah and Grosz 1998b: 27). It also involves, as Cornell discerns, an 'ontologisation', which she rejects. 'Her highly idealized writing on heterosexuality as the reflection on the limits of one's gender that becomes the basis of wonder in the Heideggerian sense, in which you are confronted with the other as the basis of a whole new engagement with difference, is fundamentally conservative to me. Irigaray is in awe of this flowering within heterosexuality' (Cornell in Cheah and Grosz 1998b: 30). It is quite obvious that this development in Irigaray's work is distasteful to both Butler and Cornell, though it is not clear in the interview whether they have read Irigaray's further development of her spiritual ideas in *I Love to You* (1996). But this is perhaps beside the point, as neither Butler nor Cornell gives any indication that she is willing to extricate Irigaray from what they perceive as her ontological predicament. What is equally obvious, however, is the fact that Irigaray does not perceive herself as in need of rescue.

In evaluating this ontological change in Irigaray's position, it is important to keep in mind that a Heideggerian ontology is but one component of Irigaray's composite model of the spiritual aspect of existence. The other is a modified Hegelian universalism. Though Irigaray never explicitly describes their merger, they interact in a intriguing manner. Originally, Irigaray posited the image of two lips as emblematic of women's open-ended and indefinite possibilities. She also connected this initial stage of women with 'self-affection'. 'This is a "self-affection" that would certainly not be reducible to the economy of Sameness of the one' (1985b: 132). But Irigaray did not stay with this image. She then developed the idea that women, by being faithful to their gender, and consciously adopting 'feminine' qualities, can realise their own particular mode of becoming. In this way, women can attain their own particular mode of Hegel's universality. This state, however, did not seem to be sufficient to reform the social fabric, for

Irigaray then introduced the heterosexual couple. In this context, the notion of 'touching upon' (1996: 124–5), expressed in the caress of another, marks the decisive gesture of sexual difference. It is by this mutual touching that the heterosexual couple, confirmed in their separate ontological realities, realise a universality that is specific to the relationship (139). Irigaray describes this dynamic: 'An encounter between a woman and a man may reach a dimension of universality if it takes place with each being faithful to their gender' (143). Often, when Irigaray discusses Heideggerian ontology, the Hegelian element is omitted, but it needs to be noted that the Hegelian realisation of spirit remains an integral part of Irigaray's philosophical and spiritual orientation, together with her Heideggerian ontological turn.

Heidegger's influence on Irigaray is again apparent in her support of 'letting be' or the non-objectification of the other. This is a form of attentiveness to the mystery of the other. While it is not thematised in I Love to You, it is apparent in her admonition to adopt a non-intrusive silence and a non-manipulative attitude towards another (1996: 117). Irigaray deepens these insights in The Way of Love (2002b):

In the exchange between two, a certain resignation must exist concerning the claim of saying everything. No one can say the whole without making exchange impossible.... The highest rule of the word would consist in not appropriating the thing but letting it be as thing. What is sought here is beyond: how to let be the other as other while speaking, speaking to them. Moreover: how to encourage the other to be and to remain other. (2002b: 28–9)

In contrast to Heidegger, however, for Irigaray it is not only Being, as word, that is revealed. This is because: 'man and woman breathe together, engender together, carnally and spiritually. Their alliance is flesh becoming word – the announcement, the question, the dialogue, the thanks, the poetry of the encounter' (1996: 124) For Irigaray, it is Being, as the fullness of the human spiritual dimension, that is disclosed.

It is exhortations like these that have exasperated former admirers, such as Drucilla Cornell. In the beginning, Cornell was in accord with Irigaray's view that something is lacking in a simple programme of equality. Similarly, Cornell invoked the need for recourse to an imaginary realm that posited utopian possibilities of new forms of gendered identity. As Cornell herself states:

Something is missing in both the limited formal equality for women found in the United States and in the social equality provided women in the socialist states.... What has been missing is the protection of each person's imaginary domain, that psychic and moral space in which we, as sexed creatures who care deeply about matters of the heart, are allowed to evaluate and represent who we are. That love and sex are personal should be obvious. (Cornell 1998: x)

Cornell agreed with Irigaray, as she first understood her, to be against any mandatory imposition of a gendered identity. But when Irigaray begins to place more emphasis on a renegotiation of a heterosexual relationship within a model of sexual difference, Cornell opts instead for a more flexible reading of gender differences, including homosexuality. As she states: 'The freedom to be ourselves must be understood as a right that cannot be displaced whenever it is economically convenient to do so. I refer to this right as the right of each person to represent his or her sexuality, or what I call sexuate being' (Cornell 1998: x–xi). In contrast, for Irigaray, sexuate or gendered identity becomes a preoccupation with a virtually compulsory heterosexual difference. It is on this issue of sexual difference as implying distinctive identities, rather than a free play of possibility, that Cornell and Irigaray part company. Cornell relates her disillusion in the interview with Cheah and Grosz:

> What I thought was so utopian was in fact conservative. I was confirmed in my view when Irigaray moved to a concept of sexuate rights at the same time that I felt politically and ethically compelled to critique legal feminism for its own conservative categories, and more specifically, the way in which it had deployed gender in equal opportunity so as to completely shut out gays and lesbians, and women of colour, transvestites, transsexuals, and on and on, from the reach of anti-discrimination. (Cornell in Cheah and Grosz 1998b: 21)

Compared to Cornell, Irigaray seems to live a very sheltered life, and her heterosexist bias is extremely problematic. There are also other forms of difference, however, that Irigaray fails to take into consideration. These are highlighted in an article, 'Divine Women and the Nehanda *Mhondoro*' (2003), by Mary Keller, a feminist scholar in Religious Studies. Keller also notes a positive influence of Heidegger on Irigaray, particularly in her refutation of oppositional differences in the postulate of a sensible transcendental. Her reservations are similar to Huntington's, however, in regard to Irigaray's narrow construal of difference, specifically its relation to female forms of subjectivity. Keller's critique, in contrast to Huntington's, is from a post-colonial perspective. She states: 'While Irigaray's sensible transcendental is a strategic response to a particularly modern and Christian problem with the figuration of women's lives, there are other important models of women's religious subjectivity found in the world's religions, models that it has taken post-colonial theories to identify' (2003: 69).

Keller narrates the story of Nehanda, a powerful Shona woman involved in Rhodesia/Zimbabwe's struggle for independence at the turn of the nineteenth century. Nehanda's subjectivity can be understood as situated at the confluence of many contexts that Keller graphically depicts, but none of them includes the western notion of women's autonomy, central to Irigaray's model of sexual difference. Keller observes: 'a more complex notion of agency is required that recognizes multiple axes of power (race, wealth, gender) and multiple networks of support that can also constrain (kinship, extended family, creative responses within the community, tradition, maintaining links to historical memory)'

(2003: 77). This notion is needed because Nehanda's religion was one that practised ancestor worship which helped to maintain a balance in the community by communication with their presiding spirits. Nehanda's agency is indicative of the influential roles that women, as spirit intermediaries, have had in such indigenous religions. Irigaray's Eurocentric model ignores this indigenous spiritual tradition. Keller takes Irigaray to task by asking which women Irigaray has in mind when she recommends a divine that is appropriate for all women. In addition, Keller notes that Irigaray's depiction of (western) women as the ones who are best suited to mediate religious differences betrays her own colonialist impulses. '[A]s Irigaray expands upon the reason women are privileged mediatrices for cross-cultural engagements, the diaphanous white veil of a Eurocentric notion of religion is drawn across the differences between women's religious bodies. What would it mean for Nehanda's life to be evaluated with reference to a 'God appropriate to the feminine' (2003: 80)? Keller's implication is that this meaning would not necessarily involve adopting the features attributed to gynocratic goddesses, as Irigaray recommends.

Cynthia Willett is another scholar with mixed feelings about Irigaray. Willett is particularly appreciative of Irigaray's location of erotic passion, in preference to reason or character, at the heart of ethical agency (*The Soul of Justice* (2001: 128)). For Willett, this relational orientation adds a needed poetic element to human activity, especially interpersonal relations. Yet Willett is troubled by the somewhat naive if not sentimental depiction of this poetic intimacy. This results, in Willett's view, from Irigaray's lack of political realism, especially of the dynamics of power that are present in most human interchanges, be they public or private. This power, while not inevitably destructive, is not always benign.[8] Willett indicates an aspect of Irigaray's thought – her unwillingness to confront the problem of power and conflict, particularly in connection with women – that several other commentators, most notably Whitford, Ziarek and Hollywood, have also noticed. One area where such power dynamics are prominent, and one which is especially urgent for Willett, is that of class. Willett observes: 'Ethical attunement does not happen in a vacuum, but in a space that is warped by asymmetries of power and social recognition' (128). For Willett, Irigaray's portrayal of an idealised heterosexual relation seems to occur in neutral territory that does not take into account those who are dispossessed of their rights because of their race, ethnicity or class. Willett is severe in her condemnation of Irigaray's blindness to class and her omission of those who labour and are exploited so that the privileged lovers may indulge at leisure in their poetic predilections.

As if in response, in *Between East and West* (2002a) Irigaray does appear to respond to criticism of her model of sexual difference. She declares that other links between nature and culture, besides that of gender, need to be taken into consideration. Unfortunately, the further recommendations that she offers are inadequate, at best, as a solution to instances of class privilege, as well as racial and religious intolerance. Irigaray's proposal is that marriages 'between a white woman and a black man, between a Catholic and a Muslim man' should occur, though she admits that they may either 'ameliorate or exacerbate the problem' (144). Even to suggest such a solution is particularly unfortunate as, in many contemporary situations, instances of callous neglect, exploitation and even extermination witness to much deeper antagonisms towards differences than any marriage relations could ever ameliorate. Thus, given the horrific dimensions of many of these events, inter-racial and inter-religious heterosexual marriage appears to be an ineffective panacea to propose. But Irigaray is unapologetic, as she is convinced that becoming conscious of the nature of sexual difference and its specific demands is 'the most civilized and spiritual [path] that presents itself to us today' (98). For Irigaray, such conscious heterosexual relations appear the most effective way to combat forms of abstract universality that foster intolerance. It is within this framework that Irigaray now promotes heterosexual family life and values as providing the cornerstone of her social and spiritual programme. She states:

Civil community is based on the family entity, this is in its turn being founded upon the union of man and woman. The duality of the sexes cuts across all races, all cultures, all traditions. It is therefore possible to organise a society starting from this difference. It represents the double advantage of being globally shared and of being able to join together the most elemental aspect of the natural with the most spiritual aspect of the cultural. (2002a: 136)

Taken out of context, such sentiments could easily be read as supportive of reactionary family values.

It is exactly this conservative application that Cornell has in mind when she dismisses this later work of Irigaray. In the previous chapter, I discussed certain troublesome presuppositions that inform Irigaray's new vision of sexual difference and its ontological essentialism. These included the assumption not only that men and women are biologically or naturally different but that they also diverge in matters of behavioural conduct that take on ontological significance in essentialised ways (2002a: 129). It is these differences that lie at the heart of the mystery of love for Irigaray. 'The human species is made of two genders, irreducibly different, attracted to one another by the mystery that they represent for each other, an undisclosable mystery that is the source of natural and spiritual life' (84). Sexual desire for Irigaray is an awakening to this mystery of sexual difference – where the corporal and the spiritual differences are to be reconciled in love.

In this spiritualisation of love, Irigaray's definition of women's difference, especially her relation to spirituality, has changed from her early attitude towards women, when she simply encouraged them to imagine themselves as divine. At that time, in repudiating the façade of 'femininity' that had been allotted to them, women were advised to adopt other 'feminine' values derived from pre-Christian gynocratic societies. Since her recent turn towards the east, however, Irigaray has come to a further conclusion regarding the 'nature' of women. Enhancing the gynocratic myth that I described in Chapter 1, Irigaray posits that in the remnants of oldest strata of eastern religions other 'feminine' traditions and values become evident. These include: 'A teaching linked to earthly life, to the sensible, to the concrete, and concerned with cultivating their other fecundity as well as their spiritual, divine, mystical qualities' (2002a: 60). This has led Irigaray to make two inferences. One is that women are divine by birth (1999b 3E), the other is that, from birth, woman has 'an almost spontaneous taste for relational life' (2002a: 87). Endowed with these innate qualities, women are extolled by Irigaray as especially suited to be spiritual initiators. It is in this way that 'The feminine divine provides a bridge between the human world and the cosmic world, between micro-cosmic and macro-cosmic nature, the body and the universe. The feminine divine never separates itself from nature, but transforms it, transubstantiates it without ruining it' (1999b: 7E). This statement illustrates Irigaray's progression from a descriptive mode of cultural or cosmic essentialism (as I outlined in Chapter 5) to an ontological essentialism which assumes an inherent spiritual nature in women. It also marks Irigaray's self-transformation from a scholar to a spiritual practitioner and advocate. Such a vision renders any further debates about the relevance of a deconstructive model of impossibility futile. This is because Irigaray now supports the enactment of a specifically spiritual worldview, with an ethics based on heterosexuality at its core.

Irigaray's evocation of a 'feminine' divine is at the heart of the divide between women scholars who engage with her work. Her original depiction of divine women could be said to identify the divine primarily with a woman's coming into her own, into personal autonomy (1993a). In many ways, this was in accord with her programme for women to attain civil rights, and for an ethics of intersubjectivity (1994). As such, this version was acceptable to secular feminists, whether of a utopian leaning or not, in that divinity as autonomy did not necessarily need to be associated with religion. It was perceived as a rejection of all traditional hierarchical structures, religion included, in the name of women's independence. Yet as a divine 'feminine' began to emerge, with its proposed idealised affinities of women with a natural world that manifested peace and love, many secular feminists, who were still in agreement with Irigaray's primary proposal for the need for sexual difference, particularly in civil and political matters, became uneasy. In response, certain scholars, such as Ziarek and Deutscher, avoid any reference to 'feminine' characteristics, and attempt to retrieve Irigaray's differential displacements for political implementation in other modes of difference. Others, such as Cornell, while acknowledging their earlier debt to Irigaray, reject this aspect of her recent work as ontological or essentialist. Feminist scholars of religion who initially found Irigaray's previous work insightful, such as Hollywood and Armour, also do not accept this evolution, with its emphasis on a spiritually inclined heterosexual difference. In a recent book, *Sensible Ecstasy*, Amy Hollywood astutely evaluates Irigaray's failure to examine critically her own idealisation of woman and sexual difference: 'Irigaray may not intend to fetishize either woman or sexual difference ... Yet I think these mistakes are symptomatic, marking a return of crucial issues repressed by Irigaray' (2002: 340). A question arises as to whether the heterosexual couple now becomes Irigaray's ultimate pronouncement on the location of the divine. I think that Irigaray has dual loyalties in this direction – as both women and the heterosexual couple, depending on the context, maintain intimate connections with a refigured idea of the divine. But lurking in the background of Irigaray's imaginative evocations of this new age of History as spirit, especially as it is depicted in *The Way of Love* (2002b), is a very traditional naturalism. Such an unreconstructed version of natural law excludes many forms of difference from its hallowed sanctuary of divine love. This segregation detracts from the overall impact of Irigaray's vision.

At the same time, Irigaray's spiritual or ontological, turn is agnostic in its stance on the existence of a god or goddess. While she uses the words 'spiritual', even 'religious', in her most recent work, her emphasis is on 'human flourishing', beyond any confines where God is 'the property of a religious community' (2003: 1). In 'On Old and New Tablets', Irigaray finally provides a definition of what she understands as religious: 'The religious, in my opinion, must correspond to a way of accomplishment of the human both as a gathering of self in oneself and as a bond with the universe and the other [as community]' (2003: 7). Such a 'gathering', with its open orientation, resonates with Heidegger's waiting for a new disclosure of Being or a God (Heidegger 1981). The exact identification of this God (for Heidegger), or the divine (for Irigaray), defines definition as it is not an entity that can be reconciled with previous philosophical and religious orthodoxies. Yet Irigaray's divine is predominantly understood as resulting from circumstances that foster human becoming, and that are the effect of human conduct. The term 'transcendent' no longer evokes otherworldly aspirations or interventions, but its spiritual dimension of self-cultivation, specifically in its 'feminine' dispensation, is contentious.

Nevertheless, Irigaray definitely needs to be credited with a number of invaluable innovations in feminist thought. In her deconstruction of male dominance – whether it involved the rational formation of knowledge, of political organizations, of legal prerogatives or of domestic authority – Irigaray brilliantly exposed its fantasies of entitlement. The theological transformations she introduced by her reclamation of the body – given its conventional debased associations with women – as a site of divine in-dwelling will continue to reverberate in positive ways. Her call for imaginative explorations – with their mythological and poetic invocations – is extraordinarily seductive. But Irigaray's unquestioning exhortation of her own proposals as the most suitable solution for the present situation of women is particularly troublesome.

Irigaray herself does not seem to be aware of the controversy that she has created with this recuperation of 'feminine' values and her capitulation to an ontological essentialism. She still warns against accepting 'feminine' stereotypes that are prescribed by the patriarchal tradition, but appears oblivious to the fact that her own description are in similar need of discriminating evaluation. This points to a curious anomaly in the work of Irigaray. While she has been incisive in her exposé of the western male-centred tradition's propensity either to incorporate women within a generalised (masculine) neutrality or to assign them to an artificial 'feminine' ethos, she is not cognisant of her own tendencies in the same direction. As late as I Love to You, Irigaray still proclaims that 'the generic universal is not transhistorical' (1996: 112), but her assignment to women of an intrinsic 'feminine' spirituality and the power to save both humankind and the cosmos belies this. At the same time, Irigaray's alignment of women or the 'feminine' with myth and spirituality, at the expense of non-dualistic modes of reflection, reiterates women's exclusion from the intellectual domain.

It would be only too easy to wrangle for hours debating the ontological and gendered meanings that arise from the work of Irigaray. Is this pantheism? panentheism? Orientalism? ethnocentrism? utopian religiosity? heterosexism? idealised 'femininity'? New Age bathos? These are designations that have been proposed, and will no doubt continue to be part of the ongoing discussions regarding Irigaray's work. Perhaps in all this debate and criticism it is still appropriate to acknowledge the positive impact that Irigaray's work, especially in its early stages, has had on those who perceive religion as something other than displaced needs for security or authority, or other than self-indulgence in sacrificial fantasies. Yet, Irigaray's positive imaginative variants of a new 'feminine' worldview, however inspiring, are in need of careful scrutiny before being unreservedly appropriated by women.

Irigaray's oeuvre has been a concerted effort to reclaim an identity and a spirituality for women. This involves a recognition of a repressed or forgotten divine heritage. In effecting this, Irigaray has enacted a process of becoming a divine women for herself, within a new spiritual order. But this presupposes both a dubious legacy and an emphatic prescription of what becoming a woman entails. The question remains: does Irigaray's retrieval of ancient myths provide women with a firm basis for acquiring a divine nature, thereby initiating a spiritual regeneration of the world, or does it revert to a religious worldview where the divine, defined in a 'feminine' mode, prevents women from achieving the infinite potential of their being? Imaginative experimentations of alternative identities can be exhilarating, even intoxicating, in their persuasiveness but, as Irigaray has admonished in her demolition of male impositions of 'femininity', such designations should never be definitive. Perhaps Irigaray's greatest achievement has been her recuperation of the dynamics of desire as love, and of the body's positive role in acts of knowing (carnal or otherwise). Her explorations of the divine – whether in a 'feminine' or a heterosexual mode – however, do leave something to be desired. Divinity may well indwell in the embrace of lovers, but Irigaray's limitation of such participation to heterosexuals is indicative of a repressive tendency in her programme. Such a denial only serves to restrict the diverse ways in which a divine can become manifest in a world that respects differences, and that does not attempt to exclude them, because they threaten one's own circumscribed worldview.

Notes

Chapter 1

1 In 'The Power of Discourse' (Irigaray 1985b), Irigaray discusses two forms of mimicry: (1) parodic mimicry, which reiterates a situation in a deliberately assumed role, and (2) a productive mimesis, which involves a creative and dynamic process (131). Naomi Schor, in 'This Essentialism which Is Not One', would envision Irigaray's work is in the service of a mimicry which 'comes to signify difference as a positivity, a joyful reappropriation of the attributes of the other that is not in any way to be confused with a mere reversal of the existing phallo-centric distribution of power' (1994: 67).

2 It needs to be observed that Irigaray does deal in vast generalizations regarding her use of the terms of 'patriarchy' and 'gynocracy', just as she does in her explorations of 'western' and 'eastern' cultures and religions. My analysis will inevitably reflect this framework, though I acknowledge the drawbacks of such unqualified ahistoric and non-contextual generalisations.

3 Irigaray describes the phallic system as one which 'shares the values promulgated by the patriarchal society and culture, values inscribed in the philosophical corpus: property, production, order, form, unity, visibility ... and erection' (1985b: 86).

4 For Freud, a fetish is associated with the penis, or rather, with the dread of its removal – castration. The fear of castration is displaced on to reassuring objects associated with women, of either a positive or negative kind. As such, the fetish serves as a protective device against men's unconscious fear of castration.

5 As Margaret Whitford notes: 'It is essential to think through again the implications of the fact that the Other is constitutive of subjectivity, whether the Other is the unconscious – that which the subject cannot master or control, or even know in himself – or whether the Other is embodied in other people who likewise constitute that which is irreducible to the subject, or whether the Other is the Lacanian Other, whose desire is located in the symbolic order' (1991: 149).

6 In her book *Jacques Lacan & Co.*, Elisabeth Roudinesco details how the structuralist ideas of Ferdinand de Saussure were to have a marked impact in Lacan's reformulation of the Freudian unconscious according to linguistic categories. She proposes two different influential readings of Saussure by Lacan. The first was that of the years previous to 1953, where his other influences were Heidegger and Lévi-Strauss. During the period from 1953 into the 1960s, the time of the crystallisation of

many of his ideas, Lacan's reading of Saussure was further affected by the work of Jakobson and Merleau-Ponty. This period was also marked by a re-evaluation of Hegel's philosophy, which, by way of Alexandre Kojève's lectures in the 1930s, also was a major influence on Lacan (1990: 297–300).

7 Irigaray would be the first to agree that, in the phallocratic system, imaginary projections have been conflated with the symbolic Other in the various expositions of God. As Lacan has observed: 'The objective of my teaching, inasmuch as it arms at that part of analytic discourse which can be formulated, or put down, is to dissociate the a [*autre*/other] and the O [*Autre*/Other], by reducing the former to what belongs to the imaginary and the latter to what belongs to the symbolic. That the symbolic is the support of that which was made into God, is beyond doubt. That the imaginary is supported by the reflection of like to like, is certain. And yet, it has come to be confused with the S(O) [Symbolic Other]' (Lacan in Mitchell and Rose 1983: 153–4).

8 For Irigaray, 'femininity' is simply a role, a pretence which women have unwittingly adopted in order to survive. The original commentary on Freudian 'femininity' as masquerade was made by Joan Rivière (1986 [1929]).

9 In so far as Lacan follows Freud, both see 'the unconscious as a consequence of primal repression, where the phallus is the preserved infantile nucleus of the unconscious, a residue of the child's primal repression of its maternal desire' (Grosz 1990: 117).

10 In both Freud and Lacan, it is the fact of women's castration that, either literally or figuratively, constitutes the reason for her rejection as defective in a phallic economy. Grosz explains the manoeuvre: 'men *have* the phallus only if some subjects (i.e., women) do not have it, because the phallus is predicted on the division of some from all. They define the others as *not all*. No-one is all. Yet women are distinguished from men by being *not-all* (men, presumably must be not *not-all*)' (1990: 138). This maladroit logic needs to be situated within the framework of Lacan's overall project so as to gain insight into its biased mind-set. 'Instead of the Freudian commitment to a phylogenetic, pseudo-biological explanation of the oedipal structure, Lacan will use social, unconscious, and linguistic explanations.... The mother is denigrated from her position as the all powerful phallic [unconscious] mother, not because of the child's perception of an anatomical lack. Instead, the child perceives her powerlessness in terms of the mother's relation (of desire for, of subordination to) the father' (70).

11 Juliet Mitchell does not view the situation as being quite so vehemently anti-woman as does Irigaray. 'Freud, and Lacan after him, are both accused of producing phallocratic theories – of taking man as the norm and woman as what is different therefrom.... To both Freud and Lacan their task is not to produce justice but to explain this difference which to them uses, not the man, but the phallus to which the man has to lay claim, as its key term. But it is because Freud's position only clearly became this in his later work that Lacan insists that we have to "re-read" it, giving his theory the significance and coherence which it otherwise lacks' (1983: 8).

12 For a general survey of the impact of Kojève see Elisabeth Roudinesco (1990: 134–47). Kojève's stress on the anthropological elements of the master/slave model has had a profound effect on the French reception of Hegel. (See also Descombes (1980: 9–54.)

13 Another facet of Lacan's modification of Hegel (by way of Kojève) so as to accommodate his revision of Freud has to do with the term 'desire'. As Roudinesco explains it: 'Through his doctrine and through the relations he entertained with his disciples and with the psychoanalytic community, Lacan put into effect the essence of that negative dialectic of human Desire and the Struggle for Recognition, as Kojève formulated them out of Hegel's discourse' (1990: 141). She elaborates further: 'He did not pit a "philosophy" against a "biologism"; he made use of philosophical discourse in order to restore its adequate meaning to Freud's endeavour. He thus effected a merger between Begièrde, [Hegel's term for desire], that is, desire founded on recognition or the "desire of the desire of the other" and a Wunsch [Freud's term for desire] unconscious in nature and bound to signs. He introduced the Freudian unconscious into a Hegelian-Kojèvian definition of Begièrde and "the struggle for recognition" into the Freudian definition of Wunsch' (146).
14 The work of Hegel will be discussed in more detail in Chapter 3.
15 Kelly Oliver describes well the ramifications of the traditional oedipal resolution: 'The mother–infant dyad is anti-social and must be prohibited and repressed by the Law of the Father so that society might exist.... The Oedipal situation is a struggle to the death between mother's body and father's name/law in which, if the resolution is successful, the father always wins. This struggle is a battle between nature and culture. The child must leave nature behind in order to enter culture. The maternal body is sacrificed for the sake of culture' (Oliver 1995: 167).
16 Irigaray describes this strategy: 'It [to play with mimesis] means ... to make "visible" by an effect of playful repetition, what was supposed to remain invisible: the cover-up of a possible operation of the feminine in language' (1985b: 76).
17 Lacan appears to taunt women from his own position of linguistic competence – not only can he decode their inarticulate yet visceral paroxysms of desire, but he would even class his own writings as of the same calibre – though he knows and can articulate exactly what's going on (Lacan in Mitchell and Rose (1983: 147)). In taking Lacan to task for his somewhat smug and tasteless ascription of jouissance to Bernini's statue of St. Teresa in ecstasy, Irigaray's acerbic response is an enquiry as to whose pleasure was actually involved in this act of voyeurism (1985b: 90–1).
18 Diane Chisholm describes Irigaray in Speculum as engaged in the imitative mimesis for subversive purposes, though it is a risky enterprise: 'Such a mimicry would systematically "unspeak" that discourse by performing a risky de(con)struction so as to clear the ground for other, less reactively reproductive, more actively productive strategies of mimesis. The problem Irigaray must confront is how to liberate the first mimesis (the productive/active mimesis) through the second (reproductive-reactive mimesis) – how to open a space for countercultural production by overblown histrionic effects of hysterical reproduction without destroying that enclave in the process' (1994: 270).
19 See Philippa Berry, 'The Burning Glass: Paradoxes of Feminist Revelation in Speculum' (1994), for an excellent description of Irigaray's combination of various traits of women mystics. Amy Hollywood also treats this topic in her chapter, 'From Lack to Fluidity: Luce Irigaray, La Mystérique' (2002: 187–210), where she criticises Irigaray for this conflation, even essentialism, of medieval mystics. She also adds that Irigaray cites male mystics, though I believe that it is the figure of the female mystic that is central to her thesis.

20 Chapter 5 will be a contrast and comparison of Irigaray's and Daly's work.
21 The term 'becoming' denotes a mode of existence that does not conform to the ontological categories of Being. Ontology, or the study of Being as an independent entity, is the backbone of orthodox western metaphysical philosophy and theology.
22 The work of Grace Jantzen in *Becoming Divine: Towards a Feminist Philosophy of Religion* (1999) and her development of the topic of natality also provides a fine example of imaginary improvisations in accord with Irigaray's suggestions. See Jantzen's full discussion of her adaptation of 'natality' from the work of Hannah Arendt (1999: 145–55).
23 Irigaray does interrogate Merleau-Ponty in 'The Invisible of the Flesh: A Reading of Merleau-Ponty, *The Visible and the Invisible*, "The Intertwining – The Chiasm"', where she reprimands him for his omission of the flesh of women (1993a: 151–84).
24 In my understanding of the relation of Irigaray's work to that of Merleau-Ponty, I am indebted to the work of Dorothea Olkowski, in particular to 'The End of Phenomenology' (2000a). Here Olkowski argues that Irigaray, though she never develops her ideas philosophically, moves beyond phenomenology as articulated by Merleau-Ponty. This is because Merleau-Ponty fails to appreciate the affectivity of women's bodies – the 'two lips' – that are 'not remote from one another; not out of touch' Olkowski (81). He also fails to develop the interval – which he tried to express in his construct of 'flesh' – as an intermediary spacing or moment that intervenes between dualities. Irigaray will explore this mediatory space. See the following chapter for further discussion of this topic.
25 Irigaray will give more specific directions in *I Love to You* (1996). These will be discussed in Chapter Four.
26 I am indebted to Luisa Muraro for this insight into Irigaray's change from a matricidal to gynocratic society. Muraro assesses it accordingly: 'It is not a question of inconsistency on Irigaray's part but of the progression of her thought' (Irigaray 1994: 321). Irigaray's work concerning the existence of gynocracies 'should not be restricted to matriarchy but should include all eras when women reigned as women' (Irigaray 1993c: 24). It is also worth noting that, besides a reference to the bibliography of Merlin Stone's book *When God Was a Woman* (1976), Irigaray does not mention the work of any contemporary Anglo-American advocates of gynocracy or matriarchy or their critics.
27 Irigaray brings other goddesses into play. In *Marine Lover* (1991a) she adopts the personae of Athena, Persephone, Ariadne as imaginative representatives of various modes of women's relation to an elemental maternal substrate. In interrogating Nietzsche's work from the perspective of Ariadne, she associates this goddess figure with water, representing the repressed element that haunts Nietzsche's work – the amniotic fluid.
28 For Bachofen, the Aphroditean or *hetaerist* stage is also described as tellurian, or related to the earth. 'This stage is characterized by unregulated sexual relation, the absence of all individual possessions or private rights of any kind, by the communal holding of women, children, and consequently all property; it is a stage of formless, orderless freedom, and the only bond between creatures is that of Aphroditean desire' (1967: 190). In contrast, in the following Demetrian stage: 'The origin not only of customs and laws, but also of cities may be traced back to Demeter. Cities

were founded amid Demetrian rites, the walls rose from the womb of the earth, and their inviolability was rooted precisely in this relation to maternal matter' (196).

29 This romantic version of myth, as bearing wisdom from the past, is but one of the theories regarding the way myth can be interpreted. For an overview of these different interpretations see Segal (1998). See also Bruce Lincoln's discussion of myth as 'ideology in narrative form' (1999: 207). The whole question of Romantic and mythic idealism, and the influence of Bachofen's own mythmaking work on thinkers such as Jung and Eliade, but especially on certain strains of goddess appropriation, is in need of critical theoretical analysis from a feminist and an interdisciplinary perspective that would include classics, history, history of religions and post-colonial theory.

30 Irigaray will make these claims in a more definitive way in *I Love to You* (1996). See Chapters 4 and 6 for further evaluations.

31 The topic of women and nature will be treated in greater detail in Chapter 5.

32 This work and Irigaray's ideas on spirituality will be discussed in Chapters 5, 6, and 7.

33 The term 'mucus' is used as a synonym for multiplicity by Irigaray. It also has other more bodily resonances such as fluidity and viscosity. It is never fully thematised in Irigaray's work. See Whitford (1991: 163) for an excellent description of this term and its further applications in the work of Irigaray.

34 Braidotti is somewhat discouraged by the fact that male postmodern philosophers have 'first sexualized as "feminine" the question of difference and, second, have turned it into a generalized philosophical item' (1994: 173).

35 Proponents of equality are generally portrayed as being in favour of women obtaining all the rights and privileges of men, while proponents of difference are characterised as supportive of women having distinct needs and properties that should be recognised.

36 In connection with the archaeological and historical investigations that are seeking an original matriarchy, Cavarero views them as having pragmatic rather than essential value: 'the truth of their findings is not so much measured by documental accuracy (did matriarchy exist historically?) as by their ability to function as images for a project, where what is lost is what we want to find' (1993: 208).

37 In this context, it needs to be noted that *An Ethics of Sexual Difference* (1993a) was published in French in 1984, three years before *Sexes and Genealogies* (1993b), though they both appeared in English in 1993. However, much of the work in both books was written over the same period. *An Ethics of Sexual Difference* contains a series of lectures given by Luce Irigaray at the University of Rotterdam in 1982. *Sexes and Genealogies* is a compilation of essays that were written during the years 1980–86.

38 In her exposition of sexual difference, Cavarero states that it is necessary today, particularly for theologians, to rethink the biblical references to the creation of the sexes. She is referring to the two stories of human creation in Genesis. One reference is Genesis 1:27, where both male and female are created in the image of God. The other is Genesis 1:21–3, where woman is formed from man's rib. The first 'feminist' to comment on this discrepancy was Elizabeth Cady Stanton in *The Woman's Bible* (1895–98). Since then much work has been done by biblical scholars and theologians. Deborah Sawyer, in *God, Gender and the Bible* (2002), gives an excellent overview of contemporary scholarship – including a discussion of Irigaray.

39 These social aspects are discussed in more detail in Chapter 4.
40 Irigaray's views on myth has been influenced by the work of Mircea Eliade. See Eliade (1978).
41 Domna Stanton has made a similar criticism (1986). Her references, however, are only in connection with *Speculum*, which does not give a sufficiently nuanced picture of Irigaray's views on the maternal.
42 It is obvious that a simplistic division between sex (as biology) and gender (as cultural) is no longer helpful. As early as 1983, Alison Jaggar had remarked that 'sex neither uniquely determines gender, nor is it irrelevant ... [Sex and gender] create each other' (52). In *Bodies that Matter*, Judith Butler states that we need to examine carefully 'those proverbial commas' that separate sex, gender, race, class, and 'that usually mean that we have not figured out how to think the relations we seek to mark' (1993: 168). This topic will be given a closer examination in Chapter 7.

Chapter 2

1 This is actually not Descartes' grave, which was ransacked during the revolution. His remaining bones are interred here. For an account of how this untoward situation came to pass see G. Rodis-Lewis (1998: 204–5).
2 Descartes' objection to the Scholastic tradition stemmed from a number of things. He distrusted the unquestioned emphasis on sense perception as a basis of knowledge. More importantly, Descartes rejected the hylomorphic union of matter and form which meant that there was an indivisible link between matter and its essential form, which provided its nature and qualities. Scholastics believed in this union and that the mind can have direct awareness of this essential form of matter. Descartes did not accept that knowledge could be transmitted in this seamless way from body to mind.
3 Descartes describes the pineal gland as 'one small part of the brain, namely the part which is said to contain the "common" sense' (1984: 59). He will also refer to it as 'gland H' and will also place the imagination there (1985: 106). The activity within the pineal gland, by which sense perceptions are transmitted, is attributed by Descartes to 'animal spirits'. Descartes describes their workings: 'The parts of the blood which penetrate as far as the brain serve not only to nourish and sustain its substance, but also and primarily to produce in it a certain very fine wind, or rather a very lively and pure flame, which is called the *animal spirits*. For it must be noted that the arteries that carry blood to the brain from the heart, after dividing into countless tiny branches which make up the minute tissues that are stretched like tapestries at the bottom of the cavities of the brain, come together again around a certain little *gland* situated near the middle of the substance of the brain, right at the entrance to its cavities. The arteries in this region have a great many little holes through which the finer parts of the blood can flow into this gland' (100). The term 'common' sense is actually a borrowing from Scholastic philosophy, which functioned there as an internal sense that that processed the impressions received from the external senses.
4 For Descartes, an innate idea is not necessary a Platonic form, nor an eternal truth. Innate ideas are 'thoughts within me which neither came to me from external objects nor were determined by my will, but which came solely from the power

of thinking within me' (1985: 303). Yet he will also state: 'And indeed it is no surprise that God, in creating me, should have placed this idea in me to be, as it were, the mark of the craftsman marked on his work' (35). In the Third Meditation, Descartes expounds his arguments for the existence of God, which are in part a variant of Anselm's ontological argument. In so doing, Descartes distinguishes between formal and representative aspects of ideas. The fact that the idea of God can exist objectively and not just formally in his mind leads Descartes to conclude that God exists. This argument depends on the rather implausible idea that there are different degrees of reality that exist between a formal abstract mode and an idea as objectively existing. Descartes then establishes that there is a cause for such a distinction. This is that the only reason that he can have this (objective) idea of an omnipotent perfect being in his mind is because God does exist. Finally, in the Fifth Meditation, Descartes extrapolates from the idea of God possessing every perfection (such as omnipotence, etc.) to the necessary existence of this perfect being. Again, this is a very suspect move, for which he was taken to task by his own contemporaries, such as Gassendi, and, since then, by many other scholars.

5 Descartes responds to criticism of this move: 'I was guilty of circularity in proving the existence of God by stating that "We are sure that God exists because we attend to the arguments" which prove this; but subsequently it is enough for us to remember that we perceived something clearly in order for us to perceive that it is true. This would not be sufficient if we did not know that God exists and is not a deceiver' (1984: 171).

6 Descartes tends to use the terms – mind and soul – interchangeably. See especially 'Comments on a Certain Broadsheet' (1985: 303). He distinguishes the brain as a physical organ from the mind or soul as the rational or spiritual dimension. 'It must be realized principally that the human soul, while informing the entire body, nevertheless has its principal seat in the brain; it is here alone that the soul not only understands and imagines but also has sensory awareness. Sensory awareness comes about by means of nerves.... The result of these movements being set up in the brain by the nerves is that the soul or mind that is closely joined to the brain is affected in various ways corresponding to the various sorts of movements' (279–80).

7 For background on Arnauld and the Jansenist connection see Jolley (1992: 400–3). One of the areas that Descartes got himself into hot water about was, unsurprisingly, theology, for Descartes believed that his method could be of relevance to this subject. Given Descartes' focus on the brain or mind alone as a thinking substance, and the somewhat obscure nature of the body's relation to it, the doctrine of transubstantiation – the change that takes place in the Catholic Mass from bread and wine into the body and blood of Christ – presented a problem. How could Descartes account for sensible material things being transformed into another substance – the matter and form of Christ? For insight into the debate on this topic see Watson (1987: 155–77).

8 In 'Maleness, Metaphor and the "Crisis" of Reason', Lloyd illustrates her position by describing a complex interweaving of different metaphors in Descartes that tend to emphasise martial modes of mental supremacy when discussing the interaction of the mind and body. These can alert a reader to the unresolved problems that lie at the heart of Descartes' treatment of the passions. While not necessarily indicative

of essentialist gendered associations, these metaphors are linked by Lloyd to deeply embedded symbols of manly attributes or activities that pervade philosophical texts (1993b: 74).

9 Irigaray's title '... and if, taking the eye of one recently dead' is a quotation from Descartes' *Optics* to which *The Discourse on the Method* was actually a preface. The aim of the exercise was a physiological and psychological treatment of vision so as to corroborate that empirical analyses can be reconciled with the indubitable facts of geometry.

10 S. V. Keeling's statement is typical of those who worry about a lack of consistency in Descartes' work: 'Nor is it easy to state briefly what sort of connection holds between Descartes' Method and his Metaphysics on the one hand, and on the other his Physics. The difficulty arises partly because he, like most philosophers who stress the importance of their method, is by no means precise as he should be in stating what he understands by it' (1934: 60).

11 Joan Scott has also detected this nature/culture paradox that at the heart of the modernist feminist movement. As she depicts the situation, women both contest the cultural ideals of equality and appeal to 'feminine' ideals. They want inclusion but not in the name of purely 'masculine' values (Scott 1996: 172–3).

12 Descartes employs different meanings of the term 'distinct'. There are modal, conceptual and real distinctions. It would seem that what he has in mind here is a real distinction, whereby 'Strictly speaking, a *real* distinction exists only between two or more substances; and we can perceive that two substances are really distinct from the fact that we can clearly and distinctly understand one apart from the other' (1985: 213). There is a debate as to what status Descartes accorded the 'union' the mind and body. In the *Sixth Meditation* Descartes begins his exploration of aspects of body/mind co-operation by saying: 'Nature also teaches me, by these sensations of pain, hunger, thirst and so on, that I am not merely present in my body as a sailor is present in a ship, but that I am very closely joined and, as it were, intermingled with it, so that I and the body form a unit' (Descartes 1984: 56). In a recent book, Marleen Rozemond comments: 'Descartes himself never calls the mind-body composite a substance, even though there are several occasions on which his doing so would have been a most appropriate means of placating his opponents. For this reason one should at the very least be sceptical towards the view that he regarded the human being as a substance, and I myself am convinced that he did not' (1998: 213). The recent biography by the Cartesian scholar Geneviève Rodis-Lewis reads this topic in a more positive light. 'The Sixth Meditation is thus the first development on the *substantial* union between body and soul ... Because the senses teach us not what objects are in themselves but only their usefulness or danger in relation to that union of body and soul, what we call "errors of the senses" has a completely different meaning: they reveal illnesses or accidental disturbances of a "nature" established by God for the preservation of life ... The union of body and soul and the possibility of dominating or correcting their disturbances once their source had been understood would be the object of extensive reflections by Descartes in his *Replies to the Objections* and in a significant correspondence that would lead to his last book, *The Passions of the Soul*' (1998: 131–2).

13 For general background information on Princess Elisabeth see Harth (1992: 67–78) and also Nye (1999). Elisabeth, Princess Palatine, at the time the correspondence

began, was exiled in The Hague. Her father, a Protestant, had claimed the throne of Bohemia, but had been deposed and killed. She had been educated by tutors, and was intellectually prepared for the interchange with Descartes. Her background, however, could not have been more different from that of Descartes. As Nye describes her: 'Elizabeth's life was different [from Descartes']. The questions she raised came not from isolated meditation but from involvement: from painful experience, emotional upset, intellectual turmoil, struggles with self, and a recalcitrant body, conflict between her own desires and the will of others. She was not concerned, as were so many of Descartes' critics, with defending an academic reputation or scoring points' (Nye 1999: 14); see also Harth (1992: 67–78).

14 In her first letter, dated 16 May 1643, Princess Elisabeth asks: 'Can you please inform me how the human soul (being as it is a thinking substance) can affect the [animal] spirits of the body so that it can undertake voluntary [willed] actions. For it seems that every instance of movement is brought about by an activity in the object that is moved to the extent that it is set in motion by something that moves it, or again depends on the nature and shape of the latter's surface. The first two conditions require contact, the third requires extension. You have entirely eliminated extension from your depiction of the soul, and contact seems to me to be incompatible with an object without extension [*immatérielle*]' (1935: 3–4).

15 The six primitive passions are: wonder, love, hatred, desire, joy and sadness. Descartes will initially define the passions in the most general sense to indicate all forms of perceptions and sensations (Descartes 1985: 336), but then he narrows the definition to refer specifically to the six emotions as belonging to a class which impinges on the soul by way of the (animal) spirits and is distinct from internal bodily perceptions (e.g., thirst) and externally caused sensations (e.g., pain) (1985: 338–9).

16 In *The Passions of the Soul*, Descartes reworks his ideas on the pineal gland to accommodate the passions. As with sense perceptions, the mind or soul is passive in the reception of the passions. The principal effect of the passions (with the exception of wonder) is to dispose the soul to want the things that nature deems good for it. 'Their [the passions'] natural function is to move the soul to consent to and contribute to actions which may serve to preserve the body or render it in some way more perfect' (1985: 376). The passions, however, must always be subject to rigorous rational scrutiny. It is only then that an act of volition sets a reverse process in motion. 'And the activity of the soul consists that simply by willing something it brings it about that the little gland to which it is closely joined moves in the manner required to produce the effect corresponding to this volition' (343).

17 Wonder alone is prereflective in the sense that it does not involve judgement.

18 As part of Irigaray's programme for women's attainment of identity, the 'love of self' is indispensable. Her initial recommendations regarding the way to achieve this, especially in 'When Our Lips Speak Together' (1985b: 205–18), have been read as an endorsement of lesbian relationships, but Irigaray then turned to focus more on the mother and daughter relationship, and after that the male and female one (Holmlund 1991: 283–308). Thus, in retrospect, it seems that it was more a form of auto-affection and self-affirmation that Irigaray supported all along.

19 Irigaray clarifies this idea in her later work, *I Love to You* (1996). 'The other of sexual difference is he – or she – towards whom it is possible to go as towards a

transcendence, while remaining in the self, and without turning transcendence on its head in the guise of soul or spirit. I will never reach this other, and for that very reason, he/she forces me to remain in my self in order to be faithful to him/her and us, retaining our difference' (Irigaray 1996: 105).

20 There are distinct Stoic influences in Descartes. In a letter to Princess Elisabeth he recommends that she read Seneca's *On the Happy Life* (Descartes 1991: 256) regarding the exercise of reason. Princess Elisabeth, however, is not overly impressed (Descartes 1935: 94–6). She quite graphically depicts situations where reason, or even the assurance of God, does not suffice to calm the mind and control the passions in certain circumstances.

21 Descartes' position is that in principle there is not a human will that does not have the capacity to order the passions (Descartes 1985: 348). All he will concede to Princess Elisabeth, who is doubtful regarding Descartes' blanket endorsement of such recommendations, is that perhaps Seneca does not express himself sufficiently clearly on certain matters. There is no admission that Princess Elisabeth's doubts may have a basis (1991: 256–9).

22 Irigaray does have her own prescription for the disciplining of the instinctive drives, which she views as different from Descartes' mastery of the passions. She will explore this dimension of her work more fully in *I Love to You* (1996). See Chapter 4.

23 As both Harth (1992) and Joan Scott (1996) demonstrate, there were women who took Descartes up on his proposition that the mind was neutral and that women were therefore equal. Perhaps the rallying cry of such women is exemplified in the life of Olympe de Gouges. 'She was best remembered most for articulating the claim that became the motto of the nineteenth-century French feminist movement: "Woman have the right to mount the scaffold; she ought equally have the right to mount the tribune"' (Scott 1996: 55).

24 The transfiguration is a doctrine in Catholicism, based on the Gospel, that witnesses to the transformation that occurred on one occasion in the presence of certain apostles, where the divinity of Jesus, the man, was fully revealed. It is the disclosure of the divine in a human form. In contrast, transubstantiation is another Catholic doctrine where it is believed that in the Catholic Mass the bread and wine – while retaining their everyday appearance – are substantially changed into the body and blood of Christ. See note 7 above for reference to Descartes' own tussle with explaining this religious doctrine.

Chapter 3

1 In this chapter, the slippage between the qualifier 'feminine', as indicative of gender and enculturated ideals, and the word 'woman', as indicative of a biological distinction, is extremely obvious. Both Irigaray and Levinas tend to blur these entities.

2 Though he does not make any explicit references, perhaps it is the criticisms of Beauvoir and, more recently, of Irigaray that Levinas has in mind.

3 Levinas relates: 'What I admire in his work is *Sein und Zeit*. It is a peak of phenomenology. The analyses are brilliant. As for the later Heidegger, I am much less familiar with him. What scares me a little is also the development of a discourse in which the human becomes an articulation of an anonymous or neutral intelligibility,

to which the revelation is subordinated' (1998: 116).
4 Levinas observes: 'I do not preach for the Jewish religion. I always speak of the Bible, not the Jewish religion. The Bible, including the Old Testament, is for me a human fact, of the human order, and entirely universal' (1988: 177).
5 In a later interview, Levinas qualifies this usage of the term 'justice'. 'In *Totality and Infinity* I used the word "justice" for ethics, for the relationship between two people. I spoke of "justice", although now "justice" is for me something which is a calculation, which is knowledge, and which supposes politics; it is inseparable from the political. It is something which I distinguish from ethics, which is primary. However, in *Totality and Infinity*, the word "ethical" and the word "just" are the same word, the same question, the same language. When I use the word "justice" there it is not in the technical sense as something opposed to or distinct from the moral' (1988: 171).
6 While it would seem consistent to refer to the infinite as 'Other' (*Autre*), and the other human being as other (*autrui*) this usage does not hold either in Levinas or in his translators. Sometimes *autre*/other is to refer to the other person. One of Levinas's translators acknowledges this: 'Levinas often uses *autre* where he could very well have used *autrui*' (Cohen 1987: viii). I have tried to be consistent in my own differentiation of these two terms, using 'other' for the other person, and 'Other' for the Infinite, but it is sometimes at odds with an accompanying quotation.
7 Levinas states: 'The God who passed is not the model of which the face would be an image. To be in the image of god does not mean to be an icon of God but to find oneself in his trace. The revealed God of our Judeo- Christian spirituality maintains all the infinity of his absence, which is in the personal "order" itself. He shows himself only by his trace, as is said in Exodus 33. To go toward Him is not to follow this trace, which is not a sign; it is to go toward the Others who stand in the trace of *illeity*' (1996: 64).
8 Levinas admits: 'Philosophy employs a series of terms and concepts – such as *morphe* (form), *ousia* (substance), *nous* (reason), *logos* (thought) or *telos* (goal), etc. – which constitute a specifically Greek lexicon of intelligibility. French and German, and indeed all of Western philosophy is entirely shot through with this specific language; it is a token of the genius of Greece to have been able to thus deposit its language in the basket of Europe. But although philosophy is essentially Greek, it is not exclusively so. It also has sources and roots which are non-Greek. What we term the Judaeo-Christian tradition, for example, proposed an alternative approach to meaning and truth. The difficulty is, of course, to *speak* of this alternative tradition given the essentially Greek nature of philosophical language. And this difficulty is compounded by the fact that Judaeo-Christian culture has, historically, been incorporated into Greek philosophy' (1986b: 19).
9 Adriaan Peperzak warns against any simplistic characterisation of Levinas's work: 'Many writers on Levinas present his work as a synthetic, hybrid or paradoxical result of Greek and Jewish culture, denying thereby the importance of other traditions like the Roman, Russian, Christian or Germanic ones.... As a Lithuanian born Jew, a Russian and French educated citizen of Europe and a philosophical member of contemporary humanity, Levinas is not only heir to (a certain) Greece and (a certain) Israel, but also to the Roman Empire with the medieval and modern transformations of its Law, to the Slavic and Germanic elements that entered into

his formation, and even to a certain form of Christianity that has marked and impregnated 2000 years of European history ... It is impossible to reduce Rome to Greece, the Germanic traditions to nothing at all, and Christianity to a subordinate heresy of Judaism or to an amalgam of Jewish faith and Hellenistic philosophy' (1991: 431).

10 Many scholars of Levinas have commented on the marked difference between the vocabulary and forms of *Totality and Infinity* (1969 [1961]), where his metaphysics is obvious, and those of *Otherwise than Being or Beyond Essence* (1981 [1974]). In the later work, Levinas has consciously striven to disassociate himself from his early more conventionally philosophic terminology, and 'otherwise' can have a number of referents. It mainly refers to an ethical mode of being as distinct from an ontological one.

11 The original article appeared as 'Le Judaisme et le feminine', in *Age Nouveau*, 107–9 (1960). An earlier translation by Edith Wyschogrod entitled 'Judaism and the Feminine Element' appeared in *Judaism* 18: 1 (1969).

12 Though he doesn't thematise this equality, there are indications in other works that Levinas perceives an appeal to this primordial equity in contemporary women's demands for equality under secular law (1987a [1947]: 86).

13 There is one sentence in *Time and the Other* where Levinas could be said to prefigure this development: 'Profanation is not a negation of mystery, but one of the possible relationships with it' (1987 [1947]: 86). Levinas, however, does not develop this statement further at this time.

14 My own nomination for one reason for the change is that, as noted in the *Cambridge Companion to Levinas*, from 1945 to 1980 Levinas studied the Talmud with the 'enigmatic Monsieur Chouchani', whose great influence on him 'should not be underestimated' (Critchley 2002: xxi). (Levinas himself refers to this man by the name of Mr. Shosani, though he professes he is not sure if this name is correct (2001: 73–5).) The evidence is the following: *Time and the Other* and *Existence and Existents* were originally published just after the Second World War. In both of these books, the notion of Woman or 'the feminine' is idealised in an unproblematic way. In *Totality and Infinity* (1969) and in the two essays 'Judaism and the Feminine' (1990a) and 'And God Created Women' (1990b), erotic relations between women and men become more problematised. Limited space prevents a more detailed study of this development. One noticeable change is Levinas's negative attitude to 'The Eternal Feminine' (1990a: 37) which he had referred to favourably in *Time and the Other* (1987a [1947]: 86).

15 This discipline, or 'labour of the negative', will be discussed more fully in the next chapter on the work of Hegel.

16 These claims have been refined and extended in more recent books, such as Koehn (1998).

17 Alison Ainley expresses the implications of this development well: 'Levinas must face the charge that the continuity of the identity via fecundity expresses not only the continuity of the Law of the Father, but also a presupposition of a heterosexual relation, albeit symbolically rather than biologically expressed.... Perhaps metaphysical desire is essentially virile' (1988: 79). It is not so much that Levinas intends to promote a 'virile metaphysics' in contrast to a 'feminine erotics', but this is where his unreflective usage of the 'feminine' has led him.

18 See Wehr (1987) for a feminist criticism of Jung's archetypes.
19 In 'Judaism and the Feminine', Levinas refers to the Midrash and how it interprets the forms of romance found in the Bible, including the Songs of Songs, 'so as to bring out the eschatological side of the romance' (1990a: 37 [1960]). Irigaray takes a different attitude to the Song of Songs. She interprets this hymn to love as demarcating the division between male and female cultures. 'The Song of Solomon harks back to the break and evokes the painful separation between she who wants to be initiated into her mother's chamber, and he who awakens her beneath the tree where her mother is said to have conceived her.... The two lovers are separated. The nations of women and men are also divided; they no longer occupy the same places, they are no longer faithful to the same genealogy, or to the same tradition. But the Song of Solomon bears the trace of the woman as lover (l'amante), for it says, and repeats: "Do not awaken my love until she please"' (1991b: 117).
20 In an article, 'Reinhabiting the House of Ruth', Katz will propose that in Levinas, though the feminine seems only to provide the condition of possibility for ethics, conditions are created where the feminine is capable ethical conduct, as illustrated by women in the Book of Ruth, specifically the excessive conduct of Ruth (2001b: 163–4). This is, however, another case of slippage between the 'feminine' and women.
21 An example of such theoretical refinement can be found in Stella Sandford, who aptly observes: 'The idea of empirical "women", ... is no more purely empirical than the idea of the "feminine" is purely metaphorical, and there is no purely empirical ground to which one can then refer the metaphor of "women" (even the idea of sexual difference would have its metaphorical element). The categories of "man" and "woman" would then be very far from being the natural kinds that we mostly tend to assume they are; sexual difference would be much more complicated than our binary presumptions would suggest' (2002: 158–9).

Chapter 4

1 Mary O'Brien does qualify this statement, observing: 'In fairness to Hegel, it should be added that he brought the boy into the "natural ethical community" of his own household with, he claimed, the full acquiescence of his wife. The fact that Hegel's own relationship with desire was less detached than his analytical intelligence suggests is less important, however, than the realities which he inverts rather than mediates' (1996: 204).
2 For Hegel, a threefold dialectic can be detected in all movements of change. As described in Hegel's *Phenomenology of Spirit*, the dialectic accounts for the coming to self-consciousness of a human being. This involves a movement from an undifferentiated awareness (*en soi*) to an encounter with another – difference or negativity – which involves a struggle for recognition. It is only with this encounter with another that self-consciousness (*pour soi*) becomes possible. Desire for consciousness or identity is the impetus for this complex interaction. Judith Butler describes the workings of desire in this development: 'Human desire articulates the subject's relationship to that which is *not* itself, that which is different, strange, novel, awaited, absent, lost.... Thus, human desire is a way of thematising problem of negativity; it is the negative principle of human life, its ontological status as a lack in pursuit

of being.... But desire is also the mode in which consciousness makes its own negativity into an explicit object of reflection, something to be labored upon and worked through' (1987: 11).

3 For an excellent discussion of this topic see particularly the conclusion of Heidi M. Raven's essay: 'Has Hegel Anything to Say to Feminists?' (1996: 246).

4 Hegel denied self-consciousness to women by confining them to familial duties. As Irigaray describes the situation: 'According to Hegel, within the family, there is no longer an individual for self (*pour soi*).... The family is a *substantial* unit in which the individual units that make up the *number* fuse and also thereby lose their individual rights' (1993b: 130). To remedy this, Irigaray believes that 'If there is ever going to be a consciousness of self in the female camp, each woman will have to situate herself freely in relation to herself, not just in relation to the community, the couple, the family' (1993b: 69).

5 Universality is another term used to describe the final stage of Hegel's dialectic. It is variously described in his works, depending on its place in Hegel's work on logic, politics and society and the movement of consciousness. The universality of self-consciousness is also referred to as the attainment of Geist or Spirit. When Irigaray refers to women attaining the universal, what she has in mind is a mode of this universality. Irigaray does not use the German term *Geist*, but translates it as *l'esprit* (spirit). While she is attracted by the notion that the spirit is progressively manifested through a conscious process of cultivation, Irigaray does not, like Hegel, restrict its operations to the rational dimension. For Irigaray, the body must be incorporated in this process. Thus the Hegelian dialectic, desire and universality must be reframed (1996: 37).

6 Initially, Irigaray uses the word 'sex' (*le sexe*) to refer to the biological nature of sexual identity. In this sense it can also refer to women's sexuality which has not been allowed free expression (Irigaray 1993a: 10). Irigaray believes that this cannot be achieved, however, without a 'morphology of a sexualized body'. Grosz explains this as 'the social/psychical representations, and lived reality of the female body' (1990: 171). This is the morphological body, and it will be subject to ascriptions of gender (*genre*). Gender, in this sense, refers to the 'index and mark of subjectivity and the ethical responsibility' of each sex. 'It constitutes the irreducible differentiation that occurs within the human race' (Irigaray 1993b: 169–70). This differentiation will be the basis of Irigaray's agenda for a sexual or sexuate ethics, where Irigaray appreciates each sex has having distinct biological as well as gendered characteristics. Irigaray uses the term *sexué* (sexuate) basically to refer to the gendered characteristics specific to each sex. 'In order to become, it is essential to have a gender or an essence (consequently a sexuate essence) as a horizon' (Irigaray 1993b: 61).

7 It is fascinating to watch Hegel's development from his early Romantic-influenced evocations of love between a man and woman, e.g., 'Love' (1948). Here Hegel acknowledged a respect and maintenance of integrity of both partners as part of the process of recognition (1948: 302–8). This non-cooptive mutual recognition also figured as part of man's (sic) relationship to the divine (1979b: 262–3). But it did not belong, even at this stage, to the province of reason or understanding. In Hegel's later works there was gradual effacement of love as the role of Geist became more prominent. In The First Phenomenology of Spirit (1979a: 231–3), Hegel strives to allow woman consciousness, though public, communal existence takes precedence

over personal attachment. By *Phenomenology of Spirit* (Hegel 1977: 267–78), love has become relegated, according to the workings of *Geist*, to a domestic ethos. Finally there is the strict regulation of love within the ethical confines of family virtue, *Elements of the Philosophy of Right* (Hegel 1991: 199–212). Irigaray concentrates only on *Phenomenology of Spirit*, and does not consult Hegel's early writings where, ironically, he had expressed sentiments that have some similarities to her own on the topic of love between men and women.

8 Irigaray will develop her understanding of the 'labour of love' as a refinement of Hegel's labour of the negative with particular reference to the interaction of a man and a woman. Strictly speaking, Hegel, in his description of the negative in *The Phenomenology of Spirit*, does not associate human love with the negative. He is even apprehensive about divine love. 'Thus the life of God and divine cognition may well be spoken of as a disporting of Love with itself; but this idea sinks into mere edification, and even insipidity, if it lacks the seriousness, the suffering, the patience, and the labor of the negative' (1977: 100). Irigaray, however, locates the labour of love as a feature of Hegel's later writings on the family. 'As Hegel writes, woman and man lose their identity in the family. The labour of love does not return a for-itself for either one: it becomes children, the ownership of goods' (2001: 82).

9 Hegel has a particularly idiosyncratic usage of the term 'History'. The complete realisation of freedom and self-consciousness was equated with the culmination of History – which Hegel identified with his own era. This also implied the disclosure of *Geist*/spirit in History. The positive attitude which permeated Hegel's depiction of the manifestation of spirit in History had unfortunate results for women. 'Citizens as a gender are cut off from their roots in the body, even as they remain bound, as bodies, to their mother-nature' (Irigaray 1993b: 136). For Irigaray, the body or nature must not be spiritualised in a way that subsumes or sublimates it to a higher principle.

10 In *The Phenomenology of Spirit*, Hegel defines woman's place in the community. 'Womankind – the everlasting irony [in the life] of the community – changes by intrigue the universal end of the government into a private end, transforms its universal activity into a work of some particular individual, and perverts the universal property of the state into a possession and ornament for the Family' (1977: 288).

11 As Margaret Whitford states: 'Women's nature has been constituted by a particular symbolic organization, in which they are "used" for the repression and sublimation of men's death drives, but are unable to sublimate or repress their own' (1991: 96).

12 When Irigaray refers to the truth of Antigone, she would appear to be referring to her own interpretation, as she is objecting to an interpretation that she had seen recently on French television where Antigone is portrayed as a type of suicidal anarchist – bent on destroying political and civil order (1994: 67–8).

13 Irigaray remarks: 'since 1970 I have regularly worked with women or groups of women who belong to liberation movements, and in these I've observed problems or impasses that can't be resolved except through the establishment of an equitable legal system for both sexes' (Irigaray 1993c: 82). In her reference to law, Irigaray has the French civil code in mind (Irigaray 1996: 131). Cornell comments: 'What's interesting about French law is that it is much more duty-oriented than

right-oriented. So I think that she is serious ... that these would be the spheres of duties and responsibilities of both men and women.... Such rights are certainly inconsistent with the way law operates now, but it is not inconsistent with the concept of the French legal system' (1998: 28).

14 In another essay, Irigaray develops these rights in more detail: '1. The right to *human dignity*, which means: a) Stopping the commercial use of their bodies and images; b) Valid representations of themselves in actions, words, and images in all public places; c) Stopping the exploitation of motherhood, a functional part of womanhood, by civil and religious powers. 2. The right to *human identity*, that is: a) The legal encodification of *virginity* (or physical and moral integrity) as a component of female identity that is not reducible to money, and not cash-convertible by the family, the State, or religious bodies in any way' (1993c: 86; see also 1996: 132).

15 As Irigaray notes elsewhere: 'Hegel clearly points to this in the development of the dialectic: the individual is estranged from natural, sensible immediacy for the sake of a spiritual becoming in which reciprocal communication is never considered a goal of spirituality' (1996: 100).

16 Irigaray associates the partial drives with those involving the senses. 'The partial drives, in fact, seem to refer especially to the body that brought us whole into the world' (1993b: 13). According to Irigaray, neither Freud nor analysis is concerned sufficiently with these drives. She believes that awareness of both drives is necessary for the type of sublimation she proposes. Unfortunately, 'According to him [Freud] and the spiritual authorities that still lay down our law, reproduction is the sole regulator of the sexual drives.' With particular reference to women, Irigaray observes that it is now their task to undertake a conscious sublimation of both primary and partial drives.

17 Margaret Whitford presents an intriguing account of Irigaray holding in tension the dynamics of the death drive and her creative alternative. 'The question Irigaray negotiates is the tension between death drive as destructive and death drive as creative, or between eros as thanatos and thanatos as eros. On the one hand the imaginary formations of patriarchy need to be broken up, for something new – some new formation – to emerge. Yet there are problems with this.... any stable imaginary formation is itself implicated in the death drive in its other sense as stasis; this makes *any* image problematic' (1994: 394). This remark was made with reference to Irigaray's work up to *I Love to You* (1996). Whether Irigaray continues to maintain this tension in her more spiritual work since that time will be discussed in Chapter 7.

18 In an interview with Irigaray, Stephen Pluháček and Heidi Bostic question her about such terms as 'natural'. In her response, Irigaray, without defending her claim to a form of naturalism (whereby she identifies the real with nature), states that as a female in an alien culture (male), she could not have access to her real or natural identity – that is, what she is by nature or biology. This use of 'real' no longer has any connection to Lacan's Real – discussed in Chapter 1. Irigaray also declares that 'a political and social order which is not founded on the real is precarious, even dangerous' (Pluháček and Bostic 1996: 344–6).

19 Irigaray continues this quotation: 'This division is not secondary nor unique to humankind. It cuts across all realms of living which, without it, would not exist. Without sexual difference, there would be no life on earth' (1996: 37).

20 The terms 'ontic' and 'ontological' derive from Heidegger, who distinguished between ontic knowledge of the empirical world of beings (*das Seindes*) and ontological knowledge which concerned itself with enquiry into the meaning and source of these beings, i.e., Being (*Sein*). See further discussions of Heidegger's influence in Chapters 6 and 7. Tina Chanter describes the manner in which Irigaray adapts Heidegger's ideas of the 'unthought' of western philosophy: 'Woman has been treated as a provider of places for men ... but the *place* of these places that women provides ... has itself remained unthought.... Woman remains the unthought in relation to man, that which is taken for granted, that to which thought never attends as such, but on which it depends' (1995: 158).

21 According to Irigaray: 'Freud is acting like a prince of darkness with respect to women, leading them into the shadows and separating them from their mothers and from themselves in order to found a culture of men-amongst-themselves: law, religion, language, truth and wisdom' (1994: 110).

22 In many ways, Nancy Chodorow, who focuses on object relations theory in *The Reproduction of Mothering* (1978), anticipated Irigaray's call for reform of mother/daughter relations. Chodorow declared that if a girl child identified only with her mother in the maternal role, she cannot but reproduce the same pattern of maternity.

23 For further amplification of Irigaray's rationale for her appeal to these particular works and their interpretation, see Irigaray (1994: 98–112).

24 Irigaray also asserts that: 'In the time of women's law, the divine and human were not separate. That means that religion was not a separate domain. What was human was divine and became divine. Moreover the divine was always related to nature. "Supernatural" mother–daughter encounters took place in nature' (1994: 10). She also states: 'The daughter ... can live with her mother without destroying either of them prior to the mediation of specific objects. To them, nature is a preferred environment; the ever fertile earth is their place and mother and daughter co-exist happily there.... This relation depends on the establishment of female lines of descent' (1994: 110–11).

25 Irigaray explains that the male form of genealogy has presented a unitary heritage where a woman is assimilated into the lineage of her husband (1993b: 139). Irigaray maintains that a separate genealogy of women – the maternal line – needs to be given equal status, as it was in pre-patriarchal Greece (1994: 6).

26 Irigaray proposes: 'To anyone who cares about social justice today, I suggest putting up posters in all public places with beautiful pictures representing the mother–daughter couple – the couple that illustrates a very special relationship to nature and culture' (1994: 9). One of the prominent examples that Irigaray suggests is that of the Virgin Mary and her mother Anne, as well as those of Greek mythology.

27 Irigaray's use of Heidegger and Hegel will be treated in Chapter 7.

28 See Irigaray (1999a: 92–104) for a development of her ideas on Heidegger and Being. This topic will be discussed further in Chapter 7.

29 This statement should not be taken as a disparagement. I consider Irigaray's work to be eminently rational. She does, however, employ her 'double' or mimetic style in a in a speculative and experimental way so as to undermine the hierarchical and exclusionary structures that she detects in traditional 'rationalist' philosophy.

30 As Heidi M. Raven observes in her article 'Has Hegel Anything to Say to Feminists?'

(1996): 'It is interesting and important to note that the contemporary temptation to read Hegel's account of women and man in terms of the dialectic of lordship and bondage is not true to Hegel's intention. It is surely tempting to reify lordship and bondage as an absolute depiction of freedom (or the possibility of freedom) and then attribute it to women because in society women have been recognized as occupying servant status, and then apply it to what Hegel says of women elsewhere. We might say that lordship and bondage has some important lessons for women, but they are not lessons that Hegel thought applied to women' (Raven 1996: 242–3). Raven, in a footnote, does acknowledge Irigaray's 'daring interpretation' of Hegel, and also admits that she would not be quite so hard as Irigaray on Hegel (Raven 1996: 249–50). Both Beauvoir's and Irigaray's emphasis on the master/slave dynamic can be attributed in part to the influence of Alexandre Kojève, whose stress on the Marxist reading of the master/slave model influenced French twentieth-century reception of Hegel – particularly the concept of negativity. See Butler (1987: 61–79) and discussion in Chapter 1.

31 Sara Heinämaa clarifies Beauvoir's meaning of transcendence. 'One needs to realize first what Beauvoir means by transcendence here is not just any overcoming of state of affairs or a given condition of life. Rather, what she means is a radical mode of overcoming in which one questions, not just this or that goal or value, but life itself as the horizon for the realization of all values and goals, all activities and practices' (2003: 108).

32 Irigaray has recently been taken to task for her treatment of Beauvoir by Toril Moi, a defender of Beauvoir. See Moi (1999: 71–7).

33 Naomi Schor, in her 1995 article 'French Feminism Is a Universalism', is helpful in situating Irigaray's employment of the universal statements. She writes: 'What is certain is that whereas in American feminist theory there has been a tendency to extrapolate from the falseness of phallocentric universalism the notion that all universals are false, in French feminist theory the universal remains, despite all its misappropriations, a valorized category to be rethought and refashioned. Though French feminists reject the imperialistic universalization of masculine particularity, like so many French intellectuals they remain wedded to the concept of the universal' (1995: 21). Warning against the conflation of essentialism and universalism, Schor continues by confirming that, as Irigaray affirms, philosophy is the mark of the universal (Irigaray 1993b: 147) and that this universal is not transhistorical (1996: 112). Thus for Schor, Irigaray, as a late twentieth-century woman, perceives her task as one of inscribing for this age 'the mark of gender onto the alleged neutrality of the universal handed down by the Enlightenment and post-Enlightenment philosophers' (1995: 34). Yet it is evident that, in her promotion of a distinct female identity from *Ethics of Sexual Difference* onwards, Irigaray strays perilously close to the type of essentialism criticised in her early work that Grosz and Braidotti defended her against. This topic is discussed further in Chapters 4, 6, and 7.

34 Irigaray acknowledges that there will always be a third term between a woman and man in love (1996: 117), but she believes that 'belonging to a gender might, in part, serve as a third term in the constitution of adult identity' (106). This is Irigaray's response to Freud's use of this term where it is only 'the father, law, Name of the Father or something else – This third term supposedly avoids the fusion that would lead into the chaos of psychosis, and is said to guarantee order' (1993c: 42).

35 This avowal is the concrete development of the thoughts that she expressed regarding the 'sensible transcendental' as the location of the divine in *Ethics of Sexual Difference* (1993a).
36 From a psychoanalytic perspective, Margaret Whitford describes what she appreciates in Irigaray's task. 'In her attempt to rewrite a founding myth for the new era, she wants to bind the death drive with eros. Eros is also an unbinding force; there might seem to be a paradox here. But I think Irigaray would argue that this is because it remains primitive, 'uncivilized', unsublimated, a purely private affair, when it should be a civil and social recognition of two generic identities' (1994: 394).
37 Irigaray is quite explicit in her directions for men: 'he himself has to accomplish the task of being this man he is by birth and a model of humanity, a model that is both corporeal and spiritual. It is not right to leave himself to the woman's cultural maternal care, especially as she, not being him, cannot take responsibility for him. He has to become a man by himself, to grow without her and without opposing himself to her in the process. He must be capable of sublimating his instincts and drives himself, not only his partial but his genital' (1996: 27).
38 Irigaray clarifies this notion of transcendence in her book *To Be Two*. She states: 'Transcendence unveils itself in the other who is here present to me, but irreducible to my rational perception, if not as other' (2001: 93).
39 As Irigaray states elsewhere: 'The only possible way of reconciling objective spirit and absolute spirit seems to be to rethink the notion of gender, of the genders and of their ethical relationship' (1993b: 141). It is from this perspective that Cheah and Grosz concede that: '[Irigaray] is probably the only living feminist philosopher today who has articulated an elaborate program for concrete sociocultural, legal, and political transformation, "apolitical ethics that refuses to sacrifice desire for death, power, or money" [ILTY 33]' (Cheah and Grosz 1998a: 5).
40 When asked for clarification on this issue, Irigaray replied: 'It's difficult to explain, but interesting, because between a man and a woman there's a negative, a type of irreducibility that doesn't exist between a woman and a woman. Let's say that between a man and a woman the negativity ... is, dare I say it, of an ontological, irreducible type. Between a woman and a woman it's of a much more empirical type.' Irigaray then adds: 'Yes, there's an irreducible mystery between man and woman' (Hirsh and Olson 1995: 110).
41 Grosz states: 'if we focus on Irigaray for a moment, it seems that when she is talking about sexual difference as ontological difference, she is not specifying it in any way, nor can she possibly specify what it might consist in. She is claiming that each has its other and that they are irreducible' (Cheah and Grosz 1998b: 34). Grosz would claim that there is room for other differences to be inserted. This is a highly debatable reading in the light of Irigaray's later writings, and it will be discussed further in Chapter 7.
42 Irigaray states that she is not propounding truths, in the sense of logical or definitive assertions: 'The relation between man and woman, men and women, takes place on the grounds of a groundless ground. It is without definitive resolution or assumption, always becoming in the outward and return journeying between one and the other, the ones and the others, with no end or final reckoning' (1996: 107). There is an incongruity here, however, because Irigaray's irreducibility rests

on a presumption of two distinct genders, where sexual difference is not just a signal of dissimilarity but an ontological principle.

43 In *Bodies that Matter* (1993), Judith Butler explores, in particular, the notion of a lesbian phallus both as a critique of Lacan's monolithic system and as a speculation of what the phallus, as a free-floating signifier, could entail.

44 As Cornell also notes: 'Irigaray cannot grapple with someone who is a woman whose "feminine difference" is inseparable from imposed personas that she has to live with in a racist society like our own [US].... A complex ethical and political field has to be opened up that would allow us to see ... that our categories of traditional gender-understanding simply cannot grapple with the kinds of oppression an that are mandated by a sense of "being woman"' (Cornell in Cheah and Crosz 1998b: 40). The question of race as it pertains to Irigaray's work will be discussed in Chapter 7.

45 Despite her encomium to the delights of heterosexuality and its innovative polymorphous potential, Irigaray is no defender of the patriarchal household. Sexual desire is cultivated for its own development, its own realisation. 'Sexed desire, sexual desire, should not have its end, its effectivity, in the family as such, nor in the State, nor in religion, for then it perverts the truth and spirit of the community. Sexual desire demands a realisation appropriate to its matter, its nature. This realisation takes place in the body proper and in the couple that man forms with the other sex – woman' (1996: 28).

Chapter 5

1 In order to emphasize the points of comparison between Daly and Irigaray, especially the dates of the publication of their books, I will insert the dates of Irigaray's French publications as well as the separate dates of Daly's revised introductions.

2 In this passage, Daly's use of upper and lower case letters is one of the keys to her provocative playing with conventions. This will be evident in most of the quotations from her work.

3 Daly does not employ the term 'lesbian' either.

4 Within Christianity, it was Aristotle's metaphysical formulations that influence the medieval theology of Thomas Aquinas (1224–74). It is his ontology that Daly has in mind.

5 In a biographical essay in *The Church and the Second Sex*, Daly describes her seven years of taking doctoral degrees in both philosophy and theology at the canonically approved University of Fribourg, Switzerland, where this form of philosophy or theology was the orthodox tradition of the Catholic Church (1985b: 7–9).

6 Daly describes her revision of this process: 'Unlike the so-called "First Coming" of Christian theology, which was an absolutizing of men, the women's revolution is not an absolutizing of women, precisely because it is the *overcoming* of dichotomous sex stereotyping, which is the source of the absolutizing process itself' (1974: 97).

7 Daly will concede that this new vision can also be discovered by men who are willing to hear women's voices, but she does not dwell further on their possible participation in it (1974: 169).

8 Daly's 'cosmic covenant' (1974: 177) will include in time stellar and interplanetary excursions. See particularly *Outercourse* (1992: 27–8).

9 This definition of the symbol was borrowed from Paul Tillich.
10 On the flap cover of her book *Quintessence* (1998), Daly is pictured wielding the labrys.
11 For a clear idea of how the workings on the unconscious became associated with semiotic and semantic theories of Ferdinand de Saussure and Roman Jakobson see Kaja Silverman (1983: 87–125).
12 Macey continues: 'Lacan's own classifications are uncertain: in "Fonction et champ" both metaphor and metonymy were "semantic condensations", but in the Seminar of 9 May 1956 condensation, displacement and representation are all said to belong to an order of metonymic articulation which allows metaphor to function. A week earlier, Lacan had been insisting that metonymy is the opposite of metaphor and had established a polarity between the two' (1988: 157).
13 Daly states in the preface to *Gyn/Ecology*: 'There is no way to remove male/masculine imagery from God. Thus, when writing/speaking "anthropomorphically" of ultimate reality, of the divine spark of be-ing, I now choose to write gynomorphically. I do so because *God* represents the necrophilia of patriarchy, whereas *Goddess* affirms the life-loving be-ing of women and nature' (1978: xi). She will nevertheless qualify the usage of the term 'Goddess'.
14 Daly describes elemental powers in the following way: 'Elemental spirits/angels/demons may be understood as Metaphors manifesting the essential unity and intelligence of spirit/matter, the inherent telos of spirit/matter. They Name Intelligence ensouling the stars, animating the processes of earth, air, fire, water enspiriting the sounds that are the elements of words, connecting words with earth, air, fire, water and with the sun, moon, planets, stars. The Metaphoric language of "Elemental spirits" is crucial for the empowering of women, for this conjures memories of Archaic integrity that have been broken by phallic religion and philosophy' (1984: 11).
15 In this regard, it is quite striking that both Daly and Irigaray emphasise the element of air as perhaps the primary element that is associated with 'the creative breath of life' (Daly 1984: 17; Irigaray 1996: 148). As the spirit of life, air, for Daly, represents a primal energy, while, for Irigaray, it has close connections to the maternal as the lifesource.
16 Daly is here playing with the Catholic belief that Jesus Christ becomes fully present in the consecrated host, or Eucharist, during the Catholic Mass. This is referred to as the 'Real Presence'.
17 Daly coins the term 'biophilia' as an antidote to 'necrophilia' which she sees as pervasive in western philosophy and theology. See *Gyn/Ecology* (1978: 61–2).
18 This Heideggerian influence is particularly evident in *The Way of Love* (2002b).
19 The statement is attributed to Laleen Jayamanne, Mary Daly event, Sydney, 24 August 1981 (Morris 1988: 27).
20 The footnote to this statement in Heidegger's text reads: 'While the terms '*ontisch*' ('ontical') and '*ontologisch*' ('ontological') are not explicitly defined, their meanings will emerge rather clearly. Ontological inquiry is concerned primarily with Being; ontical inquiry is concerned with entities and the facts about them' (footnote 3, 1962: 31). Ontic thus has to do with things in a utilitarian and pragmatic way, ontology with Being and the meaning of life. In Heidegger's questioning of the Being of western metaphysics, or 'ontotheology', as he terms it – because of it

preoccupation with an Absolute or Eternal god figure – he attempts to recover a pre-Socratic awareness of Being or ontology. This awareness does not reify Being nor divide Being from the beings of the world in an ahistorical framework. The ontotheological framework, with its dualistic oppositions, served only to provide an illusion of mastery of beings as objects. It did not help to provide insight into the meaning of existence. In Heidegger's revised ontological approach 'Ontological inquiry is indeed more primordial, as over against the ontical inquiry of the positive sciences. But it remains itself naïve and opaque if in its researches into the being of entities it fails to discuss the meaning of being in general' (1962: 31).

21 Claire Colebrook will describe Heidegger's task as one of discerning the difference between Being and beings. As she states: 'Philosopher's task, for Heidegger, is not to think Being in terms of its identity; it is, rather, to recognize philosophy's historical failure. Being is such that it is only known and presented through beings; there can be no identity given to being in general. It is, therefore, in the very character of Being to fall into determination and identity in terms of beings. The project of philosophy is to think this fall by thinking *difference*: not the difference between various beings, nor the difference that can be thought in *opposition* to identity, but the difference between *difference and identity* (Heidegger 1969: 62)' (Colebrook 1997: 85).

22 There are feminist scholars who do have problems with Daly's postulate of women's elemental self. Perhaps Rosemarie Tong expresses this most succinctly: 'We are left wondering, however, whether this true, natural self is an original self that existed before both patriarchy and matriarchy, or whether it is the *counterfactual self* that would have been constructed had women and men lived in matriarchies rather than patriarchies' (1989: 107).

23 Ferguson expands on her earlier definition of this form of essentialism: 'When you take some more or less stable category as your unity, the point of reference from which your analysis can proceed, at what point do you remind yourself of what you have disregarded in order to do so? What signposts do you build into your accounts to serve as reminders? What posture do you take toward that which does not or will not fit even into the most liberation-bound of categories?' (Ferguson 1993: 87–8).

24 Colebrook, in her Heideggerian reading of Irigaray, understands essentialism as impossible within this approach. 'There is also an attempt to move from feminist critique to feminist philosophy. This would, presumably, begin to think beyond the terms of identity and representation. Whatever the feminine is, it could not be thought as that which thought sets before itself in a moment of self-determination and ideality ... A *certain form of essentialism* [ontological] would therefore be anathema to Irigaray's position' (1997: 90).

25 There seems to have been a merger of sorts between Merchant's work and Susan Griffin's *Woman and Nature* (1978). An excellent overview of this naturalist movement and its relation to witchcraft can be found in Ronald Hutton's *The Triumph of the Moon* (1999).

26 Ferguson is not sympathetic to the purported historical reality of the era of the Goddess. 'A prominent example of cosmic kitsch is Riane Eisler's popular and much translated book, *The Chalice and the Blade* ... Eisler tells a cosmic feminist story of resurrection and return. The earliest societies of Europe, Eisler tells us, were

"partnership" societies – egalitarian and goddess worshipping. Then "nomadic invaders" from the "peripheral areas of our globe" (anywhere that is not Europe) "swarmed down" and overthrew the partnership societies in favour of patriarchy. The racial implications of centring "our globe" in Europe, while designating non-white people as those who "swarm" go uninvestigated. Eisler promises a return to partnership, fulfilment of a telos that predicts renewal of the good and a defeat of the bad' (1993: 111–12).

27 The interpretations of Irigaray's theory of difference by Kelly Oliver and Ewa Płonowska Ziarek will be examined in Chapter 7.

Chapter 6

1 'New Age' religions are in many ways not particularly novel, absorbing and adapting many currents that have been part of western esoteric thought. See Hanegraaff (1996). Irigaray is indebted to this tradition for her idea on the three ages of Father, Son and Spirit, which can be traced back to the work of a German mystic, Jacob Boehme (1575–1624).

2 The term 'Oriental' is one that has come under scrutiny in recent years, especially since Edward Said's *Orientalism* (1978). In France, there has been a serious tradition of Oriental Studies (Gardaz 2000). Irigaray employs this term in keeping with the school of French thinking. Commencing with the publication of Said's book, the study of other cultures has been assessed as a product of European colonialism and imperialism. Said's thesis has not gone unchallenged. See Said (1986).

3 Irigaray does list a bibliography of the books that she has read in connection with this study, which includes the *Yoga Sutras of Patanjali*, and a French edition of the *Upanishads* (2002a: 71).

4 In this book I have chosen not to use diacritical marks when using Sanskrit terms, as Irigaray does not employ them. The exceptions occur in quotations and titles of books and articles.

5 Eliade has described the influence of women in Tantrism accordingly: 'One must never lose sight of this primacy of the Shakti – in the final instance, the Divine Wife and Mother – in Tantrism and all the movements that derive from it. This was the road by which the great subterranean current of the autochthonous popularity emerged into Hinduism' (1969: 178–9).

6 *Chakras* are centres of energy that can be mobilised by directing the breath (*prana*) during specific meditative practices. As Feuerstein states: 'These major configurations of our "subtle anatomy" are especially responsive to mental manipulation and therefore are often made the focal point of meditation and visualisation. Many tantric teachers speak of seven principal psychoenergetic centres, but some list five, and others name nine, ten, eleven or very many more' (Feuerstein 1998: 149).

7 In a response to a paper that I wrote earlier on this topic, Irigaray has since replied: 'For my work, the *Upanishads* of yoga, for example, are more important than more recent texts, because they belong to an early feminine tradition. Certainly later Tantric texts do allude to these earlier texts and thus signify that the feminine traditions are still alive in them, as Mircea Eliade reminds us' (Irigaray 2002b: 200).

8 In his recent book, *The Integrity of the Yoga Darśana* 1998), Ian Whicher relates yoga to its earliest metaphysical principles, which date from the Vedas: 'I suggest that

Patanjali's Yoga can be seen as a responsible engagement, in various ways of "spirit" (*puruṣa* = Self, pure consciousness) and "matter" (*prakṛti* = the source of psychophysical being, which includes mind, body, nature), resulting in a highly developed, transformed, and participatory human nature and identity, an integrated and embodied state of liberated selfhood (*jīanmukti*)' (1998: 2).

9 See the Introduction by David Gordon White to the volume *Tantra in Practice* (2000) for a comprehensive coverage of the multiple aspects of Tantra.

10 Tringham and Conkey present a nuanced and critical evaluation of the interpretation of archaeological material and the way that 'facts' have been taken out of context.

11 I do not address the work of Gayatri Spivak in this work, but I have done elsewhere. See Joy (2000a).

12 In France, new religions are not burgeoning in quite the same way as in other European and North American countries. This is both because France is highly secularised and because the State is proactive in 'anti-cult' control. (Introvigne 2004: 206–20).

13 Miranda Shaw writes of a time from the seventh to twelfth centuries CE when it appears that many women were active practitioners in Buddhist Tantrism. Shaw writes: 'Women participated in this tradition at every level, from the practice of magic, ritual, yoga, and meditation through the attainment of enlightenment and assumption and the role of *guru*.... women helped to shape the emerging movement by introducing meditations, doctrines, Deities (including some of the Goddesses), and practices' (1997: 128). Tsultrim Allione also relates the biographies of a number of renowned women teachers and practitioners from the eleventh to thirteenth centuries (2000). See also Simmer-Brown (2001: 182–233).

14 Vasudha Narayanan would qualify this observation. She states that the *Dharma Shastras* 'were not well known and utilized in many parts of India' (1999: 34). She also allows that it was more custom and habit, rather than these specific legal texts, that maintained the low status of women. The seeming pervasiveness of such laws is credited by Narayanan to the British colonial emphasis on the brahmanic tradition to the neglect of other heterodox elements of Hinduism.

15 It needs to be observed in this context that, while the counter-tactics of the Hindu right, Hindutva, are diverse, one obvious fact cannot be ignored – this is the agenda to essentialise the definition of Hindu womanhood. In its appeals to the *Vedas* and the *Manusmrti* as normative texts, a single idealised vision of womanhood is constructed, ignoring the divergences of caste, class, regional or historical variants during a long history. Ironically, this standardisation has obvious parallels to the British artificial acclamation and promotion of the brahmanical tradition as the defining element of Hinduism. See Roy (1995) and Joy (2000b).

16 In later works, Said (1986) did respond to his critics on this issue. Consequently, to leave the impression that he is simply a dualistic thinker is false. Post-colonial scholars themselves have been extremely eloquent in problematising Said's early formulas of Orientalism and its accessory, colonialisation. Their positions are diverse. A principal concern is that: 'the organization of the immediate past under the rubric of colonialism tends to reduce the contingent and random diversity of cultural encounters and non-encounters within that past into a tired relationship of coercion and retaliation' (Gandhi 1998: 171–2).

Chapter 7

1 In her analysis of 'male' and 'female' imagery, Anderson refers to the insightful work of Geneviève Lloyd that was discussed in Chapter 2. The slippage between 'female', as an adjective, and 'female', referring to a woman is, as indicated in this chapter, problematic. Irigaray becomes less clear on this distinction as her work progresses, so it is no wonder that Anderson cannot remedy the situation.
2 See Freud (1984).
3 Arendt discusses her views on natality in The Human Condition (1958).
4 Jantzen is explicit that the mode of relatedness refers to all human beings, and does not confine it to women.
5 In describing *fantasia* as both critical and creative, Huntington allows that the critical aspect opens up space for new expressions and discoveries. There is no implication, however, that either Heidegger or Irigaray is self-critical of their own imaginative expressions.
6 Huntington adopts Deborah King's definition of monism as 'the claim that social relations can be distilled down to one dimension that underpins all other forms of oppression' (Huntington 1998: 246).
7 Peng Cheah does acknowledge the potential for actuality in Irigaray's work: 'I think we often miss the beautiful simplicity of her point: sexual difference is not an ideal separated from the real. The interval of sexual difference may be slippery and impossible to pin down. But in this world, it is a concrete "mechanism" for structural change. If her critique of the patriarchal family can ever be put into practice, it will have immense repercussions for the restructuring of the market, and the state in all nations throughout the globe' (Cheah and Grosz 1998b: 37–8). I would be interested to hear Cheah's views in the light of Irigaray's latest work. It seems to me that, here, Irigaray loses the interval of the sensible transcendental and, especially in The Way of Love (2002b), could even be said to reinforce the patriarchal family.
8 Willett argues that Irigaray establishes a false dichotomy in her description of power when she attributes a form of political power (*le pouvoir*) to men and procreative power (*la puissance*) to women (2001: 128–44; Irigaray 1993b: 12; 60). Willett charges that this distinction, grounded in Irigaray's postulate of sexual difference, falsely aligns maternal power with a divine cosmic force which deprives the mother of subjectivity and does not recognise the other elements of power that feature in a woman's life. Willett would prefer to see power admitted as a component of each person's struggle for recognition, and to understand power as not necessarily distinguished on the basis of sex. This model would none the less allow that power may not be equally distributed in certain cultures.

References

Afzal-Khan, Fawzia, and Kalpana Seshadri-Crooks, eds (2000), *The Pre-occupations of Postcolonial Studies*, Durham, Duke University Press.
Ainley, A. (1988). 'Amorous Discourses', in R. Bernasconi and D. Wood (eds), *The Provocation of Levinas: Rethinking the Other*, trans. M. Whitford, London, Routledge.
Allione, Tsultrim. (2000), *Women of Wisdom*, Ithaca, NY, Snow Lion Publications.
Amsberg, Kiki, and Aafke Steenhuis. (1983), 'An Interview with Luce Irigaray', trans. Robert vam Krieken, *Hecate*, 9:1–2, 192–202.
Anderson, Pamela Sue. (1998), *A Feminist Philosophy of Religion*, Oxford, Blackwell.
Arendt, Hannah. (1958), *The Human Condition*, Chicago, University of Chicago Press.
Armour, Ellen. (1997), 'Writing/Reading Selves, Writing/Reading Race', *Philosophy Today*, 41, 110–17.
Armour, Ellen (1999), *Deconstruction, Feminist Theology, and the Problem of Difference: Subverting the Race, Gender Divide*, Chicago, University of Chicago Press.
Aziz, Razia. (1992), 'Feminism and the Challenge of Racism: Deviance or Difference', in H. Crowley and S. Himmelweit (eds), *Knowing Women: Feminism and Knowledge*, Cambridge, Polity Press.
Bachofen, Johann J. (1967), *Myth, Religion and Mother Right: Selected Writings of J. J. Bachofen*, trans. R. Manheim, London, Routledge.
Bagchi, Jasadhara, ed. (1995), *Indian Women: Myth and Reality*, Hyderabad, Sangam Books.
Baier, Annette. (1985), *Postures of the Mind: Essays on Mind and Morals*, Minneapolis, University of Minnesota Press.
Baier, Annette. (1986), 'The Ambiguous Limits to Desire', in J. Marks (ed.), *The Ways of Desire*, Chicago, Precedent Publishers.
Behdad, Ali. (2000), '*Une Pratique Sauvage*: Postcolonial Belatedness and Cultural Politics', in F. Afzal-Khan and K. Seshadri-Crooks (eds), *The Pre-Occupation of Postcolonial Studies*, Durham, Duke University Press.
Berghoffen, Debra. (1997), *The Philosophy of Simone de Beauvoir*, Albany, State University of New York Press.
Berry, Philippa. (1994), 'The Burning Glass: Paradoxes of Feminist Revelation in *Speculum*', in C. Burke, N. Schor, and N. Whitford (eds), *Engaging with Irigaray*, New York, Columbia University Press.
Bordo, Susan. (1987), *The Flight to Objectivity: Essays on Cartesianism and Culture*, Albany, State University of New York Press.

References

Bordo, Susan. (1999), *Feminist Interpretations of Descartes*. University Park, PA, Pennsylvania State University Press.

Braidotti, Rosi. (1991), *Patterns of Dissonance: A Study of Women in Contemporary Philosophy*, New York, Routledge.

Braidotti, Rosi. (1994), *Nomadic Subjects: Embodiment and Sexual Difference in Contemporary Feminist Theory*, New York, Columbia University Press.

Brodribb, Somer. (1992), *Nothing Mat(t)ers: A Feminist Critique of Postmodernism*, Toronto, James Lorimer.

Butler, Judith. (1987), *Subjects of Desire: Hegelian Reflections in Twentieth Century France*, New York, Columbia University Press.

Butler, Judith. (1990), *Gender Trouble*, New York, Routledge.

Butler, Judith. (1993), *Bodies that Matter*, New York, Routledge.

Butler, Judith. (1994), 'Gender as Performance: An Interview with Judith Butler', *Radical Philosophy*, 67, 32–9.

Butler, Judith. (2001), 'The End of Sexual Difference?', in E. Bronfen and M. Kavka (eds), *Feminist Consequences: Theory for the New Century*, New York, Columbia University Press.

Campbell, June. (1996), *Traveller in Space: In Search of Female Identity in Tibetan Buddhism*. New York, George Braziller.

Cavarero, Adriana. (1992), 'Equality and Sexual Difference: Amnesia in Political Thought', in G. Bok and S. James (eds), *Beyond Equality and Difference: Citizenship, Feminist Politics, Subjectivity*. London: Routledge.

Cavarero, Adriana. (1993), 'Towards a Theory of Sexual Difference', in Sandra Kemp and Paola Bono (eds), *The Lonely Mirror: Italian Perspectives on Feminist Theory*, London, Routledge.

Cavarero, Adriana. (1993), 'Towards a Theory of Sexual Difference', in Sandra Kemp and Paola Bono (eds), *The Lonely Mirror: Italian Perspectives on Feminist Theory*, London, Routledge.

Chakravarti, Uma. (1989), 'Whatever Happened to the Vedic Dasi? Orientalism, Nationalism and a Script From the Past', in K. Sangari and S. Vaid (eds), *Recasting Women: Essays in Indian Colonial History*, New Delhi, Kali for Women.

Chalier, Catherine. (1982), *Figures du féminin*, Paris, La Nuit Surveillée.

Chalier, Catherine. (1991), 'Ethics and the Feminine', in R. Bernasconi and S. Critchley (eds), *Re-Reading Levinas*, trans. M. Whitford, Bloomington, Indiana University Press.

Chanter, Tina. (1988), 'Feminism and the Other', in R. Bernasconi and D. Wood (eds), *The Provocation of Levinas: Rethinking the Other*, London, Routledge.

Chanter, Tina. (1995), *Ethics of Eros: Irigaray's Rewriting of the Philosophers*, New York, Routledge.

Chanter, Tina. (2001), *Feminist Interpretations of Emmanuel Levinas*, University Park, PA, Pennsylvania State University Press.

Cheah, Peng, and Elizabeth Grosz. (1998a), 'On Being Two: Introduction', *Diacritics*, 28:1, 3–18.

Cheah, Peng, and Elizabeth Grosz. (1998b), 'The Future of Sexual Difference: An Interview with Judith Butler and Drucilla Cornell', *Diacritics*, 28:1, 19–42.

Chisholm, Dianne. (1994), 'Irigaray's Hysteria', in C. Burke, N. Schor and M. Whitford (eds), *Engaging with Irigaray: Feminist Philosophy and Modern European Thought, Gender and Culture*, New York, Columbia University Press.

Chodorow, Nancy. (1978), *The Reproduction of Mothering: Psychoanalysis and the Sociology of Gender*, Berkeley, University of California Press.

References

Christ, Carol P. (1991), 'Mircea Eliade and the Feminist Paradigm Shift', *Journal of Feminist Studies in Religion*, 7, 75–94.

Clarke, J. J. (1997), *Oriental Enlightenment: The Encounter between Asian and Western Thought*, London, Routledge.

Cohen, Richard. (1987) 'Translator's Introduction', *Time and the Other*, Pittsburgh, Duquesne University Press.

Colebrook, Claire. (1997), 'Feminist Philosophy and the Philosophy of Feminism: Irigaray and the History of Western Metaphysics', *Hypatia*, 12:1, 79–95.

Conkey, Margaret W., and Joan M. Gero. (1991). 'Tensions, Pluralities, and Engendering Archaeology: An Introduction to Women and Prehistory', in Joan M. Gero and Margaret W. Conkey, (eds), *Engendering Archaeology: Women and Prehistory*, Oxford, Blackwell.

Conkey, Margaret W., and Ruth E. Tringham. (1995), 'Archaeology and the Goddess: Exploring the Contours of Feminist Archaeology', in D. Stanton and A. J. Stewart (eds), *Feminisms in the Academy*, Ann Arbor, University of Michigan Press.

Cornell, Drucilla. (1991), *Beyond Accommodation: Ethical Feminism, Deconstruction and the Law*, New York, Routledge.

Cornell, Drucilla. (1993), *Transformations*, New York, Routledge.

Cornell, Drucilla. (1998), *At the Heart of Freedom: Feminism, Sex & Equality*, Princeton, Princeton University Press.

Cottingham, John, ed. (1992), 'Cartesian Dualism: Theology, Metaphysics, and Science', in *The Cambridge Companion to Descartes*, Cambridge, Cambridge University Press.

Cottingham, John. (1996), 'Cartesian Ethics: Reason and the Passions', *Revue Internationale de Philosophie*, 50, 193–216.

Critchley, Simon. (2002), 'Introduction', *Cambridge Companion to Levinas*, Cambridge: Cambridge University Press.

Daly, Mary. (1968), *The Church and the Second Sex*, Boston, Beacon Press.

Daly, Mary. (1974), *Beyond God the Father: Towards a Philosophy of Women's Liberation*, Boston, Beacon Press.

Daly, Mary. (1975), 'Feminine PostChristian Introduction', *The Church and the Second Sex*, Boston, Beacon Press.

Daly, Mary. (1978), *Gyn/Ecology: The Metaethics of Radical Feminism*, Boston, Beacon Press.

Daly, Mary. (1984), *Pure Lust: Elemental Feminist Philosophy*, Boston, Beacon Press.

Daly, Mary. (1985a), 'Original Reintroduction', *Beyond God the Father*, Boston, Beacon Press.

Daly, Mary. (1985b), 'New Archaic Afterwords', *The Church and the Second Sex*, Boston, Beacon Press.

Daly, Mary. (1992), *Outercourse: Be-Dazzling Voyage*, London, The Women's Press.

Daly, Mary. (1998) *Quintessence* (1998), Boston, Beacon Press.

De Beauvoir, Simone. (1975), *The Second Sex*, trans. H. M. Parshley, New York, Knopf.

De Lauretis, Teresa. (1990), 'Upping the Anti [sic] in Feminist Theory', in M. Hirsh and E. Fox Keller (eds), *Conflicts in Feminism*, New York, Routledge.

Denton, Lynn Teskey. (1991), 'Varieties of Hindu Female Asceticism', in J. Leslie (ed.), *Roles and Rituals for Hindu Women*, Rutherford, Fairleigh Dickinson Press.

Denton, Lynn Teskey. (2004). *Female Ascetics in Hinduism*, Albany, State University of New York Press.

Derrida, Jacques. (1979), *Spurs: Nietzsche's Styles*, trans. B. Harlow, Chicago, University of Chicago Press.

Derrida, Jacques. (1981), *Positions*, trans. A. Bass, Chicago, University of Chicago Press.

References

Derrida, Jacques. (1991), 'At this very moment in the work here I am', in R. Bernasconi and S. Critchley (eds), *Re-Reading Levinas*, trans. M. Whitford, Bloomington, Indiana University Press.

Descartes, René. (1935), *Lettres sur la morale: Correspondance avec la princesse Elisabeth Chanut et la reine Christine*, ed. J. Chevalier, Paris, Boivin.

Descartes, René. (1970), *Les passions de l'âme*, ed. G. Rodis-Lewis, Paris, Vrin.

Descartes, René. (1984), *The Philosophical Writings of Descartes*, 2, eds J. Cottingham, R. Stoothoff and D. Murdoch, Cambridge, Cambridge University Press.

Descartes, René. (1985), *The Philosophical Writing of Descartes*, 1, eds J. Cottingham, R. Stoothoff, and D. Murdoch, Cambridge, Cambridge University Press.

Descartes, René. (1989), *The Passions of the Soul*, trans. S. M. Voss, Indianapolis, Hackett Publishing Company.

Descartes, René. (1991), *The Philosophical Writings of Descartes*, 3, eds J. Cottingham, R. Stoothoff, D. Murdoch and A. Kenny, Cambridge, Cambridge University Press.

Descombes, Vincent. (1980), *Modern French Philosophy*, trans. L. Scott-Fox and J. M. Harding, Cambridge, Cambridge University Press.

Deutscher, Penelope. (1996), 'Irigaray Anxiety: Luce Irigaray and Her Ethics for Improper Selves', *Radical Philosophy*, 80, 6–16.

Deutscher, Penelope. (2002), *A Politics of Impossible Difference: The Later Work of Luce Irigaray*, Ithaca, Cornell University Press.

Eliade, Mircea. (1958), *Yoga: Immortality and Freedom*, trans. W. R. Trask; 2nd ed., Bollingen Series LVI. Princeton, NJ, Princeton University Press.

Eliade, Mircea. (1969), *Patanjali and Yoga*, trans. C. L. Markmann, New York, Funk & Wagnalls.

Eliade, Mircea. (1978), *Myth and Reality*, New York, Harper & Row.

Ferguson, Kathy E. (1993), *The Man Question: Visions of Subjectivity in Feminist Theory*, Berkeley, University of California Press.

Feuerbach, Ludwig. (1957), *The Essence of Christianity*, trans. G. Eliot, New York, Harper & Row.

Feuerstein, Georg. (1989), *Yoga: The Technology of Ecstasy*, Los Angeles, Jeremy P. Tarcher.

Feuerstein, Georg. (1998), *Tantra: The Path of Ecstasy*, Boston, Shambala.

Foley, Helene. (2001), 'A Question of Origins: Goddess Cults Greek and Modern', in Elizabeth A. Castelli, (ed.), *Women, Gender and Religion*, New York, Palgrave.

Freud, Sigmund. (1918), *Totem and Taboo*, trans. A. A. Brill, New York, Random.

Freud, Sigmund. (1984). *On Metapsychology*, trans. James Strachey, New York, Penguin.

Gandhi, Leela. (1998), *Postcolonial Theory: A Critical Introduction*, New York, Columbia University Press.

Gardaz, Michel. (2000), 'The Age of Discoveries and Patriotism: James Darmesteter's Assessment of French Orientalism', *Religion*, 30, 353–65.

Georgoudi, Stella. (1992), 'Creating a Myth of Matriarchy', in Pauline Schmitt Pantel (ed.), *A History of Women in the West*, vol. 1, *From Ancient Goddesses to Christian Saints*, Cambridge, MA, Harvard University Press.

Gilligan, Caroline. (1982), *In a Different Voice*, Cambridge, MA, Harvard University Press.

Gimbutas, Marija. (1991), *The Civilization of the Goddess: The World of Old Europe*, New York, Harper Collins.

Goodison, Lucy and Christine Morris, eds, (1998), *Ancient Goddesses: The Myths and the Evidence*, Madison, University of Wisconsin.

References

Grene, Marjorie. (1985), *Descartes*, Brighton, Harvester Press.

Grene, Marjorie. (1991), *Descartes among the Scholastics*, Milwaukee, Marquette University Press.

Griffin, Susan. (1978), *Woman and Nature: The Roaring Inside Her*, San Francosco: Harper & Row.

Gross, Rita. (1978), 'Hindu Female Deities as a Resource for the Contemporary Rediscovery of the Goddess', *Journal of the American Academy of Religion*, 46:3, 269–92.

Gross, Rita. (1997) 'Some Buddhist Perspectives on the Goddess', in Karen L. King (ed.), *Women and Goddess Traditions*, Minneapolis, Fortress Press.

Gross, Rita. (2000), 'Is the Goddess a Feminist?', in A. Hiltebeitel and K. M. Erndl (eds), *Is the Goddess a Feminist?: The Politics of South Asian Goddesses*, New York, New York University Press.

Grosz, Elizabeth. (1987), 'The "People of the Book": Representation and Alterity in Emmanuel Levinas', *Art and Text*, 28, 32–40.

Grosz, Elizabeth. (1989), *Sexual Subversions: Three French Feminists*, Sydney, Allen & Unwin.

Grosz, Elizabeth. (1990), *Jacques Lacan: A Feminist Introduction*, New York, Routledge.

Grosz, Elizabeth. (1994), 'The Hetero and the Homo', in C. Burke, N. Schor and M. Whitford (eds), *Engaging with Irigaray*, New York, Columbia University Press.

Gulati, Leela. (1995), 'Myth and Reality: In the Context of Poor Working Women in Kerala', in Jasodhara Bagchi (ed.), *Indian Women: Myth and Reality*, Hyderabad, India, Sangam Books.

Gupta, Sanjukta. (1991), 'Women in the Śaiva/Śakta Ethos', in J. Leslie (ed.), *Roles and Rituals for Hindu Women*, Rutherford, Fairleigh Dickinson Press.

Handleman, Susan. (1991), *Fragments of Redemption: Jewish Thought and Literary Theory in Benjamin, Scholem and Levinas*, Bloomington, Indiana University Press.

Hanegraaff, Wouter J. (1996), *New Age Religion and Western Culture: Esotericism in the Mirror of Secular Thought*, Leiden: Brill.

Harth, Erica. (1992), *Cartesian Women: Versions and Subversions of Rational Discourse in the Old Regime*, Ithaca, Cornell University Press.

Hawley, John Stratton, and Donna Wulff. (1996), *Devī: Goddesses of India*, Berkeley, University of California Press.

Hegel, G. W. F. (1948), *On Christianity: Early Theological Writings*, trans. T. M. Knox, New York, Harper & Brothers.

Hegel, G. W. F. (1977), *Phenomenology of Spirit*, trans. A. V. Miller, Oxford, Clarendon Press.

Hegel, G. W. F. (1979a), *System of Ethical Life (1802–3) and First Philosophy of Spirit*, trans. H. S. Harris and T. M. Knox, Albany, State University of New York Press.

Hegel, G. W. F. (1979b), 'Two Fragments of 1797 on Love', trans. H. S. Harris, Clio, 8:2, 257–65.

Hegel, G. W. F. (1991), *Elements of the Philosophy of Right*, ed. A. W. Wood, trans. H. B. Nisbett, Cambridge, Cambridge University Press.

Heidegger, Martin. (1962), *Being and Time*, trans. John Macquarie and Edward Robinson, New York, Harper & Row.

Heidegger, Martin. (1969), *Identity and Difference*, trans. J. Stambough, New York, Harper & Row.

Heidegger, Martin. (1981 [1966]), 'Only a God Can Save Us', in T. Sheehan (ed.), *Heidegger the Man and Thinker*, Chicago, University of Chicago Press.

Heinämaa, Sara. (1997), 'What Is a Woman? Butler and Beauvoir on the Foundation of the Sexual Difference', *Hypatia*, 12:1, 20–39.

References

Heinämaa, Sara. (2003), *Toward a Phenomenology of Sexual Difference: Husserl, Merleau-Ponty, Beauvoir*, Lanham, MD, Rowman & Littlefield.

Hiltebeitel, Alf, and Kathleen M. Erndl, eds (2000), *Is the Goddess a Feminist? The Politics of Asian Goddesses*, Sheffield, Sheffield University Press.

Hirsh, Elizabeth, and Gary A. Olson. (1995), '"Je – Luce Irigaray": A Meeting with Luce Irigaray', *Hypatia*, 10:2, 93–114.

Hoagland, Sara L. (1990), 'Some Concerns about Nel Nodding's Caring', *Hypatia*, 5:1, 112.

Hollywood, Amy. (1998), 'Deconstructing Belief: Irigaray and the Philosophy of Religion', *Journal of Religion*, 78, 230–45.

Hollywood, Amy. (2002), *Sensible Ecstasy: Mysticism, Sexual Difference, and the Demands of History*, Chicago, University of Chicago Press.

Holmlund, Christine. (1991), 'The Lesbian, the Mother, the Heterosexual Lover: Irigaray's Recodings of Difference', *Feminist Studies*, 17:2, 283–308.

Huntington, Patricia. (1998), *Ecstatic Subjects, Utopia, and Recognition: Kristeva, Heidegger and Irigaray*, Albany, State University of New York Press.

Hutton, Ronald. (1999), *The Triumph of the Moon: A History of Modern Pagan Witchcraft*, Oxford, Oxford University Press.

Inden, Ronald. (1986), 'Orientalist Constructions of India', *Modern Asian Studies*, 20, 401–46.

Introvigne, Massimo. (2004), 'Something Peculiar About France: Anti-Cult Campaigns in Western Europe and French Religious Exceptionalism', in James R. Lewis (ed.), *The Oxford Handbook of New Religious Movements*, Oxford: Oxford University Press.

Irigaray, Luce. (1983), 'An Interview with Luce Irigaray', Interview with Kiki Amsberg and Aafke Steenhuis, trans. R. van Krieken, *Hecate*, 9:1–2, 192–202.

Irigaray, Luce. (1985a) [1974], *Speculum of the Other Woman*, trans. G. C. Gill, Ithaca, Cornell University Press.

Irigaray, Luce. (1985b) [1977], *This Sex Which Is Not One*, trans. C. Porter with C. Burke, Ithaca, Cornell University Press.

Irigaray, Luce. (1991a) [1980], *Marine Lover of Friedrich Nietzsche*, trans. G. C. Gill, New York, Columbia University Press.

Irigaray, Luce. (1991b), 'Questions to Emmanuel Levinas', in R. Bernasconi and S. Critchley (eds), *Re-Reading Levinas*, trans. M. Whitford, Bloomington, Indiana University Press.

Irigaray, Luce. (1992) [1982], *Elemental Passions*, trans. J. Collie and J. Still, New York, Routledge.

Irigaray, Luce. (1993a) [1984], *An Ethics of Sexual Difference*, trans. C. Burke and G. C. Gill, Ithaca, Cornell University Press.

Irigaray, Luce. (1993b) [1987], *Sexes and Genealogies*, trans. G. C. Gill, New York, Columbia Press.

Irigaray, Luce. (1993c) [1990], *Je, Tu, Nous: Toward a Culture of Difference*, trans. A. Martin, New York, Routledge.

Irigaray, Luce. (1994) [1989], *Thinking the Difference*, trans. K. Montin, New York, Routledge.

Irigaray, Luce. (1996) [1992], *I Love to You*, trans. A. Martin, New York, Routledge.

Irigaray, Luce. (1999a) [1983], *The Forgetting of Air in Martin Heidegger*, trans. Mary Beth Mader, Austin, University of Texas Press.

Irigaray, Luce. (1999b), *The Age of Breath*. Rüsselsheim, Christel Göttert.

References

Irigaray, Luce. (2001) [1997], *To Be Two*, trans. M. M. Rhodes and M. F. Cocito-Monoc, New York, Routledge.

Irigaray, Luce. (2002a) [1999], *Between East and West: From Singularity to Community*, trans. Stephen Pluháček, New York, Columbia University Press.

Irigaray, Luce. (2002b), *The Way of Love*, trans. Heidi Bostic and Stephen Pluháček, London, Continuum.

Irigaray, Luce. (2002c), 'Luce Irigaray's Questions', Irigaray, *Dialogues* (special edition on Luce Irigaray), 25:3, 199–201.

Irigaray, Luce. (2003), 'Introduction: On Old and New Tablets', in Morny Joy, Kathleen O'Grady and Judith Poxon (eds), *Religion in French Feminist Thought: Critical Perspectives*, London, Routledge.

Irigaray, Luce. (2004), 'What Other Are We Talking About?', *Yale French Studies*, No. 104, New Haven: Yale University Press.

Jaggar, Alison. (1983), *Feminist Politics and Human Nature*, Totowa NJ, Rowman & Littlefield.

James, Susan. (1997), *Passion and Action: The Emotions in Seventeenth-Century Philosophy*, Oxford, Clarendon Press.

Jantzen, Grace. (1999), *Becoming Divine: Towards a Feminist Philosophy of Religion*, Bloomington, Indiana University Press.

Jolley, N. (1992), 'The Reception of Descartes's Philosophy', in J. Cottingham (ed.), *The Cambridge Companion to Descartes*, Cambridge, Cambridge University Press.

Jones, Serene. (1995). 'Divining Women: Irigaray and Feminist Theologies', *Yale French Studies*, 87, 42–67.

Joy, Morny. (1990), 'Equality or Difference: A False Dichotomy?' *Journal of Feminist Studies in Religion*, 6:1, 9–24.

Joy, Morny. (1994), 'Levinas: Alterity, the Feminine and Women – A Meditation', *Studies in Religion/Sciences Religieuses*, 22:4, 463–85.

Joy, Morny. (1995), 'And What if Truth Were a Woman?', in M. Joy and E. Neumaier-Dargyay (eds), *Gender, Genre and Religion*, Waterloo, ON, Wilfrid Laurier University Press.

Joy, Morny. (1998), 'What's God Got to do with It?' in K. O'Grady, A. Gilroy and J. Gray (eds), *Bodies, Lives, Voices: Essays on Women and Theology*, Sheffield, Sheffield Academic Press.

Joy, Morny. (2000a), 'Beyond a God's Eyeview: Alternative Perspectives in the Study of Religion', *Perspectives on Method and Theory in the Study of Religion*, Adjunct Proceedings of the 17th Congress of the International Association for the History of Religions, eds A. W. Geertz and R. T. McCutcheon, Leiden, Brill.

Joy, Morny. (2000b), 'Love and the Labour of the Negative: Irigaray and Hegel', in Dorothea Olkowski (ed.), *Resistance, Flight, Creation: Feminist Enactments of French Philosophy*, Ithaca, Cornell University Press.

Joy, Morny. (2002), 'Divine Love', *Dialogues* (special edition on Luce Irigaray), 25:3, 189–203.

Kanna, Madhu. (2002), 'Righteous Violence and Non-Violence: An Inseparable Dyad of Hindu Tradition', in Durre S. Ahmed (ed.), *Gendering the Spirit*, London: Zed.

Katz, Claire Elise. (2001a), '"For Love as Strong as Death": Taking Another Look at Levinas on Love', *Philosophy Today*, 45:5, 124–32.

Katz, Claire Elise. (2001b), 'Reinhabiting the House of Ruth: Exceeding the Limits of the Feminine in Levinas', in Tina Chanter (ed.), *Feminist Interpretations of Emmanuel Levinas*, University Park, PA: Pennsylvania State University Press.

Katz, Claire. (2003), *Levinas, Judaism and the Feminine: The Silent Footsteps of Rebecca*, Bloomington: Indiana University Press.

References

Kearney, Richard. (1998), *Poetics of Imagining: Modern to Post-modern*, New York, Fordham University Press.

Keeling, S. V. (1968), *Descartes*, Oxford, Oxford University Press.

Keller, Mary. (2003), 'Divine Women and the Nehanda Mhondoro: Strengths and Limitations of the Sensible Transcendental in a Post-colonial World of Religious Women', in M. Joy, K. O'Grady and J. Poxon (eds), *Religion in French Feminist Thought: Critical Essays*, London: Routledge.

King, Karen L. ed. (1997), *Women and Goddess Traditions*, Minneapolis, Fortress Press.

Koehn, Daryl. (1998), *Rethinking Feminist Ethics: Care, Trust and Empathy*. London and New York, Routledge.

Kojève, Alexandre. (1969) [1947], *Introduction to the Reading of Hegel*, trans. J. H. Nichols Jr, New York, Basic Books.

Kumar, Pushpendra. (1974), *Śakti Cult in Ancient India*, Varanasi, Bhartiya Publishing House.

Lacan, Jacques. (1977), *Ecrits: A Selection*, trans. A. Sheridan, New York, W. W. Norton.

Lacan, Jacques. (1983), *Jacques Lacan and the Ecole Freudienne*, J. Mitchell and J. Rose (eds), New York, Pantheon Press.

Leacock, Eleanor Burke. (1981), *Myths of Male Dominance: Collected Articles on Women Cross-Culturally*, New York, Monthly Review Press.

Lefkowitz, Mary. (1986), *Women in Greek Myth*, London, Duckworth.

Leslie, Julia. (1991), 'Sutee or Satī: Victim or Victor', in J. Leslie (ed.), *Roles and Rituals for Hindu Women*, Rutherford, Fairleigh Dickinson Press.

Levinas, Emmanuel. (1969 [nd]) *Totality and Infinity: An Essay on Exteriority*, trans. A. Lingis, The Hague, Martinus Nijhoff.

Levinas, Emmanuel. (1981) [1974], *Otherwise than Being or Beyond Essence*, trans. A. Lingis, The Hague, Martinus Nijhoff.

Levinas, Emmanuel. (1985) [1982], *Ethics and Infinity: Conversations with Philippe Nemo*, trans. Richard A. Cohen, Pittsburgh, Duquesne University Press.

Levinas, Emmanuel. (1986a) [1967], 'The Trace of the Other', in Mark C. Taylor (ed.), *Deconstruction in Context: Literature and Philosophy*, Chicago: University of Chicago Press.

Levinas, Emmanuel. (1986b), 'Dialogue with Emmanuel Levinas: Emmanuel Levinas and Richard Kearney', in R. A. Cohen (ed.), *Face to Face with Levinas*, Albany, State University of New York Press.

Levinas, Emmanuel. (1987a) [1947], *Time and the Other*, trans. Richard A. Cohen. Pittsburgh, Duquesne University Press.

Levinas, Emmanuel. (1987b), *Collected Philosophical Papers*, trans. A. Lingis, The Hague, Martinus Nijhoff.

Levinas, Emmanuel. (1988), 'The Paradox of Morality: An Interview with Emmanuel Levinas', in Robert Bernasconi and David C. Wood (eds), *The Provocation of Levinas: Rethinking the Other*, interviewed by Tamra Wright, Peter Hughes and Alison Ainley, London, Routledge.

Levinas, Emmanuel. (1990a) [1963], 'Judaism and the Feminine', in *Difficult Freedom: Essays on Judaism*, trans. S. Hand, London, Athlone.

Levinas, Emmanuel. (1990b) [1973], 'And God Created Woman', in *Nine Talmudic Readings*, trans. Annette Aronowicz, Bloomington, Indiana University Press.

Levinas, Emmanuel. (1996), *Basic Philosophical Writings*, A. Peperzak, S. Critchley, R. Bernasconi (eds), Bloomington, Indiana University Press.

Levinas, Emmanuel. (1997), *Qui dirait Eurydice? / What Would Eurydice Say? Emmanuel Levinas in/en Conversation with/avec Bracha Lichtenberg-Ettinber*, Paris, BLE Atelier.

References

Levinas, Emmanuel. (1998) [1991], *Entre Nous: Thinking of the Other*, trans. Michael B. Smith and B. Henshaw, New York, Columbia University Press.

Levinas, Emmanuel. (1999) [1995], *Alterity and Transcendence*, trans. Michael B. Smith, New York, Columbia University Press.

Levinas, Emmanuel. (2001) [1984], *Is it Righteous to Be?*, ed. Jill Robbins, Stanford, Stanford University Press.

Lévi-Strauss, Claude. [1949] (1969), *The Elementary Structures of Kinship*, trans. J. H. Bell et al., Boston, Beacon Press.

Lincoln, Bruce. (1999), *Theorizing Myth: Narrative, Ideology and Scholarship*, Chicago, University of Chicago Press.

Lloyd, Genevieve. (1993a) [1984], *The Man of Reason: 'Male' and 'Female' in Western Philosophy*, Minneapolis, University of Minnesota Press.

Lloyd, Genevieve. (1993b), 'Maleness, Metaphor and the "Crisis" of Reason', in L. M. Antony and C. Witt (eds), *A Mind of One's Own*, Boulder, CO, Westview Press.

Lorde, Audre. (1981), 'An Open Letter to Mary Daly', in Cherrie Moraga and Gloria Anzaldúa (eds), *This Bridge Called My Back: Writing by Radical Women of Color*, Waterton, NY, Persephone Press.

Macey, David, (1988), *Lacan in Contexts*, London: Verso.

Manu. (1969), *The Laws of Manu*, trans. G. Bühler, New York, Dover.

Merchant, Carolyn. (1980), *The Death of Nature: Women, Ecology and the Scientific Revolution*, San Francisco, HarperCollins.

Merleau-Ponty, Maurice. (1954). *The Visible and the Invisible*, trans. A. Lingis, Evanston, Northwestern University Press.

Miller, Barbara Stoller, ed. and trans. (1995), *Yoga: Discipline of Freedom, The Yoga Sutra Attributed to Patanjali*, Berkeley, University of California Press.

Mills, Patricia Jagentowicz. (1996), 'Hegel's Antigone', in P. Jagentowicz Mills (ed.), *Feminist Interpretations of G.W.F. Hegel*, University Park, PA, Pennsylvania State University Press.

Mitchell, Juliet. (1983) 'Introduction 1', in J. Mitchell and J. Rose (eds), *Jacques Lacan and the École Freudienne*, New York, Pantheon Press.

Mitchell, Juliet, and J. Rose, eds (1983), *Feminine Sexuality: Jacques Lacan and the Ecole Freudienne*, New York, Pantheon.

Moi, Toril. (1985), *Sexual/Textual Politics: Feminist Literary Theory*, London, Methuen.

Moi, Toril. (1999), *What Is a Woman?* Oxford, Oxford University Press.

Morris, Meaghan. (1988), *The Pirate's Fiancée: Feminism, Reading, Postmodernism*, London, Verso.

Nabar, Vrinda. (1995), *Caste as Woman*, New Delhi, Penguin Books India.

Narasimhan, Sakuntala. (1990), *Sati: Widow Burning in India*. New York, Anchor Books.

Narayan, Uma. (1997), *Dislocating Cultures: Identities, Traditions and Third-World Feminisms*, New York, Routledge.

Narayanan, Vasudha. (1999), 'Brimming with Bhakti, Embodiments of Shakti', in A. Sharma and K. K. Young (eds), *Feminism and World Religions*, Albany, State University of New York Press.

Noddings, Nel. (1984), *Caring*, Berkeley, University of California Press.

Nye, Andrea. (1999), *The Princess and the Philosopher: Letters of Elisabeth of the Palatine to René Descartes*, Lanham, MD, Rowman & Littlefield.

O'Brien, Mary. (1996), 'Hegel: Man, Physiology, and Fate', in P. Jagentowicz Mills (ed.), *Feminist Interpretations of G.W.F. Hegel*, University Park, PA, Pennsylvania State University Press.

References

Ochshorn, Judith. (1997), 'Goddesses and the Lives of Women', in Karen L. King (ed.), *Women and Goddess Traditions*, Minneapolis, Fortress Press.

Oliver, Kelly. (1995), *Womanizing Nietzsche: Philosophy's Relation to the 'Feminine'*, New York, Routledge.

Oliver, Kelly. (2001), *Witnessing: Beyond Recognition*, Minneapolis, University of Minneapolis Press.

Olkowski, Dorothea. (2000a), 'The End of Phenomenology: Bergson's Interval in Irigaray', *Hypatia*, 15:3, 73–91.

Olkowski, Dorothea. (2000b), 'Chiasm, the Interval of Sexual Difference Between Irigaray and Merleau-Ponty', in Lawrence Hass and Dorothea Lokowski (eds), *Rereading Merleau-Ponty*, Amherst, NY, Humanity Books.

Peperzak, Adriaan. (1991), 'The One for the Other: The Philosophy of Emmanuel Levinas', *Man and World*, 24, 427–59.

Pintchman, Tracy. (2000), 'Is the Hindu Goddess Tradition a Good Resource for Western Feminism?' in A. Hiltebeitel and K. M. Erndl (eds), *Is the Goddess a Feminist?: The Politics of South Asian Goddesses*, Sheffield, Sheffield Academic Press.

Pluháček, Stephen, and Heidi Bostic. (1996), 'Thinking Life as Relation: An Interview with Luce Irigaray', *Man and World*, 29, 343–60.

Porter, E. J. (1991), *Women and Moral Identity*, Sydney, Allen and Unwin.

Poxon, Judith. (2003), 'Corporeality and Divinity: Irigaray and the Problem of the Ideal', in Morny Joy, Kathleen O'Grady and Judith L. Poxon (eds), *Religion in French Feminist Thought: Critical Perspectives*, London, Routledge.

Ragland-Sullivan, E. (1991), 'The Sexual Masquerade: The Lacanian Theory of Sexual Difference', in E. Ragland-Sullivan and M. Bracher (eds), *Lacan and the Subject of Language*, New York, Routledge.

Raven, H. (1996), 'Has Hegel Anything to Say to Feminists?', in P. Jagentowicz Mills (ed.), *Feminist Interpretations of G. W. F. Hegel*, University Park, PA, Pennsylvania State University Press.

Ricoeur, Paul. (1997), *Autrement*, Paris, Presses Universitaires de France.

Rivière, Joan. (1989), 'Womanliness as Masquerade', in V. Burgin, J. Donald and C. Kaplan (eds), *Formations of Fantasy*, New York: Routledge. (Originally published in the *International Journal of Psychoanalysis*, 9, 1929.)

Roach, Catherine. (2003), *Mother/Nature: Popular Culture and Environmental Ethics*, Bloomington, Indiana University Press.

Rodis-Lewis, Geneviève. (1998), *Descartes: His Life and Thought*, trans. J. M. Todd, Ithaca, Cornell University Press.

Rorty, Amélie Oksenberg. (1986), 'Cartesian Passions and the Union of Mind and Body', in A. Oksenberg Rorty (ed.), *Essays on Descartes' Meditations*, Berkeley, University of California Press.

Rorty, Amélie Oksenberg. (1992), 'Descartes on Thinking with the Body', in J. Cottingham (ed.), *The Cambridge Companion to Descartes*, Cambridge, Cambridge University Press.

Roudinesco, Elisabeth. (1990), *Jacques Lacan & Co.: A History of Psychoanalysis in France*, trans. J. Mehlman, Chicago, University of Chicago Press.

Roy, Kumkum. (1995), '"Where Women Are Worshipped, There the Gods Rejoice": The Mirage of the Ancestress of the Hindu Woman', in T. Sarkar and U. Butalia (eds), *Women and Right-Wing Movements: Indian Experiences*, London, Zed Books.

Roy, Kumkum. (1999), *Women in Early Indian Societies*, New Delhi, Manohar.

References

Rozemond, Marleen. (1998), *Descartes's Dualism*, Cambridge, MA, Harvard University Press.

Ruddick, Sara. (1989), *Maternal Thinking*, Boston, Beacon Press.

Said, Edward. (1978), *Orientalism*, New York, Vintage Books.

Said, Edward. (1986), 'Orientalism Reconsidered', *Literature, Politics and Theory*, eds Francis Barker *et al.*, London, Methuen.

Sandford, Stella. (2000), *The Metaphysics of Love*. London, Athlone Press.

Sandford, Stella. (2002), 'Levinas, Feminism and the Feminine', in S. Critchley (ed.), *Cambridge Companion to Levinas*, Cambridge, Cambridge University Press.

Sawyer, Deborah F. (2002), *God, Gender and the Bible*, New York, Routledge.

Schor, Naomi. (1994), 'This Essentialism which is Not One', in C. Burke, N. Schor and M. Whitford (eds), *Engaging with Irigaray*, New York, Columbia University Press.

Schor, Naomi. (1995), 'French Feminism Is a Universalism', *Differences*, 7:1, 15–47.

Scott, Joan. (1996), *Only Paradoxes to Offer: French Feminists and the Rights of Man*, Cambridge, MA, Harvard University Press.

Segal, Robert A., ed. (1998), *The Myth and Ritual Theory: An Anthology*, Oxford, Blackwell.

Shaw, Miranda. (1997), 'Worship of Women in Tantric Buddhism: Male Is to Female as Devotee Is to Goddess', in Karen L. King (ed.), *Women and Goddess Traditions*, Minneapolis, Fortress Press.

Silverman, Kaja. (1983), *The Subject of Semiotics*, Oxford, Oxford University Press.

Silverman, Kaja. (1992), 'The Lacanian Phallus', *Differences*, 4:2, 84–115.

Simmer-Brown, Judith. (2001), *Dakini's Warm Breath: The Feminine Principle in Tibetan Buddhism*, Boston, Shambala.

Smith, Jonathan Z., with W. Burkhert and R. Girard. (1987), *Violent Origins: Ritual Killing and Cultural Formation*, Stanford, Stanford University Press.

Soper, Kate. (1995), *What Is Nature?* Oxford, Blackwell.

Spivak, Gayatri Chakravorty. (1987), 'Subaltern Studies: Deconstructing Historiography', *In Other Words: Essays in Cultural Politics*, New York, Routledge.

Spivak, Gayatri Chakravorty. (1990), 'Criticism, Feminism and The Institution', in S. Harasym (ed.), *The Post-Colonial Critic: Interviews, Strategies, Dialogues*, New York, Routledge.

Stanton Domna C. (1986). 'Difference on Trial: A Critique of the Maternal Metaphor in Cixous, Irigaray, and Kristeva', in Nancy K. Miller (ed.), *The Poetics of Gender*, New York, Columbia University Press.

Stanton, Elizabeth Cady. (1895, 1898, two parts), *The Woman's Bible*. New York: European Publishing Company.

Starhawk. (1979), *The Spiral Dance: A Rebirth of the Ancient Goddess Tradition*, San Francisco, Harper & Row.

Starhawk. (1982), *Dreaming the Dark: Magic, Sex and Politics*. Boston, Beacon Press.

Stockton, Katherine Bond. (1994), *God Between Their Lips: Desire Between Women in Irigaray, Bronte, and Eliot*, Stanford, Stanford University Press.

Stone, Merlin. (1976), *When God Was a Woman*, New York, Harcourt, Brace, Jovanovitch.

Sutcliffe, Steven J. (2003), *Children of the New Age*, London, Routledge.

Thapar, Romila. (1988), 'In History', *Seminar*, 342 (February), 14–19.

Tong, Rosemary. (1989), *Feminist Thought: A Comprehensive Introduction*, Boulder, CO, Westview Press.

Tringham, Ruth, and Margaret Conkey. (1998), 'Rethinking Figurines: A Critical View from Archaeology to Gimbutas, the "Goddess" and Popular Culture', in Lucy Goodison and Christine Morris (eds), *Ancient Goddesses: The Myths and the Evidence*, Madison, University of Wisconsin Press.

Varenne, Jean. (1976), *Yoga and the Hindu Tradition*, Chicago, University of Chicago Press.

Watson, Richard A. (1987), *The Breakdown of Cartesian Metaphysics*, Indianapolis, Hackett.

Wehr, Demaris. (1987), *Jung and the Feminine: Liberating Archetypes*, Boston, Beacon.

Whicher, Ian. (1998), *The Integrity of the Yoga Darśana: A Reconsideration of Classical Yoga*, Albany, State University of New York Press.

White, David Gordon, ed. (2000), *Tantra in Practice*, Princeton Readings in Religions, Princeton, Princeton University Press.

Whitford, Margaret. (1991), *Luce Irigaray: Philosophy in the Feminine*, London, Routledge.

Whitford, Margaret. (1994), 'Irigaray, Utopia and the Death Drive', in C. Burke, N. Schor and M. Whitford (eds), *Engaging with Irigaray: Feminist Philosophy and Modern European Thought*, New York, Columbia University Press.

Willett, Cynthia. (2001) *The Soul of Justice: Social Bonds and Racial Hubris*, Ithaca, Cornell University Press.

Wright, Tamra. (1999), *The Twilight of Jewish Philosophy: Emmanuel Levinas' Ethical Hermeneutics*, Amsterdam, Harwood Academic Press.

Wyschogrod, Edith. (2000) [1974], *Emmanuel Levinas: The Problem of Ethical Metaphysics*, New York, Fordham University Press.

Ziarek, Ewa Płonowska. (2001), *An Ethics of Dissensus: Postmodernity, Feminism, and the Politics of Radical Democracy*, Stanford, Stanford University Press.

Index

absolute 56, 59, 61, 96, 100
agape 27, 72, 76
Age of Breath, The (Irigaray) 118, 124, 136
alterity 56, 61–3, 65, 75, 76, 81
Anderson, Pamela 142–3
angels 103, 106
Antigone 83, 86–90
Armour, Ellen 120, 148, 151, 157

Bachofen, J.J. 27, 28, 130
    Mutterrecht, Das/Mother Right 27–8, 130
Beauvoir, Simone de 56, 67, 81, 94
becoming 20, 25, 27, 34, 52, 54, 55, 84, 94, 102–4, 108–10, 120, 122, 125, 136, 152, 158, 159, 164
    divine 25, 124, 144, 159
    infinite 29
    metaphysics of 15, 19
    ontology of 51
    spiritual becoming 93
    a virgin 70
    of women 105
Be-Friending 109, 110
Being
    Archaic Being 117
    Daly's Be-ing 104–6, 110, 112–13
    divine, the 25, 112
    God as 19, 20 103, 114
    Heidegger 60, 114–15, 145–6, 152–3, 158
    Levinas 57, 59, 63–4, 72, 77
    Meta-Being 113
    ontology of 59, 63, 115

    see also ontological essentialism; ontology
belief
    Anderson 142
    Daly 105
    divine women 25
    Hollywood 143
    Irigaray 90, 143, 144, 151
    Starhawk 118
    traditional 97
Between East and West (Irigaray)
    eastern spirituality 29, 124, 127, 131, 136
    gynocratic cultures 29, 130
    ontological essentialism 32, 118, 122, 136
    sexual difference 155
    yoga 127
binaries 33, 18, 106, 115, 145
body
    desire 13, 15, 16, 46
    the divine 79, 92, 127, 157–8
    essentialism 117
    God/Other 20, 29
    gynocratic culture 27, 92
    love 52–3
    maternity 40, 73, 92, 143
    mind 37–45, 47, 49–54
    nature 112
    passions 15, 50–1, 52, 53, 55, 137
    physical 32, 37, 41, 80, 83, 88, 93
    sexualised 21, 30, 71, 100, 127–9
    spiritual 52, 83, 128, 131

Index

transcendence 20, 29, 46, 47, 52, 79, 134
virginity of 88
yoga and Tantrism 127–9, 134
see also embodiment
Bordo, Susan 40, 41, 44
Braidotti, Rosi 18, 30, 31, 32, 33, 122, 136, 147
breath 25, 127–8, 136
Buddha 136
Buddhism 129, 132, 134, 138, 140
Butler, Judith 3, 13, 99, 116, 152

Campbell, June 134
Cavarero, Adriana 31–3, 122
Chakravarti, Uma 130, 134
Chalier, Catherine 64, 70, 73
Chanter, Tina 56, 57, 64, 72, 81, 87
Cheah, Peng 97, 116, 148, 149, 152, 154
Clarke, J.J. 137–9
Cogito 39, 40, 42, 54
Conkey, Margaret 27, 130, 133
Cornell, Drucilla
  Beyond Accommodation 145, 147
  essentialism 157
  heterosexuality 152–4, 156
  on Irigaray 43–4, 91, 147, 152
  motherhood 91–2
  sexual difference 99, 121, 145, 147, 148, 153–4, 156
couple 4, 64, 71, 76, 78, 85, 95–8, 112, 125, 148, 153, 158
  see also divine, divinity
culture
  gynocratic 126–7, 130
  Hindu 126, 127
  mother/daughter 91–2
  nature 90–1, 112, 150, 155
  patriarchal 28, 94
  western 33, 40, 119, 126
  of woman 29, 84, 86–94, 119, 124, 126
  see also nature/culture distinction

Daly, Mary 5, 102–7, 109–23
  Be-ing 104–6, 110, 112–13
  essentialism 111–15, 117–18, 121–2
  female friendship 109–10

God 102, 103–4
goddesses 110–11, 118
lust 102, 103, 105–6, 110–11
metaphor 106–7, 109, 110–11
ontology 103–4, 112–15, 122
patriarchy 102, 103, 109, 112, 122–3
racism 119–22
deconstruction 15, 29, 30, 41–2, 59, 115, 147
Derrida, Jacques 7, 12, 15, 59, 115
Descartes, René 36–55
  ethics 51–4
  God 37, 38, 39, 42, 54
  Irigaray's interpretation of 36–8, 41–5, 53–5
  love 49, 52
  mind/body dichotomy 36–40, 43–4, 49–54
  passions 36–7, 45, 47, 49–51, 53
  rationality 37–9, 43, 53–4
  reason 36, 44–6, 54
  sexual difference 37, 47–9, 51–2
  wonder 36, 45–9, 51–2, 54
desire 11–13, 15–20, 46, 48, 49, 53, 63, 83, 87, 105–6, 159
  transformed into love 49, 71
Deutscher, Penelope 148–9, 151, 157
dialectic
  in Hegel 83, 86, 87, 90, 94, 100
  in Irigaray 2, 9, 88, 95–6, 98
  Levinas 81
difference
  biological 32
  equality 94–5
  female subjectivity 148, 154
  'the feminine' 79–80, 81, 88
  feminism 122
  heterosexuality 151–2, 154, 156, 158
  Lacan 10, 14
  Levinas 61, 65, 66, 75, 80, 81
  otherness 20, 37
  race 121, 147, 148, 150–1
  sexual 29–31, 37, 99, 147, 149
  wonder 47–8, 52
  see also gender difference; sexual difference

Index

divine, divinity
  Being 112
  couple 4, 111, 125, 126, 129
  Daly 103, 112
  desire 15, 21, 53, 159
  in Eastern religions 124–32, 136–7, 157
  essentialism 120, 122
  feminine 7, 15, 20, 21–4, 34, 115, 157
  God 7–35, 58, 70, 79, 103, 125, 158
  heterosexual love 49, 77–9, 83, 95–8, 109, 111–12, 125, 151
  Huntington 144–5
  Jantzen 144–5
  Levinas 75–9, 82
  mother/daughter relationship 20, 92
  nature 25, 27, 157
  sexual difference 70, 115, 120, 125, 144, 156
  through love 37, 48, 49, 53, 100, 157
  transcendence 4, 29, 48–9, 53, 79, 128, 158
dualism 23, 34, 53–4, 65, 99, 108, 138, 156

eastern religion 124–41
elements 25, 33, 92, 105, 111
Eliade, Mircea 127–30, 137
embodiment 23, 26, 27, 54, 100
  see also body
equality 3, 65–6, 88, 94–5, 153
eros 27, 66, 67–72, 81, 124–41
essentialism 4, 18, 30–2, 95
  Butler on 121
  cosmic 112–14, 117–18, 121–2, 137, 157
  Daly 112, 114
  feminine characteristics 18, 32, 41–2, 95, 122, 137, 159
  feminist studies on 115–19, 121–2, 145–6, 148, 157
  lips, 'two lips' 18, 30
  metaphysical 32, 136
  nature 111, 117–19, 136, 151
  ontological 32–3, 95, 122, 136–7, 151, 157, 159
  sex/gender 32–3, 95, 116, 121–2

sexual difference 30–3, 95
ethics
  Descartes 51–4
  Levinas 57–65, 70, 72–5, 78–9
  love 49, 52, 78, 85
  o/Other 61, 64–5, 70, 78–82
  sexual difference 1, 52, 60, 65, 82, 85, 97
  subjectivity 73, 82, 157
Ethics of Sexual Difference, An (Irigaray)
  breath 127
  divinity 144
  heterosexuality 115, 125
  love 54, 111
  sex/gender 57, 111, 148, 149
  sexual difference 3, 94, 144, 148, 149, 152
  sexual ethics 85, 88
  wonder 36, 47

face 56, 61–3, 69, 70, 72, 75, 77, 78, 110, 171, 172
  alterity 56, 61–3
  feminine, the 69, 72, 75, 78, 110
fecundity 33, 40, 52, 72–5, 126–7, 152, 157
female, feminine
  characteristics 18, 32, 41–2, 95, 122, 137, 159
  divine 7, 20–4, 33–4, 100, 103, 111–12, 115, 131, 137, 156–60
  eastern spirituality 29
  the 'feminine' 7, 18–20, 29, 32, 41, 64–81, 131, 145, 159
  femininity 2–3, 11, 18, 41, 43, 54, 90–1, 122, 152, 156–7, 159
  friendship 109–10
  ideal 8, 24, 34, 80, 128
  identity 3, 7, 86–9, 110, 111, 113, 149, 159
  mythology 27
  nature/natural 26–7, 33, 86, 90–1, 112, 140, 157
  spirituality 90–3, 100, 126–8, 133–4, 140, 151–9
  subjectivity 19–20, 25, 30, 40–3, 81–2, 89, 91, 95–6, 154

201

Index

universal, universality 12, 41, 43, 80, 83, 86, 91–7, 100, 152, 174
feminism, feminists
  cosmic 117, 122
  difference 30, 33, 81, 98, 122, 154
  essentialism 41–2, 114–15, 117–19, 122
  feminine, the 80–1
  Levinas 57, 67
  maternity 74
  post-colonial 134
  religion 81, 122, 152
  white 148
Ferguson, Kathy 116–17, 121–2, 136
Forgetting of Air, The (Irigaray) 115
Freud
  God-the-Father 9
  patricide/oedipal theory 26, 34, 91–2, 140
  phallus 11–12, 14, 91, 108
  repression 11, 18, 112, 143

genealogy 9, 20, 89, 92
gender 43, 58, 89, 120
  biological 21, 18, 116, 148
  as cultural 3, 18, 93, 116
  difference 3, 30, 44, 98–9
  essentialism 32, 95, 116, 121–2
  ethics 65, 85
  female 22, 30, 32, 84, 86
  heterosexuality 71, 85, 97–9, 115, 154
  Irigaray's definition of 21–2, 57
  Levinas 57, 75, 81
  male 3, 21, 30, 82
  nature 90–1, 155
  ontological identity 95, 110, 146
  race 121, 148, 150, 152, 154
  sex 18, 21–2, 31, 116, 154
  sex/gender debate 23, 27, 41, 43, 146–7
  universality 90–2, 95, 96, 98, 152–3
  women 20–2, 30, 56
gender difference 3, 30, 44, 98–9
Gilligan, Caroline 73
God
  as Absolute 9, 59, 60–1, 100
  Being 10, 19–20, 24, 37, 58, 63, 64, 77, 100, 103–6, 114
  of Christianity 9, 29, 100
  Daly 103
  Descartes 38, 39, 42, 54
  desire 11–12, 15–20
  divine, the 21, 22, 49, 69, 78, 125
  God-the-Father 9, 15, 15, 17, 26, 48
  heterosexuality 60, 78, 109
  Irigaray 25, 53, 125, 158
  Levinas 58–66, 69, 77–82
  o/Other 7, 9, 12, 20, 29, 53, 59–61
  paternal 8–9, 16, 70, 79, 102, 126
  woman 7, 9, 22, 82, 92, 114, 136, 155
goddess/es 25, 27–9, 92, 110–11, 118, 127–9, 133–5, 140
Grene, Marjorie 38, 39
Grosz, Elizabeth 9–10, 14–15, 16–17, 19, 81, 117, 148–54
gynocracy 26–7, 29, 31, 92–3
  gynocratic culture 4, 26–34, 126–7, 130–2

Harth, Erica 43–5
Hegel, Georg Wilhelm Friedrich
  civic identity 86–9
  couple 95–7
  culture of women 89–90, 93–4
  dialectic 83, 86, 87, 90, 94, 100
  equality 94–5
  heterosexism 97–8
  Irigaray on 83–6, 99–101
  labour of the negative 13, 83–96, 150
  o/Other 10, 90, 93, 94
  spirit 9, 86, 89, 100, 153
  universality 83–4, 86, 89, 100, 152–3, 155
Heidegger, Martin
  Being/God 60, 114–15, 145–6, 152–3, 158
  imagination 145–6
  ontology 58–9, 94, 112, 114–15, 145–6
heterosexism 97–8, 151, 154, 159
heterosexuality 3, 60, 71, 78, 83, 85–6, 95, 97–100, 103, 109, 115, 125, 151–8
  couple 4, 95–8, 103, 112, 153, 158

Daly on 5, 103
divine 4, 109, 115, 158, 160
ethics 56, 60, 72, 155, 157
love 4, 95
other 60, 97, 152
sexual difference 34, 99, 115, 125, 152–4, 156–8
universality 86, 95, 153, 156
Hinduism 126–7, 129, 131–3, 137–8, 140
Hirsch, Elizabeth 1, 2, 135, 149
Hollywood, Amy 24, 26, 142, 143–4, 157–8
homosexuality *see* heterosexism; same-sex relations
Huntington, Pamela 121, 142, 144–6, 147, 148, 154

I Love to You (Irigaray)
divine 4, 53, 109
eastern spirituality 124
Hegelian universality 87, 94, 152, 159
heterosexism 97, 109, 151
heterosexuality 83, 97, 109, 152
race 120–1
sexual difference 3, 52–3, 94, 120, 125
yoga 127, 130–1
imaginary
in Anderson 142, 144
in Cornell 153
feminine (in Irigaray) 3, 7, 10, 18, 22, 23, 29, 142, 146, 153
in Jantzen 144, 164
in Lacan 3, 10, 13, 16, 17, 19, 22, 26, 91, 124, 162, 176
imagination 22, 23, 124, 145–6

James, Susan 36, 50 51, 53
Jantzen, Grace 142, 144, 145, 164, 185
Je, Tu, Nous (Irigaray) 130
Jones, Serene 24, 53
jouissance 8, 12, 15–20, 21, 163

Katz, Claire Elize 64, 76–7, 78
Kearney, Richard 146

Keller, Mary 154–5

Lacan, Jacques
desire, *jouissance* 12–14, 16
metaphor 107–8
o/Other 10, 13, 57
phallus/penis 9, 11–12, 14–15, 108
language 56, 99, 114, 148
lesbian 97, 110, 137, 149
Levinas, Emmanuel 56–82
Being 58–9, 63–4, 72, 77
difference 61, 65, 66, 75, 80, 81
divine 75–9, 82
eros 67–72, 76, 81
ethics 57–60, 70–3, 77, 81–2
'the feminine' 64–82, 157
feminism 57, 67
gender 57, 75, 81
God 58–66, 69, 77–82
Irigaray on 56–8
Jewish influences 75–7
love 64, 66–9, 72, 74, 76, 78
maternity 72–5, 77
o/Other 56–67, 75, 78–81
sexual difference 57, 66, 77
lips, 'two lips' 17–18, 19, 21, 29, 30, 108, 110, 152
Lloyd, Genevieve 34, 41–3
love
agape 27, 72, 76
carnal 26, 52–3, 83, 96, 100, 159
Descartes 49, 52, 103
desire 11, 49, 70–1, 159
divine 4, 96, 100, 151, 156, 157, 158
in Eastern culture 29, 126
eros 27, 66–72
gynocracies 26–7, 29, 126
heterosexual 64, 77–9, 95–8, 102–4, 111–12, 151
homosexual 102–4, 110
labour of the negative 83–101
Levinas 64, 66–9, 72, 74, 76, 78
maternity 72, 74, 85
natural immediacy 89, 95
sexual difference 66, 125, 156
transcendence 4, 46–9, 79, 97
wonder 37, 49, 52–3

Index

lust 102, 103, 105–6, 110, 111

male, masculine
   divine, the 48, 79, 100, 112, 120
   dominance in history 28, 86, 90, 92, 103–4, 158
   in Eastern cultures 128, 133–4, 138
   feminine, the 18, 65, 66–8, 79
   gender 21, 30, 65, 71, 75, 99
   God as 8, 9–10, 15, 19, 104, 114
   gods 25, 92, 126
   heterosexuality 71–2, 86, 95, 97–100, 103
   language 12, 56
   maternity 72, 73, 74, 91
   o/Other 10–11, 15, 47, 65, 79, 81–2
   phallus/penis 12, 11–16, 48, 91, 99, 108
   rationality 34, 40–1, 54, 100, 140
   sameness 8, 9, 11, 12, 81, 88
   sex 21, 48, 71, 81, 126–9
   sexual difference 3, 66, 85, 99
   transcendence 24, 48, 67, 79
master–slave dialectic 48, 83, 87, 94, 145
maternity 33, 40, 72–5, 85, 91–2, 94, 114, 143–4
matriarchy, primordial 27
Merchant, Carolyn 118
Merleau-Ponty, Maurice 23–4, 146
metaphor 106–8, 109, 110–12
mimesis 2, 7, 11, 15, 17, 19, 42, 161, 163
mimetic
   double play 87
   mode 42, 112
   reading 37
   subversive 22
   style 107, 177
mirror, mirror-stage 9, 10, 42, 103
Mitchell, Juliet 12, 16, 34
mother/daughter relations 20, 33, 73, 91–3, 140
mother-goddess 130
myths, Greek myths 26–9, 92, 124, 133

Nabar, Vrinda 133
Narasimhan, Sakuntala 133–4
natural immediacy (Hegel) 89, 90

nature/culture distinction 33, 39, 90–3, 111–12, 117–19, 140–1, 157
nature, natural
   body 39–40, 44
   divine 25–7, 65, 128, 157–9
   essentialism 117–19, 122
   fecundity 75, 157
   female identity 86, 90–1, 131
   gynocracies 26–7, 92–3, 157
   identity 27, 86, 90–1, 119, 157
   immediacy 89, 90–1, 95, 97, 137
   sexual difference 99, 120, 141, 156
   women 25, 39, 89–93, 111–12, 117–19, 140–1, 157
negative, negativity 3, 13, 14, 21, 83–96, 125, 150, 163, 172, 173–4, 179, 185
   labour of 85, 90
Nietzsche, Friedrich 49, 104, 138
Noddings, Nel 73–4

Oedipal theory 8, 9, 91, 108, 140
Oliver, Kelly 13, 121, 147–8
Olson, Gary A. 1, 2, 135, 149, 150
ontological essentialism 32–3, 95, 122, 136–7, 151, 157, 159
ontology 32–3, 47, 51–4, 58–60, 94, 102–4, 112–15, 122, 145–6, 151–3
   see also Being; ontological essentialism
orientalism 124, 126, 137–9
other/Other 10, 11, 47, 52, 56–67, 75–82, 85, 91–4, 96–8, 102, 125, 152
   desire 13, 17, 83
   divine, the 20–4, 136
   feminine, the 65–8, 80–1
   God as 7, 9–10, 20–1, 53, 79, 100
   heterosexuality 152–3
   Lacan 10, 13
   Levinas 56–67, 75, 78–81
   love 49, 70–1
   male-focused 9–10, 102
   maternity 4, 94, 114
   negativity 90, 96
   sexual difference 57, 66, 77, 97, 125
   transcendence 78–9, 96–7, 102

woman 10, 11, 56, 70, 81–2, 85, 91
wonder 51, 52, 152
see also alterity

passions 15, 36, 37, 45, 47, 49–53, 55, 137
patriarchy 7, 27, 33, 89, 92–3, 121–3, 125–6
penis 12, 14, 91
  see also phallus
phallus/es 9, 11–16, 18, 48, 99, 108
  see also penis
Plato 8–9, 13, 44, 54, 115
post-colonialism 130, 134, 137–9, 154
postmodern 30, 59
projection 2, 9, 24, 27, 91
psychoanalysis 2, 9, 22, 40–1, 90, 91

racism 119–22, 148, 151, 155–6
rationality 34, 37–42, 45–6, 100, 131, 140
  see also reason
Real 16, 112
reason
  Descartes 36, 44–6
  feminine, the 67
  Heidegger 115, 145
  as masculine 41–2, 46, 54
  woman 8, 39, 40, 41, 44, 73
  women scholars 34, 73, 111, 142–3
recognition 1, 13, 43, 60, 83, 84, 85, 96, 125, 137, 147, 151, 155, 159, 163, 173, 174, 179, 185
  divine, the 159
  Hegel 13, 83, 96
  love 85, 96
  mutual 1, 17, 174
  political 31
  race 120, 155
  sexual difference 84, 125
religion 7, 29, 33, 125, 126, 134, 139–40, 157, 159
  divine, the 7, 54–5, 100, 144, 145, 157, 159
  eastern 130–1, 138, 157
  Irigaray 2, 33, 123, 125, 130–1, 138–59

male-centred 2, 9–10, 33, 43, 99, 112, 140
mythology in 29, 92, 118, 130
New Age 118, 125, 131, 138, 159, 183
philosophy of 142–4
sexual difference 84
spirituality 125, 131
women 24, 119, 132, 134, 142–9
women philosophers 147–60
repetition 15, 40, 91, 106
repression
  by traditional God 9, 11, 48
  maternal role 11, 33, 40, 143
  natural immediacy 90
  western philosophy 43
  of women in India 132–5
Roy, Kumkum 127, 130, 134
Rozenzweig, Franz 63, 76
Ruddick, Sara 73, 74

Said, Edward 138
same, sameness 3, 8, 9, 11, 65, 148, 152
same-sex relations 97
  homosexuality 102–23, 149, 151
  lesbian 97, 110, 137, 149
Scott, Joan W. 98
self 9–10, 15, 53, 71, 112, 119, 128
  see also subject, subjectivity
sensible transcendental 4, 23, 47–9, 52, 79, 128, 154
sex, sexuality
  biological 18, 21, 84, 116
  body 16–17, 21, 30, 71, 127–9
  ethics 47, 52, 56–7, 154
  female 69, 71, 81, 89, 99, 153
  gender 18, 21, 23, 27, 31–2, 41, 43, 57, 71, 75, 84, 146–7
  heterosexism 97–8, 149, 154
  jouissance/desire 16–17, 52, 71
  Levinas 56–7, 69
  male 16–17, 21, 48, 81, 99, 126–9
  other 52, 56, 75, 98
  Tantrism/yoga 126–7, 129
  'two lips' 17, 21
  wonder 47–9, 52
  see also heterosexuality

Sexes and Genealogies (Irigaray)
   belief 25
   Daly 105
   eastern spirituality 126
   feminine divine 20–1, 23
   gender 22
   gynocracy 26–7, 29, 31
   imagination 124
   sexual difference 87
sexual difference 1, 3, 8, 30–4, 37, 42, 47–9, 51–3, 57, 60, 65–6, 70, 77, 82, 84–5, 87, 94–5, 97, 99, 115, 120–1, 125, 140–1, 144–5, 147–9, 152–8
   Descartes 37, 47–9, 51–2
   divine, the 115, 120, 125
   essentialism 30–2, 95
   feminine, the 34, 42, 95, 145
   heterosexuality 3, 97, 100, 115, 125, 153–5
   Levinas 57, 66, 77
   love 52, 66, 125, 156
   men 8, 29–33, 65
   ontological essentialism 136–7, 156
   o/Other 66, 77–8, 125
   race 119–21, 155–6
   universality 84, 86–7, 97, 99, 121, 156
   woman 8, 31, 42, 52, 84–5, 140–1
   women philosophers 8, 31–2, 143–54
   wonder 47–9, 52, 55
   yoga 126, 132
Silverman, Kaja 14
Soper, Kate 118–19
Speculum of the Other Woman (Irigaray)
   couple, the 95
   Descartes 36
   essentialism 117, 145
   feminine imaginary 7–8, 22, 29, 124, 145
   Freud 12
   God 7–8, 15, 17
   imaginary, the 22, 124
   jouissance 8, 15–17
   male dominance 2, 16, 87
   religion 7, 134
   sameness 65
   subjectivity 19–20

spirituality 4, 47, 90–4, 126–8, 131–6, 152–60
   see also divine, divinity
Spivak, Gayatri Chakravorty 116, 130
Starhawk 118
Stone, Merlin 110, 130
subject, subjectivity
   divine 20, 25, 58, 79
   ethics 73, 81–2
   feminine, the 71, 73, 19–20
   gender 22, 43, 58, 89, 91–2, 120
   God 42, 58, 100
   heterosexuality 71, 95
   Levinas 58, 71, 73
   rationality 39–40, 44
   sexual difference 30, 147, 154
symbolic 9–11, 16, 17, 31, 33, 34, 41, 99–100, 107

Tantrism 126–30, 132, 134–5, 138
technology 111
Thinking the Difference (Irigaray) 26, 88
This Sex Which Is Not One (Irigaray)
   essentialism 117, 145
   feminine imaginary 7–8, 22, 29
   God 7–8, 12
   jouissance 15–16
   male-centred tradition 2, 7, 109
   metaphor 109
   phallus 12, 108, 109
   subjectivity 19
   'two lips' 29, 108
Tillich, Paul 104
To Be Two (Irigaray) 65
transcendence, transcendental 4, 20, 24, 29, 46–9, 52–3, 67, 79, 96–7, 102, 128, 134, 158
   divine 4, 29, 48–9, 53, 79, 128, 158
   feminine, the 65–7, 69, 70
   God 20, 21, 24, 29, 53, 61, 79
   Levinas 59–61, 65–70, 78–9
   male 8, 24, 47–8
   o/Other 61, 65, 78–9, 96–7, 102
   sexual love 46–9, 79, 97
   transcendental idealism 23
   transcendental imagination 146
   universality 94, 95

see also sensible transcendental
Tringham, Ruth 27, 130, 133
truth
   Antigone 88
   divine, the 4, 15
   Heidegger 114
   historical 28, 38, 142–4
   Irigaray 42
   'two lips' 110

unconscious
   Daly 103, 112
   desire 71, 87
   God/Other 9–12, 93, 107
   racism 120
   rationality 131
   Real, the 16
   virginity 93
universal, universality 12, 41, 43, 80, 83, 91–7, 174
   gender 84, 86
   Hegel 83–4, 100, 152–3, 155
   heterosexism 156
   negativity 83–4
   sexual difference 94, 153
   spirit 93, 94, 152
universal statements 12, 41, 43, 80, 117, 119, 121, 148, 178

virginity 57, 69, 70, 89, 91, 93

Way of Love, The (Irigaray) 2, 4, 153, 158

'whitefeminism' 120, 148
Whitford, Margaret 22, 23, 29, 155
Willett, Cynthia 155
woman, women 7, 8, 9, 10, 11, 22–2, 24, 30, 31, 39, 40, 41, 42, 44, 52, 56, 70, 73, 81–2, 84–5, 91, 92, 119, 132, 134, 136, 140–9, 155
   civil identity 87–9
   culture of 29, 84, 89–94, 119, 124, 126, 150
   equality of 94–7
   gender 20–2, 30, 56
   God 7, 9, 22, 82, 92, 114, 136, 155
   in India 132–5
   nature 25, 39, 89–93, 111–12, 117–19, 140–1, 157
   o/Other 10, 11, 56, 70, 81–2, 85, 91
   reason 8, 39, 40, 41, 44, 73
   religion 24, 119, 132, 134, 142–9
   sexual difference 8, 31, 42, 52, 84–5, 140–1
   universality 86–7
   see also female, feminine
women scholars 34, 73, 111, 142–3, 147–60
   see also under individual authors
wonder 36, 37, 45–52, 55, 152

yoga 4, 126–30, 132

Ziarek, Eva Płonowska 121, 149–50, 151, 155, 157

EU authorised representative for GPSR:
Easy Access System Europe, Mustamäe tee 50,
10621 Tallinn, Estonia
gpsr.requests@easproject.com

www.ingramcontent.com/pod-product-compliance
Ingram Content Group UK Ltd.
Pitfield, Milton Keynes, MK11 3LW, UK
UKHW021835140426
5217IPUK00021B/1455